JULIAN BREAM
A LIFE ON THE ROAD

JULIAN BREAM
A LIFE ON THE ROAD

TONY PALMER

with photographs by
Daniel Meadows

Macdonald & Co
London & Sydney

First published in Great Britain in 1982 by
Macdonald & Co (Publishers) Ltd
London & Sydney

Maxwell House
74 Worship Street
London EC2A 2EN

ISBN 0 356 07880 9

Filmset, printed and bound in Great Britain by
Hazell Watson & Viney Ltd, Aylesbury, Bucks

Contents

1 The loneliness of the long-distance guitar player?

The tour was not going well. Six major concerts in ten days would be enough to frighten most people. But for Julian Bream this lunatic schedule, repeated month after month, year after year, has become a way of life. What is even more extraordinary is that, almost alone among international virtuosos, Bream makes all his own travel arrangements, selects the concert halls, supervises the lighting and presentation of his recitals, sometimes negotiates his fees, often collects the money, chooses his programmes and decides when and where he will play. On this tour, in Italy, he has decided to drive himself from concert to concert. He is alone, apart from one suitcase and one guitar. 'Never go anywhere without the old box,' he says cheerfully.

The journey from Milan to Rome had been particularly unpleasant. Seven hours in filthy weather and Italian traffic, both apparently intent on putting Bream into a foul temper. Still, the prospect of a warm bath and a comfortable hotel room in 'Claridge's', not to mention a touch of the spag bols and Chianti classico, had spurred him along. We arrived after dark and were immediately trapped in one of those Roman traffic jams which Fellini might have invented, all honk and not much movement. No, no one had ever heard of Claridge's Hotel. 'Better have another tube of joy,' said Bream, lighting his sixth cigarette of the last twenty minutes. Round and round, back and forth, and eventually, two hours later, home sweet home in the shape of Claridge's, an ordinary pension, almost in Milan, so it seemed to Bream, on a major road out of the city along which passed a stream of ten-ton lorries rattling the very foundations of the hotel. Yes, they were expecting a Mr Breemo, but no his room did not have a bath, only a shower. 'But it is a very *nice* shower,' said the concierge.

'Are there any messages for me?' asked Bream.

'Ah no, signor, except that the young lady is waiting, when you are ready.'

'Bit of a turn up this,' Bream said. 'Trouble is, I don't know where the concert hall is, or what time tomorrow's concert is supposed to start.'

The young lady was indeed waiting, and had been doing so for some hours. She was from the local concert management and wanted to show Bream the hall. 'Tomorrow,' he said, 'domani. At 5'—a few hours before the concert started, so that he could try out the lighting and the chair they proposed he should sit on during his recital. 'OK,' she said, and flashed out, not bothering to enquire if

'*All honk and not much movement. . . .*'

Bream needed anything, whether the hotel was adequate, what the ticket sales were like or what his programme was to be. Nor was she too helpful when Bream eventually visited the hall the following day. The lighting facilities were almost non-existent, not even suitable for the cinema screen which was the hall's regular entertainment. Bream's dressing room looked like an extension of the public lavatory, and the hall's acoustic was the worst he could remember in a long time. He had not played in Rome for ten years and was already terrified. 'This hall is as dead as a dodo,' he said to me gloomily. 'At least they could draw back the proscenium curtains which may liven this deadly place up a bit. Where's that woman? I can't go through with it. The acoustics here are absurd.'

Another woman, from the British Council, appeared and apologized that no one was here to greet him. 'We've got eight Members of Parliament in town,' she said as if by way of explanation. 'And I'm afraid there will only be a small audience tonight, mostly the aficionados and their friends.' The lady from the local agency disappeared as Bream became more and more irritable. In his anxiety about the lights, or lack of them, he had clambered up into the wings of the stage to see if anything could be moved, but in doing so had damaged a nail on his right hand, one of the nails which plucks the strings on his guitar. His ear had also begun to trouble him, no doubt aggravated by the chaos—he had been suffering from acute labyrinthitis (an inflammation of the middle ear) for over six months now; it affects his walking, although not apparently his concentration.

The agency lady now reappeared with a broad smile. 'The concert begin at 9,' she said, 'and my mother will come at 8 to pick you up from the hotel.'

Back at Claridge's, Bream is now almost suicidally depressed. Grimly, he takes his guitar out of its case, and suddenly in a cry of anguish notices that, in the back of his instrument, a hairline crack has appeared. 'Bloody mountains,' he says. 'Went up to the bloody mountains in Switzerland for a few days' respite last week and look what happens! Must have been the high altitude and the dry air. Dry air or damp can often do terrible things to the old box, you know. Still—it's still in one piece so I should count myself lucky for that.'

I remark that his guitar is somewhat smaller than I expected, and extremely light. 'In fact,' he says, 'it's so light you can pick it up with one finger. It's about half the weight of many of the instruments that are in use today, although it's only about five per cent smaller. The string length is just over 64cms, whereas the string length of some modern instruments can be as much as 66 or 67cms. It was made specially for me in 1973 by José Romanillos, a Spaniard who came to England a good many years ago and now lives virtually next door to my home in Wiltshire.

'Great instrument makers are a special breed and often a bit eccentric, you know, most probably because they're dealing with the unknown, in a sense. They're working with a living medium— wood. So, although the wood is fashioned to very fine measurements, you've finally got to feel the wood for its appropriate thicknesses. Literally. You can't just say to yourself, well, I'm going to make *this* sound-board an eighth of an inch thick because I made the *last* one an eighth of an inch thick and that worked well. Each piece of wood is unique and must be treated separately for its innate characteristics. You can't really teach a person how to understand wood, to feel the density of the grain, to feel what humidity is left in the wood, to feel the tensile strength of the wood when you bend it. These are things that come from an inner knowledge, which is almost impossible to learn. And that's why there are very few great makers. It's a question of the intuitive process, largely in contrast to the intellectual one.

'The fact that my guitar is a little smaller than average, however, does not mean that it lacks a strong bass resonance. It does not always follow that the bigger the instrument, the greater is its bass resonance. The important considerations are of proportion and balance within the integral design. The bigger the guitar, the greater can be the chance of losing that proportion, and hence harmonic balance within it. Carried to the extreme, you might even create a condition of sound-distortion. Also, it's worth bearing in mind that if you're sitting in a room playing a large modern instrument, it may often *seem* to make a large sound. But when you hear it in the concert hall, it can often surprise you that the sound doesn't travel in quite the same way or have the same presence as the sound, for instance, of my own guitar. It's a question mainly of the *focus* of the sound; it's as though the sound of many modern instruments can somehow dissipate itself as it travels through the air, whereas my instrument actually sounds better and, paradoxically, even louder a little farther away than it does when you're close to it. It is rather like decanting an old bottle of burgundy. As the wine flows into the decanter, the contact through the air not only purifies it, but also helps to focus the quality of its characteristics. Moreover, there's no doubt that the best sound-quality from almost any guitar comes, approximately, when you are utilizing about 70 per cent of its volume.'

Bream places his cracked guitar carefully back in its case. 'Provided the crack doesn't get any worse, I'll probably manage,' he says disconsolately. 'I can always borrow one, I suppose, if the worst should happen. I've twice had an instrument just fall apart, you know in the terrible cold of a Canadian winter, and on both occasions I had to borrow one. On the second occasion the borrowed guitar turned out to be a rather better instrument than the one I owned, which was a bit galling because the chap who owned it could only play three or four chords. If I was really stuck, I know I could give a concert on an old orange box if need be, though I don't think either myself or my audience would enjoy it particularly. But I must say my instruments generally hold up, and in any case, you've got to simplify things when you're on the road; you can't carry around two million instruments; one instrument has to be quite enough.

'Hell's bells, life could get so complicated if you took two instruments: can you imagine you might never know which one to play; you could even get totally neurotic half an hour before the concert trying to decide which one to use. No—if you've only got one instrument with you, even if it's in bad shape, at least you know you've got to make the best of it. Get on and do the show, that's the thing. Anyway, my split nail is a bigger worry at the moment.

'You see, we are all gifted,' he said with a grin. 'I've been gifted by the Almighty with reasonably good nails. Either you are born with good nails or you are not. My nails hold up pretty well, but are a bit on the thin side. And it probably didn't help that, until I was fourteen, I bit my nails down to the quick. In those days I used to play the guitar with the flesh of the finger. My father who was very much an amateur performer but really loved playing the guitar, always made a much better sound than I did. And when I used to ask him why, he would get so mad at me and say, well, why don't you use your nails?! And so I started letting my nails grow. I found it very difficult at first to make a really good sound, because I had such thin nails, but they've improved greatly over the years. If I'm in good health, then my nails are too. But if I get a bit run down or I've got the 'flu, then my nails get thin and, d'you know, the sound gets thin also—and cold weather can also make them brittle. Which is dangerous, as they are then liable to split.

'So the sound, the actual quality of the sound, is very much affected by health. So you might think I would have to make a specific point of looking after my nails. But I don't bother unduly. Either you take reasonable risks and relax a bit, or you don't take risks and spend your life worrying. In any case, too much care and anxiety isn't quite my style. With my hands, I do take, I must confess, calculated risks. I don't like wearing gloves, for instance. The thing about gloves is, if you've got a tiny little nick in your nail and you're wearing gloves with any sort of lining, the nail will catch in the glove and tear it further. Anyway, when the air gets to the skin or the nail, it's certainly more healthy than keeping your mitts continually cosseted. Also, for the guitarist, the left hand has to be very strong. So I find myself when away from the guitar working and lifting mostly with my left hand; I don't lift or do anything strenuous with my right hand, because that's the hand that needs to be infinitely sensitive and aware.

'But, if you're going to go bald, you're going to go bald. And nails are like your hair; that's what you're given by nature. You could put lacquer on them, nail varnish and a whole lot of gunk. But ironically this affects the *quality* of sound. Because what is important is not just the thickness of the nail, but its flexibility too. If it's too thick the sound is heavy and percussive, and the possibilities of delicate nuances are restricted. So my nails do have some advantage when it comes to shade and variety of sound, because they're on the thin side and consequently flexible.

'The other problem, of course, is that nails are constantly growing, and yet there *is* an ideal length for nails. Yesterday, I filed down my nails because they were getting a bit long, and the longer they get, the thinner the sound. So yesterday it would have been

'Either you take risks and relax a bit, or you don't take risks and spend your life worrying. . . . So a difficult piece with a broken nail? Hell on wheels.'

very difficult to give a concert; when you file a nail down and reduce its length, the angle of the stroke of your finger has to be slightly different from the angle needed when the nails are longer. It might seem a small difference to you, but it can make a hell of a difference to me. Again, there are those little rough edges on newly-filed nails which a little practise on the strings will polish up. So for me the quality of sound when you've just filed your nails is generally rather poor. Yesterday, it wouldn't have been much of a concert. Today, the nails are just about okay. Tomorrow they'll be terrific; alas I've got no concert then. The next day will be fine, but the day after that they'll be getting a little bit on the long side, so I shall have to make another terrible decision. Shall I or shan't I?

'It's amazing, perhaps, but my whole concert career has depended on such a tiny detail as when I have to file my nails. But, I suppose, by way of comparison, there is also some little plastic screw

'I like to lead an ordered, organized life, although by nature I am as chaotic as they come.'

somewhere in an aeroplane on which everything depends. Much of life is like that to some extent, so I don't complain about my nails except of course when I split one, as I have done today! Then I'm destitute. I'm miserable. At worst, I can't play; at best, I can play— but a difficult piece with a broken nail? That has to be hell on wheels.

'There have been occasions when I've used a false nail. If you look in my guitar case, I've got a whole box of false nails. They're specially made for guitarists. I did a tour a year or so ago; and for the whole trip the middle nail was a false one. As a matter of fact, it sounded rather good, rather better than my real nail. I did wonder then whether to wear false nails permanently. But it's a bit of a fiddly job fixing them on; they've got to be very secure, because when you're pulling or plucking a string on a guitar, there's a terrific strain on the nail. And once I remember at a concert a false nail flew off whilst I was playing a particularly complex and passionate passage and hit a lady in the front row right in the face— she wasn't amused I can tell you.

'In fact, it's amazing the bits and pieces I have to carry around in my old guitar case. Apart from this box of false nails, I have a little leather bag in which I carry my scissors for cutting my left hand nails and a pair of nail clippers for cutting the spare ends of strings. Then there's a tuning fork and a pencil sharpener; they're all in the top compartment.' Why a pencil sharpener? I asked him. 'Well, when I'm on tour I occasionally write something, or I may be fingering or re-fingering music that I'm currently playing, or perhaps I'm arranging something; whatever it is I always do it in pencil. I like to use a very soft 3B pencil, so I have to keep the point really sharp. I always travel with a good pencil sharpener. Now, in the bottom compartment, I keep the sandpaper for filing my nails, together with two stones with which I burnish the nails, one very fine and the other not quite so fine. They're really like little pebbles.

'Then, because the top three strings are so variable in their manufacture, I always carry a micrometer. It's an extremely accurate instrument, and can gauge within tolerances of point five of a thousandth of an inch. I can actually measure the thickness of one of your hairs with it. When new strings come from the manufacturers, they're not as reliable as they should be; some are thicker, some are thinner than they ideally should be. And for me, this can be crucial because it can radically affect the balance and overall response of the instrument. Again, I have to be extremely careful. Then I have my favourite pencil and rubber, my fountain pen re-fills in case I have time to write the odd letter, and a few packets of cigarettes—tubes of joy, I call them—tucked away to keep my nerves under control—or so I think.

'In the other compartment of my guitar case I keep my collapsible foot-stool, occasionally a cheque book, and a post-card portrait of a woman by Rembrandt which I found in Los Angeles; she gives me intense pleasure, and sometimes not a little reassurance, bless her. In the end case, I keep my spare strings. I generally carry around a half a dozen of each string. And, of course, there has to be room for the loot. I like being paid in cash, and when I am I always put it in my guitar case. But recently I have had it swiped on two occasions, and so from next season it will have to be cheques and those awful plastic cards to pay the bills.

'I like to lead an ordered, well-organized life, although by nature I am as chaotic as they come. Just as I have a standard travelling kit which goes into my suitcase. I've got just one suitcase, and in it I carry one suit, a formal suit, because I occasionally have to do an afternoon concert, or go to some rather smart reception; either a dinner jacket or a tail-coat and trousers; and one ordinary jacket which has to be strong and comfortable for travelling. I have one other pair of trousers to relax, and to practise in, because I like to be comfortable when I am practising. Then I have my four white shirts for concerts and four ordinary day shirts. I take three pairs of underwear; four pairs of socks, and a roll-neck sweater to wear just in case I'm caught short with the laundry and have got no more clean day-shirts. I have one pair of black shoes for concert-wear, the same pair I've had for six years. I only wear them for concerts and they shine up a treat. I always shine them up myself; I travel with my own shine-up kit, you see. And then a pair of brown shoes, a pair of travelling slippers, a toilet bag, a white scarf, my bow ties, eight handkerchiefs, a pair of pyjamas, a dressing gown, my pocket watch and cuff-links, and finally the dots—the music. That's it. That's standard, wherever I go.

'When I'm travelling I like to keep everything as regular as possible. I usually get up around 7.30—in the morning, that is; have a quick wash, pull on my dressing gown, ring for some breakfast to be sent up and then look out the window to see what the day is going to do for me. I always practise very early in the morning; I like that. And I usually put an old red sock through the guitar strings to dampen the sound so as not to wake up the neighbours next door. Then I have a total of an hour and five minutes on technical work, just technical work, nothing to do with music, just watching my fingers plucking the strings through chromatic and diatonic scales, together with tremolo and arpeggio figurations. When the breakfast arrives I break off, even if I'm only half-way through, which is good because I don't want to tire the muscles. Usually, I like a simple breakfast on tour, coffee and orange juice, perhaps a boiled egg and a roll. Next I finish my technical exercises, and only then do I have a shower and a shave and get dressed. Finally, I start practising the difficult passages in the pieces I'm going to play at my concert that evening, slow, very slow. All morning.

'After lunch, I like to go for a walk, or I might pop into a picture gallery or a museum, and then I come back to the hotel and have a sleep. Then I do another hour of practice, which brings me to 5.30 or 6 when I always go along to the hall to check out the chair they've given me, and, most importantly, the lighting. I get more than a little agitated if the lighting equipment is not adequate. Sometimes you get the most stupid lighting men. You see, all I

Julian Bream

'*My own shoe-shine kit,*
pyjamas, three pairs of
underwear . . .' and Neville
Cardus.

OPPOSITE
'*A bit of spag bol and a little*
chianti classico.' Julian Bream
with friend.

want really is a couple of spotlights pointing down on me, but
sometimes it's almost impossible to get somebody to set even those
up. They've often got thousands of lights up there, and they want
to do something fancy like having dozens of lights blazing in at you
from the side so that your eyes get blurred; or they want to put
some fancy coloured gels in, whereas all I want is just a couple of
straightforward white lights. The lighting set up is vitally important.
Not only does it create a sympathetic atmosphere for the music, it
also helps the audience visually to concentrate on you, and more
importantly on the music.

I never take the guitar with me, because even if I don't know the
hall I can tell by just clapping my hands how the acoustics are
going to be. If they're not good, like tonight for instance, I don't
get too discouraged. If I took my guitar and played a few pieces, a
bad sound would make me totally miserable from that moment to
the beginning of the concert, which could be a disaster for me,
psychologically. So after I've been to inspect the hall, I come back,
have a shower, shave again, and then put out my clothes on the bed.
Clean up my shoes first, wash my hands. Get out my white things

14

Julian Bream

'The concert begin at 9 and my mother will come at 8.'

and my concert clothes—the old uniform. By this time I may have rung down for a sandwich or a couple of boiled eggs. I then dress, and either drive myself to the concert hall, or even walk if the hall is nearby; sometimes I may be picked up by the promoter, or occasionally I just hail a cab.

'When you're on tour, you have to pace yourself very carefully; too many parties and social gadding about saps your vitality. And then you've got to sleep. Sleep is the most important thing for me on tour. Sometimes, on a non-concert night, I'll go to bed at 10 and sleep through to about 7 or 8 the following morning. I always have a sleep for 20 minutes or so in the afternoon. I'm very lucky; I can cut right out, within a minute or two. I can sleep anywhere, and with the greatest of pleasure.'

His ear was really beginning to bother him. 'It's the first time I've been unwell in years,' he said. 'It started as a virus infection in the middle ear, apparently. Doesn't affect the hearing; my hearing is perfect, but the balancing mechanism in one ear has gone completely to pot, or so I'm told by the medics. It all started just before a tour of America. When I was seated on the stage, I was okay; until, that is, I moved my head. And when you're playing music, of course, you move your head. When I got up to bow, the same thing happened, and on a couple of occasions I very nearly fell into the orchestra pit. I completely lost my balance. It was very difficult just getting on and off the stage. But I wasn't going to let this get me down. I'd gone all this way to give concerts, many people had taken the trouble to buy tickets and come to my concert, and I wasn't going to let them down if I could possibly help it. I knew that as long as I got to my seat on the stage, if I kept absolute control of myself, I would be fine.

'Now some people may say, how can you really give of your best under those circumstances? That's the extraordinary thing. Sometimes, under difficulties, you have to focus your concentration so hard on what you're doing, that this in itself creates a certain intensity in the performance that might not have been there if all your faculties had been in perfect condition. And I found that, as the tour progressed I was naturally getting more and more anxious before each performance. But I also found out from friends who knew my work quite well, that I did some of the best performances I'd ever done in America. I was obviously much heartened by that; especially because I've always believed that concentration in music, or anything else for that matter, is the absolutely vital thing; perhaps it was this complete and utterly singular intensity of concentration that gave my music-making on this particular tour its unusual quality.

'However confident I am before a concert I'm always nervous, though probably the right word is apprehensive. But once I get on stage, and no matter what has gone wrong previously, once I've got the instrument tuned up and I've played the first minute or so of music, I really begin to enjoy what I'm doing. It is at this point that I start experimenting, trying out differing emphasis on the many aspects of the particular piece of music in hand. I am now beginning to *make* music, rather than just going through the motions of playing it. That's why I can play the same programme night in and night out, which I often do for weeks on end, because I can *always* find something stimulating and fresh in the music. In each performance I set myself new problems, new challenges, sometimes artistic ones, sometimes technical ones. And those problems worked through can metamorphosize the music from performance to performance; towards the heightened intensity and beauty that I'm pursuing. Of course, I rarely get it, but it can be a beauty of such magical evocation that even to have got a glimpse of it on occasions, makes the whole exercise supremely worthwhile. It is a continuous search for the matter and means of expression, and the way to project the revelation of that expression to one's audience. This is what keeps me on the road, and needless to say my fingers on the strings.'

The moment of departure from Claridge's to the concert hall had arrived. Bream insisted on a light snack in the hotel's coffee shop, much to the annoyance of the lady from the concert agency who had returned to collect him. 'It's no good,' he said, 'I can get so

Julian Bream

*'There will only be a small
audience . . . mostly aficionados
and their friends.'*

bloody nervous at times, that if I don't eat something before the
concert, I'll be a nervous wreck about half-way through. I really
will. I'm so jittery, I really do need some ballast in order to do the
concert at all. I would be hopeless if I was, in a romantic sense, a
poor starving artist, because I would never be able to give a
concert—not if I was starving. I'd be hopeless if I was poor; couldn't
eat, couldn't play. Half-way through a concert, if I'm getting
hungry, I get nervous, and begin to make silly mistakes. Well, that's
no way to play a concert. So there's often a constant supply of
sandwiches backstage.'

Contrary to expectations, the concert was packed, as indeed had
been every concert on this, Julian Bream's first Italian tour for over
six years. The atmosphere was dead and heavy, the humidity on
this sweltering Roman night exhausting. Not surprisingly, a bass
string broke on Bream's guitar—a rare occurrence—but, fortu-
nately, during tuning up. 'It was so hot, and the humidity so great,
that the strings felt like I was playing on elastic bands,' he told me
afterwards. The recital began with two pieces by Leopold Weiss,
then a Bach Sonata, arranged for guitar by Bream, followed by an

extended Fantasía by the early nineteenth-century Spanish composer, Fernando Sor. After the interval, a Fantasía written for him by the twentieth-century Catalan Roberto Gerhard, a stunning piece by the contemporary Spanish composer Rodrigo, and a group of descriptive sound-pictures by Albéniz of various cities in Spain, including the beautiful and evocative 'Córdoba'. The audience went crazy and demanded at least two encores. A standing ovation. A 'fantastico publico', Bream told us between puffs of a tube of joy in his public lavatory dressing room. 'I was right on the edge of things tonight,' he said. 'My chair was unevenly upholstered, as a result of which my left leg went to sleep. I changed the chair in the interval, but it still didn't help much.'

Fans begin to crowd the dressing room, begging for autographs, a word of advice. In the confusion, Bream accepts three different invitations to dinner. When the fans have dispersed, the promoter appears for the first time, bows low before Bream and produces an enormous bundle of notes. 'The loot!' Bream exclaims with a smile, the broken nail, the cracked guitar, the unbalanced ear somehow magically forgotten at the sight of the milliardi of lire. 'Sign here,' says the promoter. 'Now wait a moment,' says Bream. 'Perhaps I could count the money first.' Before long, the inevitable squabble begins about how much the promoter has had to deduct for local taxes, publicity, entertainment expenses—what are *they*? Bream asks firmly. Then there are the performing fees and music copyright forms to be filled in, what was played and its duration, so that the composers, arrangers and publishers will eventually be paid. All this Bream does himself, carefully reading each document thoroughly and asking for a detailed translation when he comes across something he doesn't understand. The formalities concluded, the promoter bows low again, and bids Bream farewell and good night.

'Did you see that string break?' Bream asks me. 'I thought that was really rough luck. I remember I was once playing my lute in France, many years ago, and the audience was rather dull and unresponsive. And, would you believe it, I had three strings break. Within two minutes. During one piece. But I was determined to just keep playing. After the second break, the audience was in a frenzy of excitement, because it didn't seem to have had any effect on the music. But luckily they hadn't realized that on a lute you have double strings tuned in unison, and that the strings which had broken were ones which had doubles as backups. After the second string broke, the audience had obviously thought, well, that must bring him to a halt. And when the *third* broke, and I just went on as if nothing had happened—a sort of Paganini act—they just went wild. It's rather French that, don't you think?

'Now, what about a spot of lasagne verdi and a little chianti classico? This is what I like about Italy, that you can go and have a good meal and a lovely bottle of wine late at night after a concert. Not like England, where the cook has gone home after 9 o'clock and you have to make do with a stale ham wodge. After a recital,

'A touch of the nose-bags.'

I'm still a bit revved up and I need to eat something. So where's our transport?' It had not occurred to either of us until that moment that we were by now in a deserted concert hall. Even the caretaker had abandoned ship. Since Bream had been brought to the concert hall, he had no idea where it was in relation to his hotel. Indeed, he had no idea where the concert hall was in relation to anything. Once outside the building, it became quickly apparent that we were in a sleazy part of town. Not a taxi in sight. Not even any public transport. There was nothing for it but to walk. And so we did. If I had not been with him, one of the world's greatest guitarists would have had to set off after a gruelling evening, not to say day, in search of Claridge's, carrying his own guitar, stuffed with milliardi of lire, into the Roman night—Italy not being the safest of countries to walk about in unaccompanied and at night, especially if you're famous and supposedly rich. 'A bit like the loneliness of the long-distance guitar player, this,' he said to me, not entirely without a hint of the ironical.

2 'A mistake to overstay your welcome.'

'A touch of the nose-bags, before we set off down the road to our next port of call?' says Bream cheerily. 'Sorry I was so late getting up, but that Rome concert—it is Rome we're in, isn't it?—that just about finished me off. I didn't do much prac. this morning either. Still, sorry to have left you. Not a very good team leader, am I?'

If, as Bream believes, his gift from the Almighty is his nails, his gift from the Devil is a sure nose for the best restaurant in town. Any town. And no day is complete without a visit to the local taverno superbo, with an often hilarious guide to the menu.

'Ossobuco can be very nice; you know what that is? Well, it's sort of rice with a chunk of ox's tail. I think that might be your style. That'll really put hairs on your chest, Tony.'

I'm not so sure.

'Well, if you're feeling homesick, there's always a Dover sole.'

'I'll try the ossobuco.'

' "Tortellini Claridge-style" must be really first-class. Although, after last night at Claridge's, I'm not so sure.'

'I fancy starting with some soup today, for a change.'

'OK, yeah, soup's OK; but what *sort* of soup do you want? You can have a Minigasci's Minestrone or a Tavania soup.'

I opt for some vegetable soup.

'He's a real healthy chap, our Tony, isn't he? I mean, if it's a good restaurant, the ossobuco could be absolutely wonderful, but all he wants is vegetable soup. I ask you!'

'You're having pasta?'

'Oh, you bet!'

'Ooh look! You can also have "vegtatbles".'

'Vegtadpoles?'

'No, "vegtatbles".'

Bream laughs. 'How lovely. Did you look at the notice on the restaurant door? You can have lunch from 7 until 10am, dinner from midday to 2pm and breakfast from 6 until 9pm. Incredible.' Then he asks the waiter: 'What is this "spaghetti carbonara"?'

'Carbonara means spaghetti with bacon, cheese and raw eggs all mixed together.'

'Christ—that would really finish me off for the day.'

'You want it?'

'No, I'm tempted by the tenderloin steak in a paper bag. And a touch of the old red linctus, *per favore*.'

'*Vino rosso*?'

Julian Bream

Cup of char and a tube of joy . . . at the local taverno superbo.

'Yeah, why not, why not. Got to have something to get the old red blood corpuscles going.'

Julian Bream was born on July 15, 1933, in Battersea. 'I'm the eldest of about eight, I think. My mother, who was related to Ernst Lottinger, the famous music hall artist of bygone years, had two husbands and a lot of children. The first four were from my father; my grandfather ran a coach-painting business in Battersea, and my old gran on my mother's side owned pubs variously in Battersea and Fulham; she was of Portuguese Jewish descent. I was very close to her. My mother was a warm but crazy, and in her younger days extremely beautiful woman. I really loved her you know—although I think she gave my father a rough time—especially when she left home: I was about 13, and my father—who remarried in the meantime—died only three years after that. I was sixteen at the time, and so I decided to leave home. Home being Hampton, Middlesex, I pushed off to London to seek a new life. I was penniless: I had nothing except my old guitar, and a couple of

22

really nice friends who kept an eye on me. The going was rough at first and at times I was very lonely, but it was also exciting. Exciting to be in the hurly-burly of the great metropolis, without a care in the world, except for the pursuit of something that I loved passionately. It was from this moment that the see-saw of my life, my career and my fortunes really began, and it's kept going ever since. Over the years I've had two wives, but most of my life I seem to have lived on my own, in and out of harness. Perhaps the wives were just substitutes for the warmth and affection I had when I was young. I have a step-son, Ben, who was the adopted child of my first wife Margaret, from a previous marriage. She was the eldest daughter of the late novelist Henry Williamson. She's a splendid woman but I don't especially keep in touch with her, or Ben now for that matter, not much at any rate. The acrimony of the divorce put paid to any civilized or normal relationship thereafter—as it does in many cases.

'I'm a bit of a black sheep—a loner you might say, in a sense. The problem is that if you're a bit of a success, and make a bit of money, you can so easily become the subject of envy, acquisitiveness or both. But I don't think, because I run a good car, have a nice house and gardens, with a tidy piece of land, that this has changed me at all. I hope it hasn't. Some people feel that I've become a different person because of all that, but I don't think so, at least I like not to think so. In a way I would be quite content to live in a two-up two-down semi-demi in Suburbiton, provided I could have my books, instruments, pictures and a few bits of furniture along. I can be really happy you know, in a very simple way. In fact possessions can be an awful bore. The care and worry of them can divert so much energy that could otherwise be used for more creative things.

'I was actually taught the guitar first by my father, who was a gifted commercial artist and, as I told you, an amateur guitarist. After a year or so, I had some lessons with an old Russian guitarist, Boris Perott, who was then President of the Philharmonic Society of Guitarists. But it became very clear to me that his style was about two hundred years out of date. My real inspiration was obviously Segovia, the great Spanish guitarist. I had heard a couple of records of his when I was a kid, while I was evacuated during the War, and on hearing these had decided to make my life with the guitar. And when, in 1947, he came to England for the first time after the War, I was absolutely spellbound by his performances. I was determined now even more to pursue in my own way the same career that Segovia had created for himself. But the possibilities of playing the guitar as an acceptable musical instrument for the performance of classical music were, in those days and in England, almost non-existent. Segovia was a Spaniard and it seemed natural therefore that he should play the guitar. But I was an Englishman. Also, I suppose it was thought all right for one freak to exist, but not an embryonic second freak such as myself.

'So when my father saw that I was interested in following such a career he had many reservations. His feeling was that there was no

Julian Bream

chance to earn a livelihood unless I played jazz or something similar. And to prove it he did say to me one day that if you take into account the whole population of the world, and given that there's only one world famous classical guitarist so far, the chance of success for a second guitarist must be very slender. But that remark made me all the more doggedly persistent. I already played the cello a bit, and was also by this time a pretty fair pianist, although clearly my hands weren't quite big enough for that instrument. I suppose I *could* have played the jazz guitar, because I did play jazz occasionally, and most people who knew me in those early days thought that I would end up doing just that. But I was so determined to play classical guitar; it was just something I fell in love with, and I could never visualize myself doing anything else ever.

'My father had wanted me to go to the Royal College of Music in London, despite the fact that, because there were no teachers,

'It would be better for all our sakes if you didn't bring it into the building again.'

24

you couldn't study the guitar there. When I went for the Entrance Examination, at my audition I played the guitar first, and only afterwards did I play the piano, very badly as I remember. But the Director of Music, Sir George Dyson, could see perhaps that I was at least musical, and here was possibly some young boy with a chance. I think he felt that somehow he'd got to find a way of giving me that chance. So I eventually got into the College, got stuck into the old piano, and studied a bit of composition. I also took up the cello again as a second string, just in case I was finally unable to make it on the guitar.

'Those early days were very bleak. The Fathers of the Royal College thought of the guitar as just a pleasant enough instrument; indeed, they were amazed that you could play classical music on it at all. I think they thought I was some kind of nut, and the Director was very, very nervous about even letting me bring the instrument into the building. Perhaps he felt that if the other students got to hear me playing it, they might want to study it also, as a second instrument. It would have been an ideal second instrument you see, because of its harmonic character; if you're a fiddle player or a clarinet player, for instance, it's the perfect "other" instrument for that very reason. But the problem would have remained of finding a suitable person to teach it—there was just nobody around.

'Eventually, of course, the Royal College and my guitar had to part company. I had started to do a few late night concerts with the guitar to earn a bit of money, and so occasionally had taken the instrument into the College to practise down in the dungeon-like basement where they had their rehearsal rooms. Inevitably, the other students had begun to peer in through the door, and couldn't believe what they were seeing, or hearing for that matter. One day, I played a piece of Bach on the guitar; the Director got to hear about it, and told me that he wished me no disrespect, but he thought it would be better for all of our sakes if I didn't bring the guitar into the building again. So I didn't, though ironically he did ask me to play at his birthday party later that year.

'I left College in 1952 and was called up into the army as a National Service man. I was drafted into the Pay Corps because they thought I was good at figures. I was sent to Devizes on the Wiltshire Plain to join my unit, and drove down in my own little van, a 1936 Austin 7, which surprised the guards when I reported for duty at the guard room. Turning up for your two years' National Service in a van—whatever next? They'd never heard of such a thing; not even officers do that, I was told. So I parked the car in the town of Devizes, thumbed a lift in a 3-ton Bedford truck back to the camp and then did my six weeks' square-bashing. But the reason I had brought the van in the first place was to transport my instruments, a lute and a guitar, which were still in the back of the van in the garage. So I managed to bribe an NCO to go and pick them up and put them under his bunk, and thus managed after three weeks to get my guitar and lute into the camp. The trouble was, however, when you do your initial army training, it's at the double for fifteen hours a day, with just no time to play.

'The Korean War was on at the time and I had heard tell that our little mob was on draft for Korea; or if it wasn't Korea, it was Singapore. And I didn't relish the idea of my instruments, even if I had been allowed to take them, melting in that humidity. So I had to find a way of getting out of this. A very good friend of mine, and a wonderful patron, Tom Goff, the harpsichord maker, had very good connections in the army. His cousin was commanding officer of all the home-based forces, or something like that. And he managed to help find a way of getting me into an army band. It was difficult, you know, with a guitar. Can you imagine a classical guitarist in a marching band? So we had to work this one very carefully. Anyway, in order to get into an army band I had to sign on for three years; I had to become a regular. I'd already done about six months before I'd signed on, so I eventually did three and a half years, three of them in the Royal Artillery Band. And that's when I took up jazz guitar again, because the Royal Artillery boasted a dance band, and they wanted an electric guitar player. Being stationed much of the time in Woolwich near London, meant that I could moonlight when I was in London, which I did regularly.

'So although I managed to keep my career going throughout my years with the colours, the strain of it all at times was absolutely awful. I loathed being inspected *every* morning either by some lieutenant-colonel or by some warrant officer; and because I was such a lousy soldier I never rose from the ranks; I was always either Private or Gunner Bream. I got one stripe eventually, which was worn upside down because it only denoted two years of service in that rank. I never got any promotion. But I was grateful for that because it meant I never carried the can back for anything. I was in any case often in trouble. I was regularly late for parade, and in shit order when I got there. My uniform, my belts and boots were always scruffy. I think I was the worst soldier the British Army had ever seen; after three and a half years they were really very grateful to get rid of me. I remember well my very last parade. We were being inspected by a Sergeant-Major. My turnout must have been less than exemplary even for me that morning, because when he came to inspect me his face appeared to change colour. He looked very, very slowly up from my boots, and when he got to my cap he just said "Well . . . Well . . . Well . . . Well, fucking fuck!"—those were the last words I heard from the authorities of the British Army.

'Nonetheless, this was probably the only time in my life I was reasonably healthy. I could almost say I was really very fit. Getting up every morning at 6.30, for example, was a discipline, and I'd never had any discipline in my life up to then. So although I hated my life in the army, it might have had some beneficial effect on me eventually because, if nothing else, it gave me some sense of order and discipline, although I must say it took a long time to sink in, if it ever did.

'After I had left the Royal Artillery, however, success in the pursuit of my career was by no means confirmed. I had never passed an examination in my life, and always did appallingly badly in my

'*Never passed an examination in my life. . . . I had two auditions for the BBC, but failed both of them.*'

exams at the Royal College. I had two auditions for BBC radio, but failed both of them. So I took any job that came my way; quite often it was background music for radio plays or similar stuff for films. I did quite a lot of music for Gène Kelly's film *Invitation to the Dance,* and also for some of the early films they did after the War at Ealing Studios, the first being *Saraband for Dead Lovers* with Stewart Granger in 1948. Sometimes it might be an American picture where there was a fairly important guitar part in the orchestra. Commercial film and recording sessions were extremely important to me throughout the fifties and even into the early sixties, while the BBC—in spite of my lack of success at the general auditions—in fact kept me going for many years, accompanying singers, and later doing specialized programmes of early lute music on the Third Programme. I had by then taken up the lute. Quite a number of new radio plays had incidental music specially written for the guitar or the lute about this time, probably because amongst other reasons it was a cheap way of supplying incidental music.

'Although I gave my first recital in Cheltenham for the Guitar Circle as early as 1947, there were really few chances of giving straight recitals in those days and that situation remained so for many years. I was lucky if I gave fifteen concerts a year, all over the country; and the audience was usually rather thin on the ground. I remember I used to drive myself about in that old Austin van often for ten hours a day in order to do the recital, and then have to sleep in the back of the van after the concert because I couldn't afford a night in a hotel. The guitar was just not treated as a serious concert instrument.'

'Shall I *Campari* to a summer's day,' he says. Lunch in our Roman restaurant was over. We wander back to the car; first stop, a petrol station before getting onto the Autostrada north to Turin. The petrol attendant comes from Manchester. To Bream, with his totally international globe-trotting career, it seems almost inevitable that she should.

He punches in the cassette in his car hi-fi; The Beatles. Bream sings, loudly, and wildly out of tune. 'I got a silver record once, for a million dollar sale of an LP or something ridiculous like that. I happened to notice that the scrolls between the different numbers bore no relationship to the original disc. I was so intrigued, I couldn't resist the temptation to play the record, so I put it on my turntable, and do you know what came out? Paul McCartney's *Band on the Run.* Isn't that amazing? At first I felt peeved; I felt slighted, because in classical music gold and silver awards are rather rare—they're thin on the ground—and to make matters worse I had ruined my brand new pick-up stylus by using it on the silver disc. But after a little thought I didn't mind one bit: after all, amid Paul McCartney's vast collection of gold and silver discs there's a faint possibility that he may also have one of mine by mistake—though I suspect he now deals only in gold.

'You know, this has been going on an awful long time now, this touring lark. Thirty years and, by Christ, you can say that again.

Three bags full. When I'm on tour, it seems I'm nearly always on my own. As much as I adore my house in Wiltshire – and I can tell you once I'm ensconced there it could sometimes take a giant shoe horn to prize me out—but once I'm out and on the road it can be marvellous just to get away from the domestic life of home, and just think entirely about the music I'm doing. Because when you're on tour, it's a very egotistical self-centred occupation. You are forever pampering yourself; you're thinking about your health; thinking about the performances and the practice, and concentrating only on the professional aspects of your life. So it's natural, for instance, that when I'm on the road I can often be planning next year's tour. And not only planning where I'm going to play, but thinking about the music that I'm going to perform. I sometimes take with me certain works that I've got to learn; for example, on this trip I've got a new piece by Peter Maxwell Davies that will need a great deal of preparation. After all, when you're on your own in a hotel room, one can really get a lot of preparatory work done for the next tour, as well as keeping up the technical and musical standard of the music that you're playing on your present tour. There are absolutely no distractions, in other words. I'm always thinking ahead; and naturally, in my profession, you've got to think ahead, sometimes as much as two years. When I'm at home, when I'm not always concentrating on my music, I devote myself to the other things that interest me, such as the garden, reading, fiddling about with the house or cricket. But on tour, I'm my own man—it's music all the way.

'I arrange my tours so that I have one travel day, one concert day, one travel day, one concert day, and so on—particularly so in America, when one has to travel vast distances by air. So if I arrive at my destination by teatime, and there's the evening ahead, I will

'I don't really like travelling. I don't speak any foreign languages. . . . Christ, I must be a bloody idiot.'

'The important thing is not to try and deceive people . . . by sweetening the pill.'

probably find a restaurant near the hotel and go off and have a bite to eat on my own. Then I will go back to the hotel, and work for a couple of hours before I turn in. For a lot of people that would be a very boring evening. But not for me. It's ideal. I can use the time to do those jobs that might seem tedious, but that have to be done, such as studying new scores. This work by Maxwell Davies, for instance; I've got to edit it first because some of it is just unplayable, or very nearly so. What most people might find tedious about this way of life, I often find rather stimulating.

'Let's take this particular tour. When I was in Germany recently, I suddenly realized I hadn't played in Italy for about six years. And I remembered that the last time I had played here, I had enjoyed it very much. I've always been a little nervous about Italy and I often wonder why; perhaps it's because in Germany you can arrange a tour two years ahead, in Italy you may have to arrange things much nearer the time, possibly not more than six months ahead. I rather like that spontaneous approach myself, but to my agent in Hanover, who looks after the whole of continental Europe for me, it all sounds a bit risky. I should perhaps explain that although I have my agent in London who looks after my English affairs—he's called Martin Campbell-White, a marvellous chap who co-ordinates my career magnificently, this fellow in Hanover, and an agent in New York who takes care of the rest of the world, all I really need them to do is to make sure I'm not taken for a financial ride, and co-ordinate my international career. I like to do all the detailed arrangements and planning myself, especially when choosing where I go and what I play. Anyway, my man in Hanover in thorough German style really likes to plan everything well ahead, so I often have to miss out Italy or Spain in favour of countries like Holland or Denmark that are prepared to offer a contract perhaps eighteen months or two years ahead of the event.

'In fact, my European tours divide up into three kinds; those I call my "car-tours", my "plane-tours" and my "train-tours", and just occasionally a mixture of all three. I plan each according to the method of conveyance I'm going to use. So on a car-tour, for example, the first thing I have to do is collect my continental car insurance documents in Salisbury close by, fill up with petrol and off I go. I might plan to take the car ferry from Dover to Ostende; well, the first place to play, if not Ostende itself, could be Ghent or Brussels. After that I might nip down the road to Liège; or I may go to Antwerp, which is pretty near. I could then push on to Cologne or Bonn and thereafter just take the Autobahn south and play Frankfurt, Stuttgart, Ulm and Munich. Having got to Munich, I'll probably make it back home slowly by way of Saarbrucken or Strasburg; finally I might just play Paris on the way home for a few extra bob and a first class blow-out, and then get the Dover thingummy-bob Boulogne ferry back to good old Inghilterra. That's a car-tour. Never more than nine or ten concerts, and never away from home for longer than three weeks.

'A plane tour, on the other hand, will take in longer distances and many more countries, and if I plan it well I may get a reasonable round trip deal with the airlines. But naturally I don't want to shell out most of my concert fee on getting there. In the old days of course, if you purchased a first-class seat, it was always possible to wangle the instruments on board in the cabin, but nowadays most airlines are totally inflexible toward such reasonableness, and our own national flag carrier is the worst of the lot in this respect. So

'A period of self-love, self-absorption, or is it self-deception?'

now I buy two seats in the chuck-out class. It costs more, and I have to cough-up for the champers, but my instruments are safe and snug. The plastic meal is only marginally worse than what's up front and the compressed companionship around a damn sight more amusing. All in all it could be worse, not by much though.

'Now to get back to the planning. First, I usually get a map out and see how best I can route myself, in the most economical way. Perhaps I may start out on the longest leg of the journey and begin the tour in Helsinki or Oslo. From there to Stockholm and then south to Copenhagen, though I may throw in Göteborg on the way. Then a short hop to Hamburg, then Hanover or Berlin, Frankfurt, Vienna, perhaps Linz, Zurich, up to Amsterdam and then home. I'm pretty flaked out after a trip like that, so I might take a breather at home for a couple of weeks before getting wound up again for the next bunch of madness. But with all this planning, I now find it makes good sense to try and look at least two if not three years ahead.

'It's a great mistake, I believe, to overstay—or overplay—your welcome. Whereas I used to play regularly in the same cities every year, I tend not to do that anymore—with the exception say of New York or London. One year I will go to major cities in Europe, and the next year I'll play smaller towns. I like playing in smaller towns, because I think that as an artist one must make some effort to visit smaller communities. International artists so often only go to the big halls in the major cities, but they don't necessarily go to smaller towns like Iserlohn, Stoke-on-Trent, Vaduz or Padua where we're going the day after tomorrow. It is in the smaller places where some of the more charming and intimate concert venues are to be found, with a public just as warm as in any great city and just as gratifying to play to.

'As for hotels, well I'm not really very fussy, to tell you the truth. Admittedly I like to stay occasionally in a tremendously grand and luxurious hotel; it's good for the morale as well as a comfort for the body, particularly if you're on a rugged schedule. But I'm quite content with a simple room, a comfortable bed, somewhere to hang my clothes and a shower. In fact, I think I prefer that, because one is not cluttered with kitsch or grandiose make-believe. But the important consideration in choosing a hotel, at least for me, can be a mundane thing like the laundry service; actually, that's almost as important in a way as choosing the music. I hate wearing nylon or any artificial fibres; so everything I have is cotton or wool, which has to be very carefully washed. Now some hotels you can get day service, but if you arrive on a Friday, you've had it till the following Monday, and you may have already checked out by that time which might be a disaster for your ideally pristine concert get-up. So I have to plan ahead, especially for my white shirts. That's one reason—believe it or not—why I have to get up early, because I've usually got to get my laundry in for the day service, at least twice a week.

'Another problem that I used to have was what you might call my cash flow, because I must be one of the very few musicians in the international market who until very recently never possessed a credit card! I really like paying with cash. But life is so perverse; particularly in America, for instance, sometimes they just won't accept cash; they just don't want it. I mean, it's crazy isn't it? I was always taught that money was the thing, but apparently it isn't these days—it's some stupid bit of plastic and a bit of paper that you have to sign. It's your *credibility*, nowadays, that seems so vital. But cash can have its snags too. And one of the problems in Italy is you can get the cash whipped very quickly if you're not especially careful. And this can become really difficult, again particularly in Italy where they often pay you before the concert in notes of low denomination. You then have to go on stage absolutely bagged out with notes, the loot stashed away in every pocket. Sometimes it can be very tricky, not to say a bit uncomfortable, because when you sit down on stage you find you're resting your guitar on a million bloody lire, and then the angle of the guitar on your knee is a little higher than you are used to, which can be somewhat embarrassing for the right hand technique. In Savona, for example, I was paid before the concert by a lady who came in with a great bag of notes, which she slapped down on the table: "Sign here and take them." Now you can imagine that in Italian money you're dealing in trillions; well my fee's not that high, but there were a lot of noughts and zeros around. I went on stage absolutely bulging; I looked as if I'd suddenly put on three stone in weight; it was ridiculous. Normally I get a little embarrassed if I'm paid before a concert. After all if you've done a service, you get paid; you shouldn't get paid before you do that service, it seems to me. I suppose in thirty years of touring, there have been one or two occasions when a local promoter has been in a difficult financial situation, and I might have waited six months for the money to come through. And there have also been one or two occasions when I've been tipped off that a certain promoter is about to go bankrupt, so that I've had to insist on cash before the concert, which I hate doing. Or in America, a certified cheque; and I hate that even more. I really do think that you should get paid when you've done the job. That's the professional way of doing things. The whole idea of getting paid before you've done the job just seems to me anti-ethical because, in the final analysis, the engagement hasn't been carried out. In any case I don't play the guitar for money; I play for pleasure. Mostly my own; but strangely the Inland Revenue doesn't believe that.

'The ironical thing is this, and you might find this ridiculous, but I don't really like travelling. I don't speak any foreign languages. For a start, I don't really have much time to enjoy the sights. But I seem to book myself up years ahead and thrive on it. In the last two years alone, I've been to the East and West Coast of the United States (I've done one or the other *every* year since 1958), Mexico, Columbia, Brazil, Argentina, Chile, Bermuda, Italy, Germany three times, Holland a couple of times, Scandinavia, France, Australia, New Zealand and Japan. Not to mention England. Christ, I must be a bloody idiot. I must like punishment, or something. I mean, for a guy who doesn't like travelling, that's a

Julian Bream

'I don't really have much time to enjoy the sights.'

hell of a large travelling bill. But I do feel it's important for me to move around. Admittedly there are other guitarists, great as well as good guitarists, that tour the world. Segovia, for instance, is at a great age and doesn't perform so much now but amazingly he is still on the road; John Williams, whom I admire tremendously and who is in many ways Segovia's natural heir, doesn't care to travel at all. So I feel almost bound to, if only to keep the instrument before the *serious* concert-going public, in that dreaded capacity of a so-called "celebrity" artist.

'Of course, from a selfish point of view, I feel that if I have a successful concert career, which can stretch to say four different continents, there's a good chance that I may be able to continue that career in at least a couple of those places if suddenly I find myself out of fashion or politically undesirable in the other two. The public can be very fickle. So can governments. Perhaps it is a sense of personal priority as well as a need for material security which keeps me on the road travelling as much as I do. I don't know. What I do know is that I've got something to communicate, something to give, and however modest it is, give it I must. I might even call it a duty. I want to say something to other people. A gentle and tiny utterance it may be, but I believe it can also be on occasions compelling and beautiful. Also, there are all those really promising young guitar players around now, and just as I remember when I was a young boy, I learned such a lot from hearing and watching Segovia at his recitals, so I believe that many of the younger generation of budding recitalists may be able to pick up quite a bit one way or another from my efforts on the concert platform.'

Bream made his first major tour of England in 1951, after his London debut at the Wigmore Hall. Recitals in Switzerland in 1954 soon led to his first European tours. He played in Town Hall, New York, in 1958 at the invitation of the great American impresario, Sol Hurok, and was such an astonishing success that he has been invited to tour the United States every year since. Bream thus became the first British guitarist to achieve international acclaim, and lay to rest the famous dictum of the late nineteenth-century Spanish violinist, Juan Manén, that 'an Englishman playing a guitar is a kind of blasphemy.'

Nor did he neglect his English public; he appeared regularly from the earliest days of the Benjamin Britten/Peter Pears festival at Aldeburgh in Suffolk, and also from the mid-fifties at the Dartington Summer School of Music at Totnes in Devon. Dartington was founded by a redoubtable American lady, Dorothy Elmhirst, and her conservationist husband, Leonard; and the Summer School of Music was run for many years by Sir William Glock. Bream's achievement in the early fifties was not simply that he introduced the guitar as a classical instrument to an ever-growing public, but that because of his own eclectic and wide-ranging taste in music, he transformed the repertoire of the guitar. From the start, his concerts were a bewildering mix of the Baroque and unknown nineteenth-century, Spanish and contemporary composers; some of the pieces he played were transcriptions he had made himself for the guitar, although many were pieces actually written for the instrument but long since forgotten.

'Nowadays I sometimes plan my concert programmes by way of preparation for my next gramophone recording. It's not that I use the public performances of these pieces as rehearsals for the recording; not at all. I'm always thoroughly prepared, or at least I always hope I am, before I ever play a piece in public. But most pieces often take me a year at least to get to know, to discover the gist of what they may want to say. In a fine piece of music, you never discover all that there is to know, of course, never. Only by playing a piece over and over again, and judging an audience's reaction to it, as well as your own, can you ever begin to understand a new piece. That's why, in a public concert, I will often risk everything as I'm going along, by suddenly changing the fingering, or the phrasing, and even sometimes the tempo, which I previously have carefully and painstakingly prepared in my practice room, just to see if I can't discover something new, some other aspect of the phrase in question, another viewpoint. Playing the guitar is a constant journey of discovery for me, an adventure when I never quite know what the outcome will be.

'Of course, my aim is always to make a varied and balanced programme for my recitals. It's rather like planning a banquet; you have different dishes which complement each other. You might have an occasional dish which is astringent, which fixes the old taste buds for the next dish. So I always try to put at least one good modern piece in my concerts, not only because I believe in performing contemporary music, but because generally speaking a whole row of familiar romantic guitar pieces tend to cloy rather than charm. Also, a lot of guitar repertory pieces are rather short, so I try and play a couple of works that are rather substantial. In fact, I plan my recitals as if they were one gigantic and extended suite, so that the mood of one piece dramatically balances out the mood of the next. But variety of spirit and texture is essential.

'However, it's not always a question of contrast for its own sake. Matters of transition are as important as it is to begin a concert with a piece that can be grasped quickly; you've got to establish the magic of the evening from the kick-off. For instance, I might start with a Passacaglia by the eighteenth-century composer Weiss; the old groundbass, continually thundering away; it's easy to follow, it's stately; it's not tearing about, as it were, and you're not expecting the audience to listen to very complicated textures. It introduces the sound of the instrument in a firm and noble way, and hopefully the personality of my own playing, as well as giving some promise to what's to come. We then might tack on to the Passacaglia a sprightly Gigue by the same composer. It's in the same key, but the boisterous nature of the two-part writing, as well as the syncopated cross-rhythms, are in perfect contrast to what has gone before. But this Gigue is also a piece that can give a fair indication of the sort of trim I am in for the remainder of the concert. Are my nails a bit on the long side? Is the sound a bit thin, so had I better play nearer the sound hole? Is the humidity too high, so is the string flexibility too great? If the humidity is dry, the bridge sound (ponticello) will be unusually bright; which is fun for the modern pieces, but a little too strident for the classical pieces, so I'll have to take care not to overdo things.

'So now I've weighed up the acoustics of the hall, and something of the quality of the audience. I'm pretty sure about how I'm going to set my tempi, because of the sound reverberation or lack of it; and, according to how I'm feeling physically, I'll have some idea how I'm going to pace myself for the rest of the concert. Sometimes, I must admit, I let the whole bloody lot go to the wall, and just get on with it.

'However, after the Passacaglia and Gigue, I reckon that with a bit of luck I've got the audience settled and I can now play an extended work, such as the Bach Sonata in A Minor. It is of course a transcription, although the fugue was in fact written by Bach for the lute before he incorporated it into the first unaccompanied Violin Sonata. I arranged the other movements myself in order to complete the Sonata for solo guitar. The whole piece is brimming with inspiration, melodically and rhythmically, and the first and third movements have a passion and yet paradoxically a dramatic stillness of such intensity that I love this piece and could play it every night of the year.

'Hopefully, by now, I have created the atmosphere for the evening, and having won the sort of attention I want and need from my audience, we're now ready for another major piece. In any concert, I don't waste time between each piece with idle chit-chat. I used to do that, but I rarely do it now because I don't want the audience's concentration to break; I want to create the maximum dramatic impact for each piece straight away. And why not let the music do that? So to end the first half, it's no good just doing a couple of studies, or a little theme and variation by a minor eighteenth- or nineteenth-century composer. I might play the *Fantasía* Opus 30 by Sor; it's about 13 minutes long, and although the music is totally different—and let's be honest, nothing like as profound as the Bach—the musical intention in its way is just as serious. It's also a very happy piece, and I'm a great believer in happy music. Then I might play the "Royal Winter Music" by Hans Werner Henze, an extended thirty-minute sonata based on characters from several Shakespeare plays, a formidable piece, both harmonically and rhythmically. In other words, something that will attack them. Something they won't know, something they've got to damn well *listen* to.

'Nobody loves tragic, romantic, and melancholy music more than I do; but I also like happy music, just as I love jokes. You know, I can never really tell good jokes; I always forget the punch line! But I get a great deal out of life simply because I find it so bloody amusing, at times tragically so—desperately funny. And I find that this Sor Fantasía, for example, actually makes people laugh, provided I play it properly. When I played it in America, at every concert about a third of the audience just broke up at a certain point, and always at the same passage. Now you rarely hear that, do you, when you go to a serious concert? Mirth, to my mind, is as great and important in life as pathos. But somehow, in classical concerts you largely get the pathos. I can go along with that, but I like to get the humour across occasionally, because apart from anything else, it makes people relax. But more importantly it adds the pertinent contrast which can lend even greater gravity to pathos, compassion or what you will. On the other hand, I wouldn't want to give the impression that I'm flip—no Sir. Although in America the audiences often laughed their heads off at a couple of passages in the Sor Fantasía, in Germany, if you got even three or four laughs, everyone would look round; in Germany, you're not *really* allowed to laugh, certainly not in a concert. No Sir—it's ten years in the camps.

'Well you can't give a guitar recital without some Spanish music, or so I'm told. As I'm making a gramophone series on Spanish music there's a fair amount of Spanish music in my programmes these days, but I try to create as much diversion and variety as possible. The problem with Spanish music, and some Spanish musicians for that matter, is that the formal element of their music or music making is not always very strong, or at best rather secondary. It's not in the Spanish temperament, it seems to me, to come firmly to grips with intellectual musical considerations, and when they do it doesn't always come off. Though I must say here and now that there are some important exceptions to that statement; the magnificent musicians of the Spanish renaissance, for instance, and not less so in the twentieth century the remarkable musical personality of Manuel de Falla. But more of them later. Usually, you find that the *form* of much Spanish music creaks a bit for the musically inquisitive—you can be aware of the stitching, though the musical overlay can be quite beautiful. Much depends on the performance element to bind the whole thing together into a homogeneous structure.

'But a composer I greatly admire without any reservation is Enrique Granados. So, I may well start the second half with his *Valses Poéticos*, an adorable set of waltzes in the classical Spanish tradition. Then, after the sweetness of those lovely little tunes, I might do a piece by Roberto Gerhard, quintessentially Spanish, but not what one might call "tourist" music. It's got the real grittiness of Spain, the arrogance, the tragedy and dignity of the whole Spanish character. It's a pretty astringent mouthwash. Not exactly a charming piece; anti-charm, one might say. Then I might do a piece by Joaquín Rodrigo, the blind Spanish composer, also modern but more traditional in outlook. It was written in memory of Manuel de Falla and called *Invocation et Danse*—it is a stunningly attractive work which I love, although I find it extremely difficult to play. Every time I perform it, it stretches me to the utmost, and although I've never yet done a complete performance that I've really liked, I'll just keep on doing it until, one day, I'll just damn well play it well. In the last fifteen months, I've probably done fifty performances of it. Each one's been quite different, but in each one I've failed to satisfy myself. But I don't get miserable about it, because I know that in each performance there are always some sections that really sound ravishing, although there might be other sections which were pretty near disaster areas. Finally, I might finish up the whole evening with some Albéniz, and in particular "Córdoba", a miniature tone poem about the Spanish city of that name which I have recently transcribed and have such affection for.

'The important thing is not to push contemporary music down people's throats, or to try and deceive them by sweetening the pill. One has to programme contemporary pieces in such a way that they are a refreshing contrast to the piece that has gone before, and yet not so out of context that it shatters the atmosphere you've struggled to create. And then, of course, no matter what comes next—particularly if it is of a more conventional type of music—to the conservative part of the audience it will sound wonderful by way of relief. I find that contemporary pieces are for me essential to keep my musical vitality alive. I will shortly be preparing a new Sonata by Henze, for instance; a new work by Maxwell Davies; Harrison Birtwhistle is writing a piece; William Walton has promised a new piece soon; Michael Tippett is writing something for me in 1983; and Michael Berkeley, Sir Lennox Berkeley's son, will be writing a new work for me to play at the Edinburgh Festival in 1982—all a refreshing change from the nice Spanish pieces which

*'To have anyone else along
would ruin it really.'*

are a tremendous pleasure to play, but sometimes limiting in their musical point of view. On the other hand, I'm not so sure that very modern music, "avant garde" music, whatever that may be, is actually gaining in popularity. I've got the feeling that in the eighties audiences are going to become more conservative, that people may actually want to *use* music more and more as a kind of escape from unpleasant upheavals and social change. For the musically initiated it may lean towards the late String Quartets of Beethoven and the Madrigals of John Wilbye rather then the pleas of Pierre Boulez or a long weekend of Stockhausen. How's Maggie Thatcher, by the way? What's she up to? Seems to me old Blighty is going to the dogs. I'm beginning to wonder if I did the right thing by voting for her.'

The car swung off the Autostrada towards the centre of Turin. Almost immediately Bream got lost. '*Links? Sempre diretto? Centrum?*' he asked puzzled pedestrians who seemed not to understand his home-made Esperanto. 'You've got to make the best of what you've got whatever country you live in,' he said suddenly, 'It's no good blaming the system. *Links? Sempre diretto?*' he shouted through the window. Eventually, he found someone who spoke English and who gave Bream exact instructions how to get to the hotel. Again, almost inevitably, the man had been in a prisoner-of-war camp not far from Shaftesbury in the south of England where Bream now lives. 'Can I visit you in Shaftesbury?' asks our guide. 'Well, no thanks, I don't think I'll be there,' says Bream, '*buones dies*'. After a pause, he adds: 'nice fellow.'

'When I'm on form, which is by no means always, I find the guitar becomes simply an extension of me and how I feel, without anything in between. It can be a perfect amalgam of thought, feeling and intent. I find the colour and exuberance of the pieces I play in a concert utterly captivating. And I suppose that's what really makes me choose certain pieces when I'm planning a concert, the extent to which I can enter into their mood and inhabit them. Music-making is intensely personal for me. That's why I love playing music by the Brazilian composer, Heitor Villa-Lobos, for instance. Now, in terms of geography and the old genetic nonsense, nothing could be more of a contrast than Battersea, and Rio de Janeiro. But I feel I understand his music, in my bones almost, just as his music seems to understand me. Which, come to think, must make this music business a pretty peculiar affair. I mean, here I am now leading this monk-like existence; a period of total self-love, self-absorption, or is it self-deception? To have anyone else along would ruin it, really. In one sense, of course, I would love it; but two people are two people, and there's intercourse and interchange between them. Lovely, if I'm going on holiday; but not on tour. I find that if it's just me, I have total control of the situation, come what may. If something doesn't work, it's my own fault entirely. I can't blame anybody. And I think, over the years, much of my life has become like that. Pretty damn selfish don't you think? Fancy a spot of linctus?'

3 'Just a few pieces of wood glued together.'

"I used to work in a lunatic asylum," he told me with a fresh faced toothy grin. José Romanillos has now become one of the most famous guitar makers in the world. "You want a guitar from me?" he asked. "You prepared to wait for twelve years, because I have twelve-year waiting list?" He lives in a rather ordinary modern bungalow with an extension on the side which houses his workshop. By coincidence, the house is across the valley from Bream's home in Wiltshire, almost within sight and sound.

"I was trained as a cabinet maker in Spain, actually, when I was about 13, just after the War. In 1956 I decided to come to England, but I couldn't get any work, so I had to take a job as a lunatic attendant in North London, in Friern Barnet. I married and went back to Spain, but after a few years I couldn't stand the claustrophobia of Franco's rule, so I finally came back to England and settled near Salisbury. But as I often felt nostalgic, I decided to learn to play the guitar. I didn't have much money, and I couldn't afford to buy one, so I decided to make one. It took me about six months and a lot of blood and sweat actually, but eventually I finished it.

"One day, I came home from work and I found a friend of a friend playing that guitar; he asked if he could buy it and could I make some more. For ten years I sweated on kitchen tables, making guitars. What I didn't realize is that I was living less than twenty miles from where Julian Bream lived. I had made a guitar which I sold to someone who played in a local Salisbury orchestra, and who knew Bream. As a result, I was introduced to Bream, and it all started from there."

'I'd always been interested in instrument makers,' Bream told me over a spot of linctus in the Turin hotel. 'I find anything to do with wood, and the craft of fashioning wood, fascinating. I love the smell of a workshop, and the care and intentness of fine craftsmen at work. Is there not a look of gentle yet resigned optimism in the eyes of a great craftsman, as indeed in those of a fine gardener? And when you think about it, it really is extraordinary that out of some old bits of wood glued together, plus some bits of animal gut for strings, you can actually touch people's hearts. Isn't that extraordinary? Bits of wood just glued together and a few strings. Unbelievably simple, yet immensely powerful within its simplicity.

'What is especially interesting about guitars, moreover, is that they can vary so much. They vary not only in design, but you can

*'The majority of composers who
employ the guitar, are far from
knowing its powers, and
therefore frequently assign it
things of little sonorousness and
of little effect.' Hector Berlioz,
1843.*

have four guitars made at the same time by the same maker with
exactly the same principles of design, and they can all be totally
different. The guitar is a mystery, some may say a miracle. The
guitar is not said to be a feminine instrument for nothing, you
know.

'Guitars are made from wood, and wood is a living material. OK,
it's been chopped down from its living source, but it still takes up
moisture, expands in humidity, and contracts when there is extreme
dryness in the atmosphere. Some of the wood used in guitar
building is extremely thin, and the instrument is therefore very
vulnerable to environmental conditions. The sound table of a guitar
(that's the flat bit on the top) is usually made of pine or spruce,
whereas the back and sides are invariably made of Bombay or
Brazilian rosewood and occasionally from maple. But it's often very
hard to get fine really mature wood, and what is unusual about my

own guitar, for instance, is that the back and sides are made from an old rosewood sideboard. The sideboard was about a hundred years old, beautifully dry and seasoned; naturally it was fabulous wood. A lot of wood used today is just far too new. Of course, the longevity of a guitar is largely dictated not only by the wood it's made from but by the sort of use it has. As an international travelling virtuoso, I put my own instrument under tremendous pressure and stress, all the time. Before I came to Italy, I was over a thousand metres up in the Alps in Switzerland, and, as you know, the back began to split. Luckily, the more humid conditions of Rome saved the day, and the split virtually came together. Like its performer, an instrument can be always on the move, and this constant movement wears it out. If I was just a Sunday guitar-player, and my instrument was always kept in pretty much the same humidity, within moderate temperatures, it might last fifty years; whereas, I'm very lucky if my instrument lasts more than ten, if that. It's just amazing to think that my present instrument has performed over 500 concerts, as well as innumerable recording and TV performances, from arctic conditions in Alaska to the hot stifling humidity of Singapore, from the mild dampness of a place like Santiago de Chile, to the roasting heat of Mexico.

'You must also remember that the guitar has developed quite late, as European musical instruments go. The violin, for instance, had found its basic design by about 1600, give or take some small variations in shape and size. But the old guitar used to be a much smaller instrument compared to its modern counterpart, as you can see from contemporary paintings as well as from the music that was played on the instrument in the seventeenth and eighteenth centuries. Guitar music in those days was generally of a light and entertaining character; mainly dance music, though a variation form such as the Passacaglia was often used. It was, in a nutshell, a light instrument, ideally suited to music of diversion and pleasure rather than music of gravity and meaningful intent.

'The instrument we know today has evolved, quite dramatically, only in the last hundred years or so. And because it has developed so late, its full potential was never at the service of composers such as Mozart or Beethoven, or any of the other great romantic composers of the nineteenth century for that matter.'

'No-one really knows the true origins of the guitar. Some think it dates back to the ancient Greek Kithara; others say they've found carvings of what look like long-necked guitars in Mesopotamia. All important plucked instruments originated from the East, though many scholars believe the guitar to be Moorish in origin; in other words, basically North African. So that when the Moors invaded Spain, they brought to that country the guitar. But there is also a theory, quite well founded, that the shape of the guitar was already present in Spain before the Moors arrived. And just to add a bit of confusion the shape has recently been discovered on a first-century-AD frieze near Termez in Uzbekistan.

'Of course, there are plenty of references to a "guitar" in

medieval European literature. In the French romance *Blanchflour et Florence*, written around 1200, we find the instrument called a "gitere". Chaucer, in *The Pardoner's Tale* describes "yonge folk" who "daunce and pleyen . . . bothe day and nyght" with "harpes, lutes and gyternes". In fourteenth-century France, the Duke of Normandy's list of musicians included Jean Hautemar, who played the "guiterre latine". Later, in 1487, Johannes Tinctoris wrote an important history of music called *De invenzione et usu musicae*, in which he describes the "guitarra", also known as the "ghiterne", as "invented by the Catalans".

'In other words, the *shape* of the guitar seems to have been a fairly common one throughout Europe, and not particularly the invention of the Moors. It was, moreover, an instrument favoured by women, although I doubt if it was this that determined the guitar's form. Mary Queen of Scots gave Riccio, her lover and secretary, a beautifully ornamented guitar which I believe is still to be found in the Donaldson Collection at The Royal College of Music.

'In the middle of the sixteenth century, the four-stringed guitar was widely used. It was much smaller than the modern instrument, and instead of an open sound-hole, it had a carved rose, with its gut frets being tied around the neck. All four strings were doubled, and could even be tuned separately. There was also for a time quite an abundance of printed music for this curious little instrument, and some of the earliest pieces are found in Mudarra's *Tres Libros*, published in 1546. In France, the instrument became so popular that one author noted that the lute had almost been forgotten. Nine books of guitar music were published in Paris between 1551 and 1555 alone. Most of the music is pretty simple, and it's obvious that it was intended for an unsophisticated public requiring light and entertaining music. None of it approaches the complexity and invention of music being written at the same time for the lute, or its cousin the vihuela.

'The "five-course" guitar, on the other hand, does seem to have evolved from Spain at the turn of the sixteenth century, and eventually became known universally throughout Europe as the Spanish guitar. It was often highly decorated, particularly Italian-made instruments. The whole soundboard would often be covered with various inlays and filigree, depicting various musical motifs or religious scenes. The back and sides were frequently made of alternate strips of ivory, ebony and tortoiseshell, and in some cases of exotically stained wood. The great violin maker, Stradivari, produced a few of these elaborate guitars, which were beautifully made though the one thing they all had in common was that they sounded pretty awful, or so I gather. Perhaps they were intended as decoration, something to have about the Court, rather than instruments of serious musical intention. Thus, when fashion changed, as inevitably it did towards the middle of the eighteenth century, the guitar passed into relative obscurity for a while. Seemingly, it has suffered more than almost any other instrument from the whims of fashion and social change.

'But the interesting result of this has been that, again unlike most other musical instruments, the development of the guitar has largely depended not just upon particular composers but more especially upon particular performers. Although the "five-course" guitar almost certainly originated in Spain, its literature was extensively developed in the first half of the seventeenth century in Italy. I think it was in 1606, in Florence, that Girolamo Montesardo published the first system of tablature, in other words the writing down of musical notes which was soon universally adopted as the "Italian *alfabeto* or alphabet". It was a fairly primitive affair with no time signatures, bar-lines or note values as such.

'The public success of the guitar, however, often depended on Royal patronage. When Charles II returned to England in 1660 to regain the Stuart throne, Pepys describes the King strumming away on the old box during his voyage across the Channel from exile in Holland. Charles's cousin, Louis XIV of France, was taught the guitar and several "Livres de guitarre dédié au roy" were published in his reign. Some of these pieces (but by no means all) were little more than elegant strumming music, music which society ladies could play without much effort, but there was also music of distinction and originality. For hereabouts two remarkable player/composers flourished and each in their way were patronized by the two kings I have just mentioned. The older of the two guitarists, Francesco Corbetta, was born near Milan in 1615. By his early twenties he had already achieved considerable fame throughout Italy and the first of his many guitar books published in 1639 was hailed instantly, and was eagerly sought after by an ever-increasing guitar-playing public. Each book successively gave evidence of a more developed technique, a greater refinement of style. Most of the music in the subsequent volumes was pretty sophisticated stuff, and not exactly music for pretty ladies to strum in courtly circles. It was too damned difficult for that.

'By this time his fame had spread throughout Europe, and Prince Charles who was at that time in exile on the Continent became an enthusiastic admirer; and it is interesting that as soon as Charles was restored to the English throne, Corbetta was already in the King's service. His sojourn in England could only be called a *succès fou*, for within months of his arrival his personal fame together with the popularity of the guitar spread like wild fire. This could have been half predicted as a reaction against the puritan austerity of the Commonwealth and the rage for things Italianate at the English Court. In the event it seems everybody was guitaring like mad. Because of his involvement in a rather suspect shady venture the legality of which seemed open to question poor old Corbetta had to flee the country and settle in France where he eventually died, but not before he published two further collections of guitar music. One *La Guitarre Royalle* published from Paris and dedicated to Charles II in 1671, justifiably his finest work, and later in 1674 *La Guitarre Royalle* dedicated to Louis XIV. He certainly had an impressive circle of chums.

'Corbetta died in 1681. In the following year a remarkable young

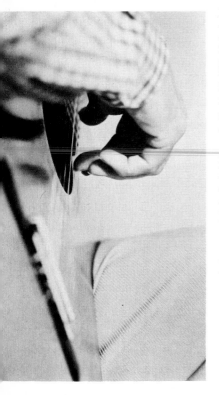

Frenchman published *Livre De Guitarre Dédié Au Roy*. His name was Robert de Visée. He was already Chamber Musician to Louis XIV, a post he may have accepted at the time of Corbetta's death. He was clearly very popular at the French Court, and although very little is known about his life, according to the diary of a French nobleman Comte de Dangeau, Robert was often requested to play for the King at his bedside during the evenings, which when you come to think of it is a charming idea, and possibly a very practical one too, as the King was known to be something of an insomniac.

'Robert de Visée, in my opinion, wrote the finest guitar music in this fascinating epoch of the Baroque guitar. Though less earthy, less flamboyant than Corbetta, his music has a refined aristocratic quality, beautifully assured in its harmonic and contrapuntal outlines. It also has immense charm which is largely what the Baroque guitar is all about.

'The change from the five-course guitar to the more familiar instrument with six single strings took place at the very end of the eighteenth century, possibly in France. The back of the instrument, which sometimes had been rounded or vaulted, now became universally flat. Double-strung courses were quickly abandoned, and lavish decoration subdued, gradually to disappear almost. Important innovations were gradually introduced, including fan-strutting the soundboard—allowing greater flexibility, thereby enhancing the bass resonance—and with that a more stable tuning at last became easier to achieve, particularly with the introduction of worm-and-drive tuning gears which quickly supplanted the old wooden peg-box. Tablature was also abandoned, and a guitar notation was introduced, on a single line of music headed by the G clef, the actual sound being an octave lower than written. This method is still in use today.

'Performers were still divided, however, as to whether to use the nails to pluck the strings, or use the tips of the fingers. Even in Spain, two great contemporary guitarists differed; Fernando Sor dispensed with nails altogether, whereas his compatriot Dionysio Aguado always used them. None the less, both of them—Sor, the sensitive and serious, Aguado, the brilliant and audacious—were very largely responsible for the sudden outburst of interest in the guitar in the early years of the nineteenth century. Again, you see, it was particular performers (actually, they were also prolific composers, particularly Sor) who revitalized the instrument.

'Sor, whose patron was for some time the famous Duchess of Alba, led a similar life to me really. Being a travelling virtuoso, he went to Paris, London, Moscow and St Petersburg, where, we are told, he even played for the Tsar.

'In Italy there were also several remarkable players, especially Mauro Giuliani, who was born in 1781. It was, however, in Vienna that he first achieved fame. There he was an established composer and famous recitalist from 1809 to 1819, the time of Schubert and Beethoven. Even so, the status of the guitar within the realm of serious music was insecure and largely ignored as far as the really great composers were concerned. Perhaps it was because the romantic image of the guitar fascinated a composer like Berlioz, more than its intrinsic musical qualities. The guitar certainly had an unmistakably romantic image about it; it was an instrument of easy conveyance, complete in itself. Being a simple yet rugged instrument, it could be played out of doors, taken on romantic rambles and serenade the ladies. The guitar symbolized a certain carefree enchantment, an ecstasy of poetry, music and nature, miraculously intertwined. It's no accident, surely, that the other important composer of the early romantic period, Carl Maria von Weber, also—like Berlioz—played the guitar, though *he* in fact did write for the instrument from time to time. It was, moreover, a useful harmonic instrument to have around as Schubert found; if you were a composer and you were travelling, for example, you couldn't travel with a grand piano, but you *could* travel with a guitar. Frankly, I'm surprised that Berlioz, Weber or for that matter Schubert, didn't write more for the instrument. Would it be that when they looked at the compositions of Sor or Giuliani, who were the recognized virtuosos, on paper the virtuosos' music looked rather dull and ordinary? It's only in performance that this sort of music really comes *alive*. You can be sure, when virtuosos such as Sor or Aguado played it, they would have infused their music with a panache, brilliance and style which obviously must have been riveting; because if it hadn't been riveting, they would have lost their beer money, wouldn't they? What I call "The Performance Factor", then as now, was vital to nineteenth-century guitar music.

'Also, you have to remember that the concert world in the nineteenth century was totally different from ours. There were few performers who could play for a whole evening and bring it off; Paganini was probably the first, Chopin perhaps the second. Most if not all recitals were shared events. You'd have a singer, perhaps a pianist, and sandwiched in between you might have a guitarist. Within that framework it would be rare for a performer to play a whole sonata, only a movement or at best two. And these evenings were held not in formal concert halls, but largely in the salons of the aristocracy. I don't think Sor or Giuliani ever gave a solo recital—it's certainly not on record. And because there was no Beethoven, Schubert or even a Chopin writing for the instrument, by about 1840 the guitar was again beginning to recede in popularity—the quality of its literature could not sustain it through. By 1850, for instance, there was not one player in France, Italy, Germany or Spain of any real eminence. In fact, eventually the guitar was hardly used at all, except as an accompaniment to the voice in ballads and music of a light, frothy character. It had become a colourful accessory to the European musical tradition. The guitar was beleaguered by its soft and tender sound—Verdi used it in his operas as such—but throughout the nineteenth century composers wanted music and their instruments to project sonorities of greater brilliance and intensity; the guitar was just not capable of supplying what was needed. The piano was, though, and did.

'But then, late in the nineteenth century, there was change in the air for the fortunes of the guitar. In 1862, a young guitarist called

Francisco Tárrega went to a concert being given by a gifted performer called Julian Arcas. Tárrega was so amazed by the sound of Arcas's instrument that he insisted on meeting its maker. Tárrega's patron was then a wealthy businessman, Antonio Canésa Mandayas, and it was he who arranged for the young Tárrega to meet one Antonio de Torres Jurado. Initially, Tárrega was shown one of the less distinguished instruments on display, but the story goes that when Tárrega began playing it, Torres was so impressed that be brought out his finest instrument, with the back and sides made from maple wood, which is unusual in a Spanish instrument. Canésa bought the guitar, and with it Tárrega began his distinguished climb to world fame, or at least world fame within the context of guitar history.

'Antonio de Torres Jurado had been born near Almeria in 1817 into a family which made guitars and had a guitar shop. As quite a young man, he developed a theory that it was the size and shape of the guitar, and in particular the soundboard, which actually affected the tone of the instrument. Thus the choice of wood for the sounding board was of crucial importance. The grain must be neither too coarse, as it might be in inferior young timber that was still growing, perhaps in the wrong soil conditions, nor too fine as it might be with old, much weathered timber grown high up on a northerly mountain slope. The soundboard should, ideally, be made from spruce or pine, from a plank about 8 millimetres in thickness which is cut into halves of equal thickness to provide the two halves of the soundboard. These are glued together to make the complete sound table. Then, to strengthen the construction and provide the maximum flexibility of the vibrating sound table, Torres devised a system of internal bracing, with a distinctive fan shape based on an earlier method sometimes used by the fine guitar and bow maker Panormo. Previously, the old system of strutting had only been used to brace the wood against the pull of the strings. But, by a modified fan shape, Torres discovered that he could achieve the same mechanical, engineering function, while giving the instrument greater clarity of tone, particularly in the bass register. This was also helped by increasing the length of the strings on the instrument by a couple of centimetres, which of course increased the proportions of the whole instrument to a size that was to become standard for many years. Torres also invented the modern bridge, on which the strings are fastened or tied. The placing of this bridge became an integral part of Torres's constructional design, in that it became the central pivot for the activation of the sound table itself.

'Tárrega soon realized that the existing repertoire for the guitar was inadequate for an instrument made by such a man, and within a comparatively short time he had transcribed for the guitar works by Chopin, Mozart, Schubert, Schumann, Mendelssohn, Verdi, Beethoven, Bizet, Berlioz and, most important of all, he was a pioneer in our rediscovery of the music of Bach. Tárrega's prodigious technique meant that no music was beyond him, in the sense of it being beyond transcription. Some of Tárrega's arrangements, like that of Beethoven's "Moonlight Sonata" or the *Pathétique*, might seem to us today a little adventurous. For the first time, however, it became apparent that the guitar was an instrument that could not be ignored by the world of serious music.

'Tárrega also toured Europe, often with very strange companions. There was one man, for instance, an Englishman, who had made a lot of money speculating in South American mines. Becoming a patron and pupil to Tárrega, just travelling round the world having a good time, was one way of spending it. Tárrega always led this sort of hand-to-mouth existence, because it was always difficult in those days to find a sympathetic patron who would support you. Especially for a guitarist. It was just a case of taking whatever came along, I guess.

'But we mustn't lose sight of the fact that although Tárrega's performances were vital in re-establishing the guitar as a serious concert instrument, it was his teaching and above all his radical re-appraisal of both left and right hand technique that singles him out as the greatest innovator in the evolution of the guitar. Before Tárrega, right hand technique for instance was largely a re-hash of the old lute system, the hand being supported by the little finger which was placed on the soundboard, and generally near the bridge, where the tactile feel of the string was tight and therefore secure.

'Tárrega was a romantic, however, and the guitar that Torres had built had given him possibilities of tonal nuance that were absent from earlier instruments. A new approach to technique was inevitable, if the full expressive resources of the new Torres guitar were to be exploited. This Tárrega worked on and developed to the day he died, but ironically he never wrote a method or tutor. He just handed down his revelations to his devoted pupils, of which the most distinguished was the Catalan, Miguel Llobet.

'It is also important that Tárrega's international fame as a virtuoso coincided with the emergence of a national school of composers in Spain, of which the best known are perhaps Granados and Albéniz. Now it may seem quite extraordinary that some of the most famous pieces in the present day guitar repertoire by these two composers were not in fact written for the guitar. Neither Granados nor Albéniz played the instrument, and many of their pieces which we now think of as so typically guitar music are in fact transcriptions by Tárrega or Llobet of their piano music.

'Tárrega died in 1909, the same year as—in Granada—the greatest virtuoso of all was making his professional debut: the sixteen-year-old Andrés Segovia. The two never met, sadly, although it was Tárrega's pupil, Miguel Llobet, who introduced Segovia to Tárrega's work. Strangely enough, Segovia had to contend at first with a fair amount of hostility from Tárrega's followers. One of them, Daniel Fortea, refused permission for Segovia to see any manuscripts of Tárrega's unpublished transcriptions. Towards the end of his life, Tárrega believed that the best guitar sound could only be achieved with the fingers, and not the nails. Segovia preferred the nails, which immediately brought a heap of abuse from the disciples of Tárrega.

'None the less, he based his early repertoire largely on the work of Tárrega. But he had a great struggle on his hands, and only his indefatigable determination to bring the guitar as a serious recital instrument to the musical public throughout the capitals of the world won him through. When he decided to go on a tour of South America in 1920, I've read somewhere that he found his repertoire contained only enough material for about two recitals. Amazing, isn't it? It was this situation that initiated Segovia's lifelong quest to build a modern repertoire for the instrument from scratch, which he has continued to do since the early twenties and with commendable success. It was slow going at first, but later on contemporary composers were literally queueing up to write works for Segovia.

'The first composer to write for Segovia was Moreno Torroba. Torroba very quickly produced a number of highly effective pieces which have formed an important part of the repertoire of every international virtuoso ever since. The famous *Sonatina* in A, for instance; the *Suite Castellana*, the *Nocturno* and his *Pièces Caractéristiques*. Indeed, the *Sonatina* was one of the first pieces that I recorded way back in the mid-fifties. It must be said that although Torroba's music makes no great demands on the listener, it has pleasant melodic invention and atmospheric charm. Formally, it is simple but well made. It is, moreover, some of the earliest music written especially for the guitar that is almost inconceivable on any other instrument. By using the guitar in an evocative manner, Torroba made sure that the guitar was firmly identified with Spain and Spain with the guitar; and his success, however limited in musical terms, inspired a host of other and perhaps more gifted composers to try their hand at writing for the instrument.

'Manuel de Falla had already written a very beautiful and significant piece for the guitar, entitled *Homenaje pour le tombeau de Claude Debussy*, composed at the request of Miguel Llobet in 1920, although Segovia has claimed that Falla had been prompted by Torroba's example. Actually, the piece has a strange history. In 1919, the year after Debussy died, the editor of *Revue Musicale*, a posh critical periodical published in Paris, had asked Falla if he would write an article in tribute to Debussy. Having thought about it for some time, Falla hit upon the idea of writing some *music* in memory of Debussy, satisfying both the editor of the *Revue Musicale* and Llobet's request for a piece. So the piece is really a tribute to Spanish music, inspired by a Frenchman who was himself much inspired by the ambience of Spanish culture; in fact, some people believe that Debussy wrote some of the finest "Spanish" music. And I must confess I am inclined to agree. It was thus Debussy's debt to Spain and Spanish folklore that inspired Falla, and gave Falla the notion of writing a piece for the guitar—the national instrument of Spain.

'Curiously enough, Falla, who was undoubtedly the finest Spanish composer of this or any other century, never wrote anything further for the guitar, not even a companion piece to go with the *Homenaje*, which is only a short elegy. Benjamin Britten, who much admired the work, told me once that he always felt that the *Homenaje* was a twenty-minute piece condensed and distilled into four minutes, which is a great tribute to Falla's remarkably concise and concentrated control of musical form. There are, as a matter of fact, one or two of his other pieces that work quite well in transcription, in particular the *Farruca* from the ballet *The Three Cornered Hat.*

'I really enjoyed transcribing this piece, because Falla in this instance has made the orchestra sound like one gigantic guitar. I went straight to the orchestral score. I didn't bother with Falla's own transcription for piano. Having made the first draft, I then studied very carefully the orchestral score of Falla's own transcription of the guitar *Homenaje*. Having studied how Falla has made the small voice of the guitar sound like a gigantic orchestra, it was musically fascinating to pursue the reverse procedure in the *Farruca*. Just to complete the picture of confusion, when I occasionally want to refer to the guitar score of *Homenaje*, for some strange but quite practical reason I look at Falla's piano version of the piece. For when the music is laid out in two clefs, it gives a much clearer linear picture of the composer's precise intentions, than the over-cluttered single stave which is the usual method of notation in guitar music.

'It can be said that the *Homenaje* was the piece that brought the romantic guitar into the twentieth century. And it was Falla too who wrote in the preface to a famous teaching method by Pujol that the guitar "was the instrument most complete and richest in its harmonic and polyphonic possibilities". The lucky coincidence that there was also around a great virtuoso, Andrés Segovia, to demonstrate these possibilities, meant that soon the repertoire for the guitar found itself augmented, one could almost say besieged, by new pieces.

'One of the composers of these was Joaquín Turina, for instance, whose powerful yet evocative *Fandanguillo* was the next major work for the guitar; and there was another Joaquín, Rodrigo, who some years ago wrote *Fantasía para un gentilhombre* for Segovia, and many years earlier that incredible old warhorse the beautiful *Concierto de Aranjuez*, dedicated to Regino Sainz de la Maza. Then there was the Florentine, Castelnuovo-Tedesco, who wrote among other things a charming Guitar Concerto. Segovia's South American tours also fired the imagination of the Brazilian composer, Heitor Villa-Lobos, whose Concerto, Studies and Preludes are among my favourite pieces by any guitar composer. He has that marvellous quality of being deeply romantic, but without being vulgar. Perhaps his music does on occasion border on vulgarity, but it is the performer who must draw back from the brink. Myself, I love throwing discretion to the winds from time to time and giving his music a bit of extra umph, which brings out the intensely Brazilian character of the music. His gestures are large, sometimes pretty humid, always warm and often very beautiful. Segovia had first met Villa-Lobos in 1924; later, when he received the *Twelve Studies* dedicated to him, he wrote in the preface to the first edition: "Villa-Lobos has made a gift to the guitar's history . . . *as vigorous and wise as that of Scarlatti or Chopin*". Unlikely bedfellows, but I know what he means.

'We must not forget the Mexican composer, Manuel Ponce, who wrote a vast amount of music for Segovia, including a concerto; Ponce was prolific—a *Sonata Clásica* (a pastiche of Sor), a *Sonata Romántica* (a pastiche of Schubert), a third *Sonata* (probably a pastiche of himself), *Tres Canciones Populares Mexicanas*, twelve Preludes, twenty variations on *Folía de España* for starters. It's breathtaking, when you think, just what Segovia managed to inspire. And all this, of course, doesn't take into account his other important achievement, really a consolidation of what Tárrega had begun—Segovia's transcriptions of Bach, Handel, Haydn, Mozart and Chopin. These caused quite a ripple among the musical cognoscenti in Europe. Indeed, his performances of Bach's great D Minor Chaconne in the twenties must have been a revelation for those who heard it. The twenties were a period in musical history when the serious appreciation of Baroque music, and attendant performing practices of that music, were just beginning to manifest themselves. There is no doubt in my mind that the greatest single influence in Baroque music at this time were the plucked strings of Wanda Landowska's harpsichord, and it was therefore natural that the ravishing plucked sound of Segovia's guitar should fall upon eager and sympathetic ears.

'The whole idea of a solo recital was also at this time becoming a newly accepted part of the concert world. Segovia was among the very first virtuosi to tour the world as a solo recitalist, and whatever the merits of other guitarists around at that time, they were left out to grass in the provinces by comparison.

'Some people, including I must confess myself, have been critical of Segovia for encouraging what are best rather conservative composers of the twentieth century to write for the guitar, with the result that for a long time the guitar repertoire has seemed a bit undistinguished. After all, all the pieces written for Segovia were composed way after Stravinsky's *The Rite of Spring* and the early atonal piano pieces by Schoenberg. And as charming and effective as the best music is by Ponce, Castelnuovo-Tedesco, Tansman, Torroba and the others, the two best works written for Segovia were in my opinion *Segovia* Opus 29 by Albert Roussel, and the *Quatre Pièces Brèves* by Frank Martin, neither of which he played, though he may have given the Roussel a few airings before the War. But the point is this; the Roussel, for instance, has far more originality and intrinsic musical personality than all the very best music of the other composers I mentioned above. What is more, though it is difficult to play, it is most effectively laid out for the instrument.

'Likewise the Martin pieces. Martin had a rare and distinguished musical gift. He was a real thinker about musical form and how best to handle his inspiration and ideas within that context. The pieces themselves are not great inventions, but a fascinating resumé of musical thought and influence at the time they were written

(1933). They are a persuasive amalgam of neo-classicism, atonality, polytonality, and, just for good measure, tonality. They are pieces of great character; not show-stoppers, but fine repertoire pieces none the less.

'There *is* a guitar part in the opera *Wozzeck* by Alban Berg, and in several chamber works by Anton Webern, as well as in Schoenberg's *Serenade*. But it's sad that none of the great composers of the first half of the twentieth century wrote anything special for the guitar as a solo instrument; nothing from Stravinsky, or Prokofiev, Bartók, or Ravel.

'None the less, much of the music that was written for Segovia's guitar was eminently suited to the instrument; it captured the audience's imagination, and allowed Segovia's beautiful sound and prodigious technique to dazzle them into believing that not only was something *really* happening, musically speaking, but it was happening on an instrument that must now be taken seriously intellectually. The Spaniards are by nature, one might say, an old-fashioned and conservative people. The Spanish spirit was never thwarted by the industrial revolution and their insularity to the world outside is often arrogantly guarded. So I don't think you should be too surprised that they write conservative music; and perhaps the very identification of the guitar with Spain and with Spanish folk culture, which Segovia naturally encouraged, may have held up the guitar's progress toward a more universal musical integration. Who knows? The more neutral sound of the piano, for instance, perhaps gave composers greater scope, uncluttered by national lineage and folk-lorical considerations. For many composers, the guitar may have had too much evocative colour, too many subjective associations.

'There is also another point. If the composers who wrote for Segovia had written very avant-garde music, the audience could have been disenchanted by the originality of the music and may have blamed the musical insufficiencies of the guitar or Segovia for that matter! In which case, the maestro's crusade for the guitar could have suffered a setback. So while Segovia may not have given to the younger generation of players a repertoire of great music, he's certainly given us a repertoire of *effective* music.

'The guitar, after all, is an instrument of the senses rather than the intellect; it can convey beautifully a delicate thread of poetry. And it is the constant reminder of such a thread in this, the noisiest and most violent century in history, that I believe to be Segovia's greatest achievement. What he did not do, or was not temperamentally disposed to do, was to take the guitar and its repertoire into the second half of our century. This is perhaps an area where I myself have had some measure of success.'

'The story of the guitar, therefore, has always been linked with particular performers who, in their turn, have always been associated with particular guitar makers. We've already mentioned Julian Arcas and Torres, and the generation before there had been Fernando Sor and Lacote. For many years Segovia always used a guitar made by the great Spanish maker Manuel Ramirez. Later he used a German instrument by Hermann Hauser of Munich. So, I suppose instinctively, once I had begun my own career, I began to look around for a guitar maker who could make an instrument which really suited me. And when I moved into the country, I bought an old farmhouse for a song quite near to where I live now. This was in 1967. It was an old stone Elizabethan farmhouse which had built on to it a nice old Victorian brick cow stall which I thought would make a perfect workshop. And so I set to work on the conversion. I took out all the old cow stalls and put in some windows which opened up the magnificent views of the surrounding countryside, and had it all made very comfortable.

'Just prior to this, however, I had met a fellow called David Rubio who was just beginning to make a name for himself as a guitar maker in New York. At that time, he was doing mostly repairs, and it was in the guise of a repair man that I had met him initially. From about 1960 I had been playing French instruments made by that dear man and fine luthier, Robert Bouchet. He made three instruments for me, the second one being an absolute pearl. It had a beautiful sound, and a sustaining quality throughout its whole register rather like a small eighteenth-century organ. I treasured this instrument like no other, until in mid-December 1962 it was stolen from my car. I was shattered, and I just couldn't believe that the Gods on high could be so cruel, so thoroughly unreasonable. I asked Bouchet to make another guitar, and—fine instrument though it is—it has never had the life and magic of that earlier instrument. Nevertheless I played it for a few years thereafter, and it was this instrument that I brought to Rubio's workshop in New York for a couple of running repairs to the bridge and, as I remember, a few frets. He also had in his shop two or three damn good spruce soundboards. I was so impressed with one of them, that I had no hesitation in suggesting to him that he make a copy of my Bouchet. This he did, and quite successfully. As a result we struck up a close friendship, and both of us got very interested in the design of different instruments. He had been born in England, and when he mentioned one day that he wanted to return, I suggested that he come and settle in the neighbourhood and use the workshop that I was renovating. He was pleased with the idea, and came to work here on guitars and lutes from 1967 till about 1969. Eventually, he became so successful that he moved off and bought his own place near Oxford.

'So now I had this empty workshop, with nobody in it, and I thought what a terrible waste. About this time I managed to buy a lovely old Blüthner grand piano, very reasonably, at a local auction. It was in rather poor condition, but it obviously had, as pianos go, a beautiful quality of sound. Now as I rather like playing the piano a bit, I thought at least I must get the bloody thing in tune so I must find a tuner; and a friend in the village said oh, there's a very nice man called Michael Johnson who lives in Devon and tunes pianos, why don't you get him? So he arrived one day and he too thought it was a marvellous old piano. "As a matter of fact," he said, "I also do a bit of piano restoration. If you want that restored, I'd absolutely love to do it." So I said, well why don't you go ahead and do it? And he did.

'One day, he was complaining that Devon was really too far from London; he was finding the travelling too much, and he would someday have to find a workshop nearer to the city, where, hopefully, he could attract more business. So I said to him, well why don't you come and use the workshop I've got here! He didn't take much persuading. Whereas there had been lots of guitars and lutes made in the workshop, now there were lots of dusty old grand pianos anxiously waiting for the restorer's hand. Johnson also had a great yen to build a harpsichord. I was a bit dubious at the time about the wisdom of building a harpsichord, but he stuck to his guns and today he's one of the very finest harpsichord builders.

'So, like David Rubio, Johnson became successful and moved off to start his own business a couple of valleys away. But before Johnson's move José Romanillos turned up. At last, I thought, the workshop will be used for what I had always intended: a place in which to make guitars and lutes, and in particular an instrument or two for myself. A year or so earlier, somebody had just rung me up out of the blue and said I've got a Spanish friend who makes guitars in his spare time, and he would very much like to show you an instrument he's just finished. I often get requests to see instruments that people have made, and I was only sort of half enthusiastic. But I must have said yes, because he arrived about a week later in the pouring rain, and I said well come in. Romanillos showed me his instrument, and I could see right away that he had a great enthusiasm for the guitar, and that the instrument was quite well made, although the design of it seemed to me wrong for a really good classical instrument. It was just a good Spanish guitar, very suitable for folk music or flamenco. So I suggested some modifications to the design, and about nine months later he came back again. "I've made another one," he said; "would you like to have a look at it?" I had to admit that it was a great improvement over the earlier model, and in particular I noticed that the overall workmanship was much more refined.

'At that time, I was giving my Bouchet a rest and was playing a recently acquired German guitar, just like Segovia's, made by Hauser. There is something extraordinary and special about them; at their best, magical instruments. The one I'd acquired was a good instrument, but it was made in 1936 and needed a few minor repairs. So I said to Romanillos, look here, why don't you repair my Hauser? But before you repair it, I want you to do a very difficult thing. I want you to take the back off very carefully and make accurate drawings of the whole inside design so that we can try to copy it. I also said that now is the time he should decide whether he was going to be a guitar maker full time, because if he really wanted to I could let him have some space in the workshop. But I added that he'd better ask his wife about this—because I knew he had a family—and I just didn't want to put him in a position whereby he would go broke; because then I would have an understandably irate wife at my throat for encouraging José to leave his regular job in order to make guitars, and I'd naturally be in one hell of a state. I'll tell you what I'll do, I said to him, after giving the matter some thought; I'll commission six guitars from you, if you'll make copies of that old Hauser. I asked him how much he was earning as a builder's carpenter, which I think in those days was £15 a week. And so I said to him, well, I'll just keep you going while you're making these guitars, because they can't possibly be all bad; we'll sell a few off at a reasonable commercial price, and you can have the profit. And if one of those instruments is *really* good, I'll buy it from you at a fair price. So he said he'd talk it over with his wife, and next day he rang me back and he said they'd both agreed to the idea and he'd like to start in a month's time. And so he did.

'Eventually, he made those six guitars, and one of them turned out really quite good, another was reasonably good, and the other four were undistinguished but quite acceptable. We managed to sell off three of the instruments quite reasonably. I kept one and he kept one and we lent one to a mutual friend. He then proposed to make two more, and the *eighth* guitar he made was an unusually good instrument. So I began to use this instrument for some of my concerts, and very soon guitarists were wondering who this chap was, Romanillos, who'd made such a splendid instrument. His name eventually got around, and he gradually picked up enough business to keep him going on a permanent basis.

'So now there was Romanillos making guitars, Johnson making harpsichords, and soon I was introduced to a very nice chap in California called Anton Smith who wanted to make lutes and who also wanted to come to Europe. He had previously trained as a lute maker in Germany, but he appeared keen to work with me. About four months later he just turned up; nowhere to live, of course, very Californian. So I arranged to get an old caravan which I put next to the workshop and he lived in the caravan. By this time I just loved the idea of this workshop, because our little corner of England is inhabited largely by retired people. The real industry of the countryside is of course farming; but the populations of village farming communities have fallen in recent years as the influx of larger and more sophisticated machinery has replaced human toil. It seemed to me that some revitalization of village life would be no bad thing, and why not with craftsmen making musical instruments? Now not only had I an instrument workshop right on my doorstep, which gave me interest as well as pleasure, but these craftsmen were a pleasant bunch of chaps.

'The next step, of course, was setting up a Festival where all these craftsmen could put their work on display before the public. So with my friend George Malcolm, the harpsichordist, we set up a festival in the village church, which was not only a showcase for the chaps in the workshop to show off their wares, but also an attempt to give the village some idea of what was going on in this crazy cow stall. I remember, my new lute made by Smithy was finished just two days before the opening concert. The polish was still tacky.

'Sadly, not long after, I ran into some financial difficulties; my domestic life was characteristically in upheaval; I was in the throes of divorce, and in every other way everything seemed to be going wrong. I was also badly in arrears with my income tax. I felt as though I was in the grip of some terrible destructive force and without the necessary tenacity to combat it. So I had to sell this old farmhouse with the workshop in order to raise some money. I was broken-hearted, and not least because I felt I'd let the chaps down. But they took it very well, and José, the guitar maker, managed to use a small corner of a workshop which Michael, the harpsichord maker, had luckily found nearby. So they were all right. As for "Anton the Lute", I have lost contact with him, sadly; he was a remarkable craftsman, and whenever he pulled his finger out he made a damn good lute. Today, although the instrument workshop no longer exists as such, one good thing that came out of that experiment is my present guitar as well as my lute.

'Every player I suppose has an ideal sound that he wants to make, and with luck he gets an instrument made or purchases an instrument which helps him towards that ideal. I was brought up on a real mixture of guitars. When I was young I played Panormo or Lacote guitars, which were originally made around the 1820s. They were small instruments and I used gut strings which produced a tone that was fine and clear, although not strong enough to fill a medium-sized concert hall. Thereafter, and for the next twenty years of my performing career, I largely favoured instruments made by Hermann Hauser Senior, from Munich. I say Senior, because his son also makes instruments.

'Hauser, who I believe started as a maker of zithers, was very clever in the way he approached the building of a guitar. His finest instruments were made in typical mid-nineteenth-century Viennese style, instruments that were not really suitable for romantic or Spanish—or for that matter modern music, in that they were too inflexible and characterless in their sound. But when, in the early 1920s, Hauser heard Miguel Llobet giving a recital in Munich, he asked afterwards to see his guitar. Llobet was playing at that time a marvellous old Torres guitar, and Hauser asked Llobet if he could borrow the instrument in order to study its construction with a view to copying the instrument. The Torres guitar usually had a rich, deep velvet quality in the bass, but the response on the treble strings could be patchy and in the higher register even less *consistently* vibrant. So Hauser brought his Teutonic engineering principles to bear on the problem, and the final result—after a long, painstaking apprenticeship—was a magnificent instrument that nobody has been able to reproduce since. Several guitar makers, including Romanillos, have taken apart Hauser's instruments to find out what made them so special, but have then failed to reproduce exactly their special qualities. Even Hauser's son, who inherited his father's design templates, wood, tools and presumably some genes, failed to make a comparably great instrument.

'The older I get, the more I realize that each maker somehow builds into his instrument quite a lot of his own personality. And a great instrument maker to my mind has to be somewhat crazy, a bit round the bend. For example, I was told by somebody who knew Hauser well, that his greatest pleasure in life was to sit at home after a hard day's work with his feet in a tub of very hot water, drinking a Stein of strong Munich brew, while listening to his latest instrument being played by whoever was around. I mean, that's quite eccentric isn't it?

'I've never possessed a great Hauser guitar myself, although I do own two very good ones. The German instrument has what I can only describe as the very essence of classicism in guitar sound; the integration of the different registers of the instrument, whether in the extreme high positions or in the low, achieves a balance which is remarkable. The bass is deep but finely focused; it is sustained but has great clarity. The treble strings have a bell-like quality and a sweetness of tone that is never cloying. The third string which, on most instruments, can sound tubby and lacking a true centre, on a great Hauser has a profound ring about it, and when played softly is quite magical. And because of this concentrated focus and clarity of sound, and its consequent fine separation of detail in both contrapuntal and chordal music, this type of guitar is ideally suited for use as a concert instrument.

'Strangely, many guitarists find this type of instrument rather cold, even a little impersonal. But the real secret of it is this: it will produce whatever sound the performer wants, providing he or she knows how and where to find it. The instrument demands that the player should have a strong musical point of view in realizing everything he does, as well as the imagination to distill this point of view through his heart, his head, and above all in his finger ends.

'I suppose it is natural, however, that most people tend to think that a Spanish guitar must be the best; but it always surprises me that, for instance, no one thinks the Irish should make the best harps or the Balinese the best flutes. Certainly there have been, and are some fine makers in Spain, but they tend to construct instruments which have a preponderance of bass resonance over the treble. The treble sound on the Spanish guitar so often tends to drop away in quality, although I must confess that the modern Spanish instruments, most notably those by Fleta or even Ramirez do seem to achieve a better balance. Many Spanish guitars, however, are prone to an unevenness of response. On one string, for example, two or three notes can be of really inferior quality, while most of the others can have an almost ecstatic beauty. But if you're playing a Bach fugue, or any other contrapuntal piece for that matter, you cannot afford to take risks with an instrument of uneven response, however lovely it may be for playing Granados!

'I think Segovia realized this in the 1930s. So when Hauser produced a really magnificent instrument for him in 1937, Segovia gave up playing his old Ramirez guitar in favour of the German instrument. Naturally this caused a huge furore among the nationalistic aficionados, and not a little contempt for their Hispanic hero. But it is an interesting reflection on human nature when harnessed to extreme nationalism, that many of those people who objected to

Segovia playing on a German instrument in 1937, may well have approved the import of German bombers and bombs in order to desecrate each other and their country with a bit of style—a weird inconsistency somewhere!

'Segovia's instrument was very lightly made. The wood thicknesses, for instance, were exceptionally thin. With Hauser, everything was pared down to its absolute minimum. You can imagine that a guitar must have a lot of strength to hold itself together; so Hauser, with a typically German scientific approach, managed to find out how to pare away the wood keeping only enough to make the instrument strong and strong in the right places. The instrument is so delicate that you almost feel it will explode if you play a loud chord. As I've mentioned elsewhere, it's a false assumption that the bigger or the heavier the instrument, the louder it will sound. In fact, the greatest guitar that I ever played *was* Segovia's Hauser. Don't misunderstand me; I'm not for one moment underestimating Segovia's way of playing it, but the instrument itself was phenomenally beautiful.

'An uninformed person might think that it's the instrument that really produces the sound; a good instrument certainly helps, of course, but the sound, the spirit of that sound, is absolutely shaped by the performer. I could get a pretty good sound out of a £10 Japanese school model, but I wouldn't want to play it in a concert. So many people believe nowadays that if you acquire the right equipment such as an expensive and shiny guitar, the finest strings, the best professor, attend the right summer class and win the most prestigious competition, then you are going to make it through. Some may, of course, succeed in doing so. But those of us who have gone through the slow agony/ecstasy of evolving an individual musical personality know that it's not always the case. Far from it.

'Alas, fine guitars don't last forever. They mature for the first five years, and may stay much the same for another five years. But then—and it might be sooner—they begin to lose their original vitality. The sound can still have a beautiful veiled quality, but the wood eventually and inevitably loses its resilience. After all, when you pluck a string on a guitar, you take an awful lot of energy out of the wood and the instrument. If you can imagine a drum top being continually hit, it will eventually begin to sag. Then you have to tighten up the rim. But with the guitar, when it begins to sag you just can't tighten it up. One is always in search of a perfect guitar, if only as a second instrument if the original one packs up. But it just seems to be elusive. Today, of course, I have my Romanillos, which is an unusually fine instrument. But one day, I know that José will make a better one. After all, it took Hermann Hauser from 1923 to 1937 to make his masterpiece; thereafter he made glorious instruments right through until 1950 or so when he retired. He died a couple of years later. Someone once said to me, why is it, with so many marvellous violins on the market, that assuming you had all the money you needed you cannot just buy a guitar that you want. I'm afraid I just don't know the answer. Perhaps that's why I took up the lute!'

'I used to work in a lunatic asylum.'

"My materials", Romanillos told me, "They come from all over the world. I get the rosewood either from Brazil or from India, which is for the back and sides of the guitar. The sounding board or table is made from spruce and that comes from Switzerland. I managed to buy a few trees some time ago, when I went to Switzerland, so I've got a plentiful supply. As you can probably imagine, acoustically the sound board has to be made from the finest wood you can possibly get. I didn't like the idea of buying it through a dealer, so I decided to go the whole hog and find it in the forests. So I did. I think I've now got enough timber to last me until I'm about 110 years old.

"I only make about sixteen or eighteen guitars a year, depending on how many holidays I take, whether I'm sick or whatever. The turnover is very small, because I'm one of those fools who likes to control everything myself. I use hardly any machinery because I treat the wood and the guitar with great respect, which is one thing that I learnt from Julian; if you're going to do something in this life, it's worth doing well. There's no compromise.

"I'm not an appendage of Julian, you know. He never wanted it that way. I mean, he would never say to me you've got to do this or that. All he did was to bring the best instrument he could find for me to have a look at and criticize. He never tried to impose his will on me, although we've had our ups and downs. True, he has been playing my instruments, but he's not playing my instruments out of charity. I'm sure that if he found a guitar that he thought was better, he would play it. It's been a very clean and straight understanding between us."

'One of the many things I've found fascinating about José', Bream told me, 'is that he has a really intuitive feel about wood and about what he wants out of that wood and therefore out of the instrument. And that's why I think that we are such close friends, why we've spent so many wonderfully creative hours together. Actually, they've not *all* been wonderful. Sometimes, when an instrument is strung up for the first time, and we think that it should be marvellous—I mean, everything is there; beautiful wood, perfect dimensions, stunning workmanship—and you string it up, and it sounds really rather ordinary. And poor old José has put his heart into that for a month at least. It's a terrible moment, when you play it and you have to say to him, look, José, you know, you haven't got it this time. But don't you worry. There are some good points, but you'll have to try again. Could I suggest you might try this or that . . .? And this is how it goes in guitar-making. The instrument he built me in 1973 is a mixture of a Torres, a Hauser, not to mention a good bit of old Romanillos. It's got breeding, you might say. But Christ knows why it works. It's mad, really; a bit like the whole history of the guitar.'

4 'Quietly excessive.'

'Squire Bream, that's me. Or so I'm told. You've no idea how happy I am when I get home, back here to Wiltshire. Especially when I've been off on a long tour in Europe or America or Japan or wherever. Mind you, I've not been back a few hours before I almost begin to regret it. The bloody telephone starts going, and look—just look here, I mean, at the mountain of mail! But I'll tell you a tiny secret. I've got a little chest over there where I put all my mail. From time to time I take a peek, but most of it is from people wanting to know when I'm doing a master class, or else requests for signed photographs, new compositions, and a hideous number of brown envelopes—household bills. It's a hell of a lot to cope with. And anyway, I'm usually just beginning to cope with one little pile of mail, when I'm off on tour again; when I get back, I've got another lot, so in fact I never win, I have never yet cleared my desk. Never got ahead. The letters at the bottom of the pile, stay at the bottom, and never get answered. Now this, just occasionally, could be unfortunate. But generally speaking, after a considerable length of time I find that most letters answer themselves. Some people get disenchanted with you, naturally, or don't write to you anymore. Anyway, I don't want to know the worst that the world has got to offer me.

'So, after I've recovered from the mountain of mail, I have to think about the garden. The flowers get fed up, I find, if I don't look at them occasionally. I get back into my old clothes, because I've got a *lot* of old clothes. I'm very stingy about throwing away old clothes, I have a lot of jackets and trousers that are 15 or 20 years old. And I feel really comfortable in these very old baggy corduroy trousers. My suits all go away to the cleaners to be pressed up and made ready for the next tour. My touring wardrobe and my home clothes never mix; it's symbolic for me. I have clothes that I travel in and work in, and another whole lot of clothes when I'm at home. It's very important for me to try and keep my private and public life separate. There was a time when I never used to like people dropping in; I think my friends got wind of it, so they never disturbed me. But then I began to miss them; crazy, isn't it? I mean, you can't have it both ways. So now I love the odd visitor dropping by, particularly if it's someone I might enjoy seeing. I love giving parties; I love having people around in my big music room, over in the stables. I've given some very big parties over the years, sometimes over 40 or 50 people. Occasionally we have a country band in, and do quite a bit of dancing! Great fun.

'But I suppose the thing I miss most on tour is my food. I mean,

it may be more exotic abroad, but I do like coming back to the grub that I grow here; plus the good local cheese and bacon, and my wine cellar. It's so lovely to come back and have a simple meal and open a nice bottle of wine; I really feel I'm home. I've got quite a big vegetable garden. I grow peas, carrots, broad beans, runner beans, dwarf beans, courgettes, lettuce, spinach, radishes, winter cauliflower, cabbage, purple sprouting broccoli, and spring greens in the outside garden. Tomatoes and cucumbers in the greenhouse, melons in the compost, and I've also got blackcurrants, redcurrants, strawberries, raspberries, gooseberries, apples, plums and pears. I did think of keeping a cow once to have my own milk, because I've got a field big enough out the back. In fact, I've about thirty acres altogether; about 7 or 8 acres of woodland which I'm gradually re-foresting, and 22 acres of pasture land. My whole idea was to have enough vegetables to be self-sufficient. There have been times when I've almost managed twelve months without buying any vegetables. And, what's more, it's all fresh. I like that. It's the sort of thing that attracts me. Speaking of which, fancy a nose-bag?'

'I've given some very big parties over the years.'

The summer of '81 was notable in Britain for a Royal Wedding and more especially for two remarkable victories—'back from the bloody dead'—by England's cricket team over Australia. Bream is a cricket fanatic. 'What *about* the test match?' Bream asked me as we sat down to lunch. 'Now that was really something. Jesus, I nearly had a heart attack. The last couple of overs when England was finally bowling out Australia, that just about finished me off. I had three cigarettes burning. I mean, two is quietly excessive, but three!

'One of the great pleasures I get in life is bowling an over or two at cricket. I bowl very badly, but I get the same pleasure as a lot of professionals, probably more so because I haven't got to earn a living at it. We have a pleasant little cricket pitch not so far from here, about two miles away. Lovely setting, and I play against a friend of mine's team. He lives in the next parish. He's the Laird of the Manor. He has his friends and I have mine, and when the weather's good we spend a lovely day on the cricket field. I can't think of a more wonderful way of spending a summer's afternoon. Cricket is a team game, but it's individuals that make the team. Take that guy Ian Botham who went out in the second innings after it looked certain that England had lost. He just clobbered the daylights out of those Australians. That type of attitude towards life is extraordinary, because when all the chips are down, I mean, you normally play safe, don't you? I wish I had that sort of temperament.

'Myself, I'm a spin bowler of devious length and direction. I'm lousy, but I'm serious about it. I have my own cricket nets which I put up at the back of the house. I have six cricket balls and I'm quite happy just bowling to nobody. I put a small stone down roughly where I think an unplayable ball should pitch. I'm fascinated, bemused almost, by the spinning ball. And I love to bowl at a batsman who's good, and being able to find the weaknesses in his technique and being able then to exploit that. Now that probably shows me to be a rather nasty character. But I find that even when I'm playing table tennis I love to exploit other people's weaknesses. I'm sure Freud would have something to say about that. Truthfully, I don't want to make my opponent look a fool, and I don't want to humiliate him; but I just want to propose a propitious point.'

'I'm a spin bowler of devious length and direction. . . . I love to exploit other people's weaknesses.'

OPPOSITE
'I did think of keeping a cow once.'

65

Julian Bream

'I'll hand pick half a dozen people who will really appreciate what I'm giving them.'

'I like plain food,' says Bream as he tosses the salad. 'I like the raw materials to be good, fresh and wholesome. I mean, to go to a restaurant and have a really nice Dover sole absolutely screwed up with all sorts of sauces, seems to me a complete waste of a very good fish. Have you ever been to a restaurant where the vegetables are absolutely fresh in texture and taste—cooked to perfection? It's an improbability! For tonight, I've prepared some English lamb cutlets; do you like that? Because English lamb is so delicious this time of the year.

'Come on, have some radishes. A once in a lifetime offer. Look how lovely they look. Want some wine? This white wine is really dry and refreshing. Sancerre; I always think it tastes like mountain water running over flints. It's important to get one's priorities right, isn't it? It's so easy to get waylaid by other considerations. And a good wine makes the whole bloody difference. I get it from the Wine Society. Get my oil and vinegar from the same people.

'I was never really interested in wine until I moved down here. I decided I ought to get some sort of a wine cellar together. It was a good time to buy, it was in the mid-sixties before there was suddenly a ridiculous rise in the prices. And so I got some lovely first growth clarets; I've still got some of them, and I'll keep them until I find the right moment to drink them. Judging the right moment is important. I mean; I've got some wines laid down for my fiftieth birthday, and I've got some other wines laid down for my sixtieth, if I get that far. Wine drinking isn't really a solitary occupation. It's an occasion to share, a ritual almost. And often the very best wines are in private collections and not necessarily in restaurants. I often like bringing out a good bottle, even if there are one or two young people around who will probably never know what they're drinking. They might even prefer plonk. Nonetheless, I like sharing these things with people. In about two or three weeks, for instance, I'm having a small Château Latour supper party; we'll drink '52, '53, '67 and '61; we'll each have four glasses, just for the fun of it. I'll hand pick half a dozen people who will really appreciate what I'm giving them. Having bought all of these wines years ago, I don't think I paid more than a fiver each for the best of them—a damn sight less for some.

'Have a hunk of cheddar, and I'll cut some bread. I find that's a very good lunch. Bit of salad—there's some lovely little toms in there, just picked out of the greenhouse—bit of cheese, bit of fruit. Couldn't be better. How's the cheese? Not too tasty? You didn't eat that tomato; there is a tomato lurking there. I think you ought to eat it up. They're called "Gardener's Delight". They're small but very tasty. Do you mind if I smoke a cigarette? Good. I mean, there's no reason why *all* things shouldn't be delightful, is there? Problem is, they very rarely are. Things do go wrong. Boy, do I know that. Three bags full, yes sir, thank you very much, sir. Still, you must accept the fact that you can't have it all your own way.'

'As you know, originally I'm a Londoner, and for many years always lived in London. I had a marvellous flat in Bolton Gardens, South Kensington, which I rented for many years. And then in the early sixties, I bought a little coach-house near Strand-on-the-Green in Chiswick, which I loved. But, as I became more successful in my work, I found that London was becoming not such a good place to be in permanently. I had a lot of acquaintances there, and friends, but it was beginning to get really difficult to shut myself up and work. There were too many distractions; I mean some of them were very worthwhile such as the theatre, concerts, the art galleries and so forth. But the round of parties and pub life were beginning to take over, and quite honestly I was getting a bit bored with the whole social razzmatazz.

'I was also getting a bit disenchanted with London itself. It was changing. The streets were now bung full of motor cars. It was becoming more international, more cosmopolitan, and suddenly a lot more expensive, and for me personally it was beginning to lose a lot of its original character and atmosphere. And in any case a lot of my chums were moving out. So I decided I would have to have an escape hole somewhere. And as I love this part of England, the South-West, I thought the best thing to do was to come down and camp here. I bought a very expensive French tent and went on an extended camping holiday to Dorset taking with me a lovely girl who was later to become my first wife, Margaret. I went to Estate Agents all over the county, until I found a little cottage, which was charming, with a most beautiful view. So we moved in. It was an idyllic weekend cottage. But I soon found that it was much better to spend the *weekdays* down here, and the weekends in London. London seemed to be a much more civilized place at weekends. So, instead of the usual thing of having long weekends in the country, I did just the reverse. And eventually I grew so much to love it here, that I decided I would give up my little house in London and move to this part of the world altogether. The cottage was a bit small to expand in and make the centre of my activities, so when this present house came up for sale, I had no hesitation in buying it.

'It had previously belonged to a charming old General and his wife. He was an excellent amateur gardener; the garden was in very good nick when we took over, although I've done a tremendous lot to both the gardens and the house throughout the last 16 years. I've made the house what I've always wanted for my work and pleasure, a place in which I have time, time to reflect. Reflection can often be for me a visual experience. Not necessarily an intellectual "Yoga" exercise at all. I can look at a hill-top, or I can look at a rose, for a long time that is, and get a lot of peace and sustenance from that experience. I have a favourite hill-top near here which I return to very often. I used to spend a lot of time there; perhaps a couple of times a week for an hour or so. I found that it helped to clarify and de-clutter my mind; and also to some extent bring me down to earth. In the loveliest possible way, of course; cut me down to size. Because there's no doubt that if you begin to absorb nature as it is, certainly around here, it can have quite a significant effect on your personality. I don't mean to imply that if you moon about in a bucolic haze, the world will become a better place or you a better person. But being among nature and natural things really does give you a resilience to combat the material and sometimes destructive—and not least phoney—world in which you have to live and work.'

'Right, a petit tour de la maison, or at least part of it. My study was originally a dairy. In fact, underneath where the grand piano now stands, is a well! I purposely made that room as simple as I could; it's got lovely oak beams, so I put in an oak floor with white walls, because when I'm working I like plain surfaces. I don't want my concentration cluttered up with the aesthetics of curves, or the

textures of wallpaper. I just like honest wood and white paint. And that gives the room a feeling of lightness and clarity, which I find a good ambience to work in. That's why I call it my sweat-shop or my crotchet factory. Because I wouldn't want to read a book in there, for instance, although I write all my business letters and do all my household accounts there. I'd never write a personal letter there. Never. I would do that in the drawing room. That's the room where I read and endeavour to think.

'I don't have a television in either room, as you can see, but I do have a television in the kitchen, because it means that you can time a meal around the programme you might want to see. In theory, I hate the idea of television and all that it stands for. But there are

Julian Bream

'There's nothing like the sound of the leather on the willow.'

times when I can't resist it, particularly when a cricket match is on. So that means that you've got the meal *and* the TV programme in, without wasting too much time. Admittedly, sharing a television programme with the grub puts both in danger of becoming a half-experience.

'Although the house looks large, it actually isn't. It's only one room thick. It's long, but I like that, because you can move from one room to the other and perhaps back again as the day progresses. A bit prissy perhaps, but I play an awful lot of notes for the facility! Each room has a different feeling and purpose, and the decor and the type of furniture in each room express this variation of purpose—somewhat precious perhaps, but that's my business and nobody else's.

'Outside, in the next building, I converted a hay-loft into my music room as I told you, and I keep it for group practice with my friends or giving little concerts. Actually, to tell you the truth, I use it more for parties. And underneath the music room are two of my prize possessions: my 1947 M.G. TC. And . . . my prized cricket bat and gear. There's nothing like the sound of the leather on the willow. But have you noticed who made it? José Romanillos, from "Emley, Wiltshire". Actually, it should be "Semley", but it was not perfectly semleyficated.

'I got more interested in the outside of the house after my first wife and I broke up. She had managed the garden and organized everything. I had worked a bit on the construction of the garden—you know, the lay-out, but she did all the planting. When she left, I didn't know a wallflower from an onion. But nature doesn't stand still; it just carries on regardless of your own personal problems. I had to work very quickly; I got every gardening book I could find and just read like crazy for about two months. Then I went to visit other gardens to see how things were done. I mean, I've still got a hell of a lot to learn, so don't look too closely. But I've got a lovely collection of old-fashioned roses, for instance, that go back to the sixteenth century. I've got some rare species of rhododendron, which is quite amazing because this is not rhododendron country at all. It's clay, heavy soil and a little bit limey, and rhododendrons hate lime; or rather they love lime so much that they become limaholics and die. I brought in tons of leaf mould and completely changed the character of the soil. I just love to fiddle, I suppose. But the whole thing with gardening, or anything else for that matter, is to accept the fallibility of it all, to be forever optimistic, and not to insist on being a perfectionist when there is no point. Compromise, yes, but never lose sight of higher aspirations.

'I'm not a great mixer, in the normal sense of the word. I'm not exactly a loner either, but I cherish solitude. Also, I find it increasingly hard to be just a natural person in a local community such as the village down the road, because everyone knows what you do. They read about you in the newspapers, or they see you on the box, so it's difficult for them to accept someone who is an international musician as natural. I don't like the idea of trying to be what I am supposed to be; it makes me self-conscious. So I feel

70

a bit shy of mixing in the village. Which is why, for some years now, I've tried to run a little annual festival at the church. It's been my tiny contribution to the village, assuming they like it. It was the only thing I could do really. I mean, I don't go to point-to-points, and I don't go off on shooting expeditions, except against my own rabbits. So, most summers for the past ten years now, I have organized concerts over a long weekend in the local parish church. John Williams has come several times; Robert Tear, George Malcolm, Peggy Ashcroft, Jill Balcon, George Rylands, Laurie Lee, my old music Consort and many others. A classy lot, you could say. But after all, it's one's chums that one enjoys making music with.

'We only charged a £1 a ticket because I wanted the locals to come and bring their kids. I only paid £50 to each chamber player and a bit more for soloists. The essence of it all was a minimum of rehearsal, and then do the show. With just enough preparation, we could make the concert an event for us too. Mind you, we had to listen to each other very carefully, because if we hadn't we might have come unstuck. Perhaps we might have a run-through in the afternoon, have a rest or a game of ping-pong, then go and do the show. So the performances had a certain cliff-hanging quality which you wouldn't normally get in rehearsed, or even over-rehearsed, performances. I mean, we are actually sitting on the edge of our seats, watching each other like hawks. But that's what I reckon to be real music-making.

'As I've got older, I found that music for me is not just a question of music and then living; it's become more and more a question of living and then music, with the music expressing the living. What you do, what you feel, and the actions you take, is the essence of what you communicate through music. And this has become of vital importance to someone like myself, who is largely uneducated in the conventional sense of the word. Music is how I express myself. So I've found that my existence here, though it's not ideal in many ways—it's such a bore having property which you are forever having to patch up and forever having to watch over, what with the rabbits and the moles and the voles and the mice and the whitefly and the blackfly and the black spot on the roses; I mean, it's a continuous fight with natural adversity—but my life here is something which has become the perfect foil to the total commitment involved in trying to voice properly and elegantly the linear counterpoint of a Bach Fugue, for instance. A perfect foil, in fact, to my life on the road.

Now if you're a passionate person, which I most definitely am, it doesn't matter what you do in life, you're going to do it passionately. You're going to work passionately, you're going to love passionately, you're going to hate passionately. So if I wasn't worrying about the house, I might be worrying about the piston rings in the engine of my car. If you're built like that, that's how it is. So you need space. I like space in music, and I like space in my life. And where that all happens to me, is here. The expression of these things, of what I feel and what I experience here, comes out in the music I make on the road. This is the base where I can regenerate and think, re-think and feel, in order to go on pursuing my ridiculous international career. I suppose I could do it from a base in Paris or in New York; I could do it even in Baghdad. I could do it anywhere for that matter. But I happen to love England very much, and I happen to love this part of England especially. It represents roots, a place where I can be, dig in, and hopefully experience something wholesome, real and worthwhile. The question is that if you believe, as I do in moments of pessimism, you're living on a sinking ship, where do you want to go down? Do you want to go down in Santa Monica, in Venice, or do you want to go down in Sydney? You've just got to choose the place where you think it'll hurt the least. God, this is getting serious!'

'Have you noticed how incredibly quiet it is here? I'm told we're in what is called military airspace. We sometimes have a little jet nonsense on a Thursday afternoon, but there are no commercial airlines around. On Tuesday, in the summer, I believe there's a flight to the Channel Islands which the Military Authorities allow on sufferance, or so I am told. Apart from that, there's no other noise at all, except an occasional train across the valley which you can hear when the wind is blowing in this direction. I find that a rather friendly sound. There's a few cows over there in the field; just a feeling of gentle movement. I mean, it's so quiet here, most people would go crackers.'

5 'Bangs and crackles.'

Not a hundred miles west of Bream's home in Dorset is the modest town of Totnes in Devon, on the edge of Dartmoor; and two miles or so above Totnes is a remarkable community known as Dartington Hall. It has become famous as the home of a summer music school at which many great contemporary musicians from Stravinsky to Leonard Bernstein have taught or performed. Its history as a summer school is comparatively recent; however, the first event being held in 1947. Dartington Ham was the first recorded Saxon settlement west of Exeter, granted by the King of Wessex in 833 to Beorgwyn in exchange, ironically enough, for her land at Shaftesbury in Dorset, land which included Julian Bream's present home.

Dartington Hall itself was first built in 1385 by John Holland, half-brother to Richard II. They ate in what is now the concert hall, and jousted in what is now the Tiltyard. The Devon family of Champernown acquired the Estate in the later part of the sixteenth-century, but eventually let the buildings decay and the grounds become overgrown. In 1925 it was bought by Leonard Elmhirst, a passionate conservationist, who, with the considerable help of his rich American wife, Dorothy, restored the property and began using the land for experiments in rural reconstruction, not for archaeological purposes but out of a profound belief that each community must become aware of itself and its potential before it can make a substantial contribution to society at large. Thus, the Elmhirsts turned Dartington into a centre of research into agricultural economics, forestry management, textiles and glass, besides founding a College of the Arts and a Music School.

The summer school combines festival, school and holiday. It offers a residential course for any one week of its three week duration, during which the participants, young and old, can attend a galaxy of concerts by international soloists such as Victoria Posnikova and Rozhdesvensky, master classes, lectures, choral rehearsals, or else just play tennis, cricket, swim and listen to the music when the mood strikes. The present musical director is the composer, some think the leading composer of his generation, Peter Maxwell Davies. Davies has been commissioned by Bream to write a new piece for the guitar. Bream has returned to Dartington for the first time in eighteen years to give the world premiere of Maxwell Davies's new piece which is called *Hill Runes*, after a Viking monument near Maxwell Davies's home on the Orkney Islands, north of Scotland. Before the concert, Maxwell Davies and Bream 'discuss' the new piece.

'The balancing mechanism in one ear has gone completely to pot' . . . So a curtsey for Peter Maxwell Davies and Amaryllis Fleming at Dartington.

'Now the thing is, Max, you haven't heard me play this yet.'

'No, and if you'd like to do so before the concert, that would be wonderful. But I'm not going to press you, or worry you. I'm just so damn glad you're doing the concert.'

'Well I'm delighted too, but I must tell you something about the piece.'

'Go on.'

'Well, I think it *will* sound lovely, but I just wondered if we could actually go through the score with a tooth comb.'

'With a tooth comb?'

'With a tooth comb. You see, the opening is a bit hairy, a bit squeaky, so I've slightly modified it. Instead of five notes that go 'di a de a di', I've taken out one of the bass notes. But I think it

'And then there's this real raspberry . . . is there any reason why it shouldn't damn well be a G♭?'

sounds full enough. And these tremolandoes; well, I've had to fix them a bit too.'

'I see. Yes, that's OK.'

'Well, I'm glad you approve. And then there's this real raspberry, at the *subito piano* point. I've just taken out one chord, and then it's all feasible; slightly simplified, but I think fine. It's rather jazzy, in fact.'

'It's a sort of Scottish tune.'

'Well it sounds a bit like that, I must say, though it's rather bluesy to my ears. I wondered whether this note shouldn't be a G♭?'

'No.'

'Is there any reason why it shouldn't damn well be a G♭?'

'Oh well . . . Come to think of it, you're right, it should be G♭.'

'Now, do you remember we had such trouble with this passage? What I've done here is just taken that triplet out, put it in there, and taken that note out. I also took one note from this chord, but I give it a great *sforzando*, which makes it sound rather juicy. Then I think in this chord we ought to put in another note, just to give it an extra zing, at the top. I'd be very pleased to discuss anything else with you.'

'How do you do the ending, with the tremolando together with the harmonics?'

'Ah, that's one of my specialities.'

'A nose job is it?'

'Well I didn't go to the Royal College of Music for nothing.'

'How's your ear, by the way?—I hear it's been pretty bad.'

'Actually, I walk on stage sideways now. My vertical world is also at an oblique angle—it's not uninteresting.'

'Oh well, we'll come and catch you if you fall over.'

'I might have to take a curtsey instead of a bow. Anyway, I must go off now to do a little prac. and get nervous. See you later. By the way, if you could organize some grub before the concert, I'll be very grateful. Perhaps some low tea; pot of cha with two lightly boiled eggs, brown, of course.'

Also present, in the later part of the conversation is John Amis, the avuncular team-member from the BBC Radio and Television Musical Quiz Show, *My Music*. He is also the organizing secretary of the Dartington Summer School of Music. 'Perhaps you'd prefer

Julian Bream

'Run-of-the-mill job. . . . A little worried . . . but very stimulated. Château Loinville '61? Or Kangaroo?' John Amis as host.

a drink? Château Loinville '61?'

'Well, actually, I'd prefer a drop of gin and tonic. But after the concert.'

'We've got some good wine.'

'It's not supermarket plonk, is it?'

'No, certainly not.'

'Kangaroo? Have you come across that?'

'No I haven't.'

'They've got Australian wine here, you know. Kangaroo and Wallaby white. Quite good mouthwash.'

'Oh incidentally, Julian, Maxwell Davies is going to make a sort of warm up speech before the concert, this being the opening event.'

'Is this the *first* concert?'

'Yes, the first thing.'

'Oh crikey, it would be. Jesus, if you'd told me that, I would have done a bit more practice. I thought this was just a run of the mill job.'

'I tell you,' Bream told me later, 'I am a little anxious about this concert. Particularly playing Max's piece for the first time and from memory too. But not only that. There's the composer sitting in the audience who has never heard it either. It's very flattering and trusting of Max I must say, but I know I'm sailing pretty close to the wind doing the first performance from memory. Still, that's the sort of thing you can bring off at Dartington. I suppose it's because Dartington has a very special atmosphere for me. I admire the ideal behind this place so much, the re-invigoration of old things brought up to the very best standards without spiritually or materially harming them. All this wood; not highly polished, but exquisitely finished. The natural freestone walls beautifully pointed in, the gables and hips of the slate roofs that are so harmonious. The cobbled paths and the wonderful lawns. Simple, right and good. And it's funny how you can miss certain places. Dartington must have had a tremendous impact on me when I first came here 25 years ago. As you know, I haven't been here for about 18 years. And it's strange how the concert hall now looks a lot smaller; the

sort of experience that happens when you visit a place as a child, and return to it as an adult. But I suppose in the last 18 years I have played in hundreds of really large halls. And some of them quite unsuitable. That's why I love the intimacy of this place, and I'm sure that halls like this are my natural habitat. It's a pity that the humidity around here is so bad, it's almost impossible to stay in tune. The strings feel so soggy I'm playing on rubber bands. And it's an absolute bugger for the left hand trills. It's incredibly humid, like breathing water. Something to do with Dartington being half-way between the sea and the moors I believe. There are some days here. I tell you, when, even if it's not raining, you can hold out a cup and fill it with water.'

'Oh Max,' says Bream, having sorted out the particular problems of *Hill Runes*, 'I was just saying that because the humidity in Dartington is so high, it's an extraordinarily bad place for trills. The tips of your fingers become very soft; it's like playing with bits of damp blotting paper. Max, where will you be sitting during the concert?'
    'At the back.'

'Just sheer showmanship, I call that. I love a first performance when the composer is in the front row, and even before the last chord has been played, he's on his feet waiting for the applause. It reminds me of a Marx Brothers quip!' "And the boy gets a big cigar!" '

'Have you ever played in the Concertgebouw in Amsterdam?'

'Yes, why?'

'Because that is Karajan's favourite hall. Do you know why?'

'No.'

'He has to enter down that long flight of steps at the back of the stage; and because he can stop to bow or wave on every step, his entrance can take as long as the first act of *Parsifal.*'

'I've known Max Davies for over 20 years now,' Bream told me later. 'And I've always had a tremendous respect for his compositional skills and his incredible integrity. But somehow I've never felt that his musical language would fit naturally onto the guitar. But I heard the First Symphony not long ago, and I became aware that there was a lot in his musical personality that seemed to have developed or changed or both, and sensed there might be a good piece he could write for the box. You see, the guitar is a very evocative instrument, and it's difficult to get away from its warm and reflective overtones. Composers of astringent yet complex textures, like Max Davies, often find the colour of the instrument too personal, too exotic, and not abstract enough for their musical language. But having heard some of Max's more recent works, I felt he was in a musical period of his life when he was writing music that might be suitable and indeed even work well on the guitar. So I wrote to him, and I commissioned a piece from him. Just a straight commission.

'It's straight forward, really, commissioning music. It's like being engaged to do a concert; somebody offers you a date and a fee. Composers have to live, like everybody else. I was simply appalled about fifteen years ago when there was a survey made of all the composers of classical music in England; the average income from the music they composed was something in the region of £7.60 a week! Admittedly, that's fifteen years ago, but it's still not very much, is it? I've been commissioning music for over 25 years now. If the piece works out well and it gets performed a lot, perhaps recorded and broadcast, the composer will earn some extra bread from that. So the commission is, as they say in modern financial parlance, money up-front. But the money you give them doesn't in any way relate to the amount of work they have to put in.

'At the moment, for instance, I've commissioned Harrison Birtwhistle to do a piece for me. Now I don't know how long that will take him; but let's say it will take him two or three months. Nobody, particularly if they're married and have a family, can live reasonably well on less than £6,000 a year, can they? So if you reckon that Birtwhistle will spend a quarter of the year writing my piece, it has to be worth £1,500, doesn't it? But I can't afford to pay him that amount. I only earn *my* money through the notes I make on the old box. I don't earn it any other way. I don't have any take home pay. No regular employment. I'm in the market place. I can get what I can get, and have to pay for a whole lot of other things besides new music. Including a huge dollop to the tax boys.

'So after I've decided who I would like to write a piece for me, I just write off to the composer, to ask him if he is interested, and if so to suggest a fee. Sometimes there's quite a bit of haggling, you'd be surprised. With Max, for instance, it finally worked out that I did this Dartington concert for nothing. In lieu of the commission; although if I told you the commission, then I told you my current fee, Dartington did pretty well! But then, why shouldn't Dartington do well? It's a fine institution, and so I had no quibbles about that at all. The VAT office may feel it's a bit tough, but on the other hand, who cares?

'There's no standard rate for the job, that's the point. A commission of a thousand pounds would be enough, in my view, even for a fairly large work. And it's important, I sometimes feel, to commission a composer who is not doing so well, or is probably not so well known. A composer who is fashionable, and so in demand, usually has a lot of commissions to fulfil. You must take that into consideration when offering your fee, because if you *want* him to take on your commission, you have to pitch your offer both intelligently and fairly. A younger composer might be more grateful for the commission than the money, if you see what I mean.

'Of course, not all new guitar works are written to commission. Some are written because the composer wants to write them. Richard Rodney Bennett, for instance, actually wrote for me—I'm never too sure whether I actually asked him—a lovely little collection of miniatures called *Impromptus*. Then I heard later he was writing a guitar concerto, without any particular performer in mind. So I wrote to him and said, if you're writing this concerto, can I be of help, and can I do the first performance? And although, eventually, he very kindly dedicated it to me, it was actually a piece Richard just wanted to do. In fact, another guitarist helped him with the guitar writing of the concerto. I just happened to do the first performance of it.

'The first piece that was written especially for me was composed by Reginald Smith Brindle who wrote a Nocturne for me as early as 1947. And while I was still at the Royal College Stephen Dodgson, who was a fellow student, wrote a Suite of three pieces for me, which were among the earliest post-war pieces written for the guitar. He's written an awful lot for the guitar since, including two good concertos; and when I left the army in 1955, he wrote a collection of pieces to celebrate my abandoning the colours. But it wasn't until the mid-fifties, when my recording career had got under way, that I could actually afford new pieces, or was even in a career-cum-financial position to be able to pay for and play them. In 1957, Lennox Berkeley wrote a Sonatina for me, although that was commissioned by the BBC; Hans Werner Henze wrote some pieces for me, in *Kammermusik 1958*; and then, in the same year, Malcolm Arnold wrote the well known Concerto.

'When I first met Malcolm Arnold, I thought his musical style was in many ways the most suitable of any composer at that time for the guitar. Not only because he was harmonically a romantic composer, and the guitar is pre-eminently a romantic instrument, but because he also had an original quality of wit and the great gift for writing good tunes. The combination of these factors made his music ideally suited for the guitar. There's also a kind of simplicity; I don't mean naiveness, but a directness about his music and the forms he uses, a directness I find that especially suits the character of the instrument no less than myself. In fact, his Concerto was the first major British Concerto ever written for the guitar—not counting the one written by a Mr Ernest Shand, who was by profession a comedian, but also played the guitar and wrote a Concerto for it some seventy years ago.

'But the extraordinary thing about the Malcolm Arnold Concerto, apart from its intrinsic musical qualities is the scoring. It's miraculous, because the guitar dominates throughout the whole concerto, without amplification. The writing is also very idiomatic for the instrument, which for most English composers can set something of a problem.

'I'm ashamed to admit that, when I commissioned it, I only offered him the sum of £50, and I think he decided to write it because he realized that my offering even such a piddling sum showed I was really serious: in those days I wasn't at all well off, and 50 quid was a princely sum for me to shell out. Sadly, it isn't played very much now, partly because Malcolm wouldn't publish it; and I own the only copy of the Solo Guitar Score, though I have lent it to John Williams. But I do believe it's still one of his finest pieces. In fact I heard it quite accidentally on the radio the other day, and thought what a bloody marvellous piece it was.

'In my younger days, Malcolm Arnold was very important to me, not so much because of the pieces he wrote for me, lovely though they are, but simply because he was around at a time when extraordinary things were happening to contemporary music. In the fifties and early sixties the serial techniques of composition really caught hold, so it was refreshing to be with a man who still wrote music in the old traditional style, albeit with originality and exemplary skill. He was very brave; he had tremendous conviction about himself and his music, so he never changed his style. Perhaps he ought to have changed a little, or rather evolved a tiny bit more; but he never did, which may have been a pity because fashions change and I always felt sure there was more to Malcolm than met the eye or greeted the ear.

'He was also a marvellous companion. I used to see him quite regularly at one time. He was a great pub and club man. He liked his booze and he knew how to hold a glass as they say. But then, I must confess, so did I. Malcolm and I loved clubs. He was a member of several; so even when the drinking laws were very tight in London in the fifties, Malcolm had it all planned. It was possible to spend the whole day imbibing legally in different clubs. Which we did, of course, with relish.

'Now, Hans Werner Henze is an altogether different cup of tea.
The *Kammermusik 1958* I mentioned was dedicated to Benjamin
Britten, and written for Peter Pears and myself. It's a big cycle of
songs, guitar solos and chamber music, reflecting the late poems of
Hölderlin. Henze is an immensely practical man. He has determined
views about many things. He's essentially a dramatic composer, but
he's also written a lot of instrumental music inspired by the drama
of words. The words not only give the musical shape, but very
much inhabit the spirit of the music.

'He's also very fecund. Do you know what that word means? I
must look it up myself, actually. Fruitful, fertile, that's what I mean.
He's that sort of person. Having the ability to let it all pour out,
which in turn just creates more and more energy. He's got so many
ideas, his brain is so quick, and it's that quickness which creates the
energy, the speed with which he assesses things. He knows exactly
what he's doing, and this generates a super-abundant creativity.
It's phenomenal. But what is attractive about Hans is that he
always seems to have time for people. When he talks to you, it's as
though you are the most important person in the world at that
time. I dropped in to see him recently, during my tour of Italy. He
has a villa just south of Rome. There he was, rushing round the
room, with a little portable radio telephone receiver, dialling places
all over the globe, fixing this, fixing that. His new Sonata has one
or two problems which I wanted to chat through with him. But I

hardly got a word in edgeways. Tea, drinks, phone calls, tour of the garden, a lecture on trees, more tea, more drinks, more phone calls and that's your lot, thank you for calling and good-bye.

'Above all, Hans is immensely professional, and knows precisely what he's doing and what the world is doing in relationship to him. He certainly has his finger on the pulse. After the *Kammermusik* performance he and I got on pretty well, and I was always hankering after another piece from him until eventually, and many years later, it arrived. It was enormous! A sonata in six movements, which lasted nearly half an hour, called *Royal Winter Music*. I still can't remember whether I commissioned him and didn't pay him, or whether I just asked him or what. I think originally I asked him; I remember saying that I wanted an important piece, something of the profound quality of Beethoven's *Hammer-Klavier Sonata*. It was half a joke really; I didn't expect him to take it seriously. Can you imagine? Six highly complicated movements, each based on a character from Shakespeare—Gloucester from *Richard III*; Romeo and Juliet; Ariel; Ophelia; Audry, William and Touchstone from *As You Like It*; and finally Oberon. I was flabbergasted. But I've since performed it in New York, Ottawa, London, Berlin, Paris, Bath, Dartington, Budapest, Zagreb, Tokyo and Sydney though it's a pretty tough nut to crack for both performer and listener alike.

'From the start, I was a little terrified of it. To hold an audience for 28 minutes in a piece of such complex modern music is not my idea of a night out, but the challenge is so stimulating and the music so fascinating, that it does give me immense pleasure to play it, particularly when I manage to bring it off well, which is not always. Recently, he has written another Sonata as a companion piece to the first, which is what I wanted to discuss with him when I was on the road. It's much shorter, and two of the three movements are really lovely, although the last movement seems to me more or less unplayable. It was very difficult musically to see what he wanted, so I wrote and suggested he might re-write this movement. He said he'd show it to another guitarist in Cologne, and I said I'd be very pleased to find out what the other guitarist thought, because composers can sometimes overstretch an instrument and an instrumentalist's technique for scant purely musical reason. Now I don't consider myself to be the final arbiter in all matters concerning contemporary music. It can often be most stimulating when a composer demands a little more from your technique than you can muster, provided of course it is for musical reasons. In fact, Hans writes well for the instrument, at times marvellously well. He gets a little expansive occasionally; his gestures can be a bit large for the guitar. But when he's really concentrating on the instrument, he writes fabulously well for it. It's when his enormous imagination comes to the fore, that he sometimes writes impossibly hard music for the instrument to play.

'On the other hand, I would much rather he did so, because at the end of the day he's got such incredible facility that he can re-write a passage on the spot if it doesn't work. He doesn't just tinker

'Play the C♯ and think of the B♭'—Benjamin Britten's advice to Bream concerning a passage in Nocturnal.

with the music and change the odd note, but he re-writes the whole passage completely. If I'm with him and I've got the guitar on my lap, and he's hearing the sound, I can show him what is possible and why a certain passage doesn't work. He understands; he can see the technical problem in a flash, and he's so quick that he can adjust the music without losing any of the original shape or inspiration. God, that's very unusual. A lot of composers rush to the piano and try out two or three versions of the same idea. Hans doesn't. He knows straight away when he sees what the technical problem is, and he adjusts the music accordingly. After I'd received the *Royal Winter Music*, for instance, I suggested that Hans come to stay for the weekend. We played table-tennis and badminton and croquet and God knows what, and I lent him my studio to work in. Not only had he re-written everything I needed for my piece, but in between the badminton, table-tennis and so on he knocked off a complete movement for a string quartet. That's absolutely incredible.'

'When I approach a new contemporary piece, I do so not just by simplifying it so that it is playable, but by providing accurate and sometimes alternative fingering; that is, specifying which fingers should play which notes. Because on the guitar, the fingering that you use can radically change the *texture* of the sound, far more so than on almost any other instrument. If you know a composer's work intimately, and you've worked with him on a particular piece so that you know his musical language, how *he* wants it to sound, the fingering is vitally important in order to reveal the character and colour of that sound. In the classical works of the late eighteenth or early nineteenth century, the fingering is not so important, although it is still vital for phrasing and articulation. But in many modern works—which rely not only on the notes but also on the texture of the sound for their musical effect—the fingering has to be the ultimate key.'

'Some people say I put too much fingering into my editions of new works. But most guitarists are still not used to playing modern music with the same facility say as a pianist, so I just assume that my fingering will give them a little help as well as saving them time. The main consideration is simply this: I have gone through the musical interpretation with the composer, and the relevant fingering is the direct reflection of that interpretation.

'Take this new work by Maxwell Davies, for instance. I was in Switzerland when he finished it, so I asked him to send it to me, which he did. And when I looked at the layout of the piece, I thought the opening was sort of grumpy and low, with all sorts of curious rhythms, two against three, which were tricky to say the least. After I'd got down to the nitty-gritty and some alternative ways of playing these tricky bits, I went to see Max and said some of these passages are just not going to work out. And he said, well, why not? He suggested some minor adaptations which weren't really much help to be honest; at least, I didn't think they sounded as convincing musically as the original almost unplayable phrases.

'So I spent a solid two weeks doing nothing else but learning that piece. I took the difficult passages and turned them into exercises for myself, because there were so many unusual figurations that I'd never come across before, certain combinations of fingers moving across the strings, that I could actually make a good study of these problems and, in doing so, improve my own technique. And as I did this, I began to get interested in the music, in the musical shape that he wanted. And then I began to see the musical colour he had in mind; the rhythmic inflections, the pathos, the melancholy, the humour, the drama—all those human feelings that have nothing to do with the abstraction of notes on a piece of paper. And only at *that* point, because I could play the piece with my fingers, because the mechanics were working, did I find out eventually what the music and what Max finally wanted to say. Admittedly, he had written down exactly what he wanted; but not until I had found a way of playing what he wanted, not just the notes, but the whole spirit of the piece, could I make the piece come alive, could I make the music communicate something to other people. And the original key to this initial understanding on my part, was finding the right fingering.

'There are no rules, no fixed patterns. Every piece is different, and demands a different, a fresh approach. What I liked about Max's approach was that he was immensely practical about the actual performance of the piece, just as Malcolm Arnold and Henze had been. I suppose in Max's case this comes from the fact that he worked a lot with children when he was a Music Master at Cirencester Grammar School, and later his experiences with his group the "Fires of London". It's an extreme practicality on his part, a very professional approach to music. Because one mustn't forget that it is the performer who is at the end of the line. He's the one who's finally got to dish it all up. If he's got a sympathetic composer writing for him, it doesn't necessarily make his job easier, but it does allow him to pitch his performance at a higher interpretative level, especially in the early performances of a new work.

'You cannot afford to let a contemporary composer down. If you're playing Schubert, or Bach, or a bit of Sor, and there's a slight slip or a lacklustre interpretation, it's not the end of the world. But with a living composer, you have a tremendous responsibility. With modern music, it's very hard to get over all the expressive qualities of a new piece in one performance. But when you consider that you only have one throw of the dice, somehow your performance of a new work has to be a distillation of all the best elements inherent in it. On a gramophone record, you have time to get everything more or less right; but in a live performance, you've got to get the character of the music across first time, because very often the audience won't want to give it a second chance. So with Max's piece, I worked on it solidly for a month, without playing any other music. I had to try and understand his language, and not screw it up with bits of Bach or Albéniz or Boccherini. Many contemporary composers feel, and I think justifiably, that their music is usually heard in juxtaposition with music which is so foreign to their own language, that their compositions rarely get an ideal hearing. Not surprisingly, they're becoming increasingly reluctant to chance their arm, not to say their reputations, with an instrument and a concert-going public that is so conservative, and—frankly—unadventurous.'

Bream is pre-eminent among contemporary British virtuosi for encouraging new music. It is often thought that his achievement has been to consolidate the guitar's reputation as a major solo instrument in the concert halls of the world, following the tradition of Tárrega and Segovia. His control of tone colour, the clarity of his phrasing, his passionate, romantic, soulful qualities as a performer, have brought the guitar's repertoire before an ever-increasing audience. But his real achievement has been more subtle, less clamorous, more long-term. A gramophone record he made in 1972 entitled *Julian Bream '70s* was almost a proclamation of Bream's intent. The record included Richard Rodney Bennett's Guitar Concerto. *Theme and Variations* by Lennox Berkeley, *Five Bagatelles* by William Walton and an Elegy by Alan Rawsthorne—works by most of the major British composers of that time, some having been commissioned by Bream. One notable exception, of course, was Benjamin Britten; but then Britten had already, in 1963, written for Bream one of the masterpieces of contemporary guitar literature, the *Nocturnal*, opus 70.

'I asked him originally in the mid-fifties, if he would write a solo piece for me,' Bream told me. 'He said he would, although in fact I waited almost ten years for it. Around that time I was giving a lot of recitals with Peter Pears, who, as you know was Britten's life-long companion, not to say inspiration. For our concerts together Britten had written us a beautiful song cycle called *Songs from the Chinese*. But I suspect that for Britten the guitar was not much more than an "interesting" instrument, almost too exotic in fact, and in those days I was a more juicier player than I am now. As a plucked instrument, the harp was much more to Britten's taste, more abstract, and his use of that instrument particularly in his chamber operas is as adroit as it is inspired. At first he thought he might write a lute piece for me. He adored the lute. I said, well, that would be marvellous, but there are not many lute players around, so if you're going to write a piece that has a chance of being heard and played regularly, then the guitar is the instrument. He too was a very practical man, and I think he got the point. He obviously thought about the piece for a long time, and obviously still had the sound of the lute in his head, because towards the end of *Nocturnal* he uses the guitar in such a way that you can almost believe you're listening to a lute. In other words, he made the guitar sound the way *he* wanted it to sound.'

Britten acknowledged Bream's discovery of and love for Elizabethan music by writing a set of variations on a song by the great Elizabethan composer for the lute, John Dowland; 'Come Heavy Sleep', No. 20 in Dowland's *First Book of Songs or Ayres of Four Parts*, published in 1597. *Nocturnal* set new standards for other guitarists to follow; indeed, so intense was it thought to be after its first performance, that for several years no other guitarist felt capable of tackling it.

'When the piece first arrived,' Bream told me, 'I found I didn't have to change anything, not one note. It's the *only* piece written for me of which that is true. Oh yes, except for one tiny blemish where Britten had contrived to place two notes on the same string, which was naturally impossible to play. When I pointed this out to him he was simply horrified! It was as though you'd pointed out some terrible gaff in his social behaviour. He said "Oh my God! Julian! How did I *do* that?" And I said, "Well, Ben, there it is. There's a B♭ and a C♯, and I've only got one A string to play them on." He looked at it, and he looked at it again, and he then said; "Look, I'll tell you what, Julian. Let's put one of those notes in brackets, so that when you come to play the piece, play the C♯ and just think of the B♭." That's rather nice, don't you think? But it was also very typical. It was simply that the inevitability of the counterpoint had to logically evolve to these two notes, and visually it was important for the continuing shape of the music. It was a visual thing; and if you look at Britten's scores, the visual aspect is obviously very important. He's absolutely clear and practical about his intentions, and visually, on the score, everything is extremely clear and his musical direction so adroitly expressed that no one could ever mistake his intention. I'll tell you, nobody ever did make a mistake if Britten was around or sitting in the audience, because if you did it could be curtains. He was saddened if things didn't work out as they should, although he was exactly the same with himself as a performer. You cannot say that he was inconsistent; it's just that his standards were so high that nothing was left to chance. "Chance" was not a word in Britten's vocabulary.

'Aesthetically, he was a remarkable man. His integrity was astounding. Many people felt in awe of him because, although he could be the most charming of men, particularly if you were in trouble and needed sympathy, at other times he could be remote and totally unconcerned, even chilly. I always put that down to the constant worry of composing. I think the world outside worried him, desperately. Composing certainly worried him. But he knew his gift so well. I think his musical world was carefully set up; he only heard music that he wanted to hear, and he didn't hear music that could muddy his sensibilities. To my mind, he rarely ventured out beyond his immense capabilities, so that a lot of his music tends to face inwards because it is constantly re-working those few things which were his musical passions. And one of those passions was undoubtedly his "Night Music"; "Midsummer Night's Dream", for instance; the *Nocturne* for Tenor and Orchestra. He was, in the early sixties, fascinated by the inspiration of the night. And the guitar, of course, is a very reflective instrument, especially of the atmosphere, the other worldly stillness and mystery of the night. I know that Britten wrote the music that he wanted to write; he adapted the guitar to *his* musical language, rather than adapting his musical language to the guitar. I'm sure he understood the instrument better than I do; in fact, I know he did!

'I wish every new work I get was as simple as Britten's; well, not simple, but at least you got the feeling that the composer had sat down and done his homework on the instrument for which he's writing. I mean, my God, everytime I come back from a tour, there are at least four or five new works that people have sent me. It seems as if anything goes; I'll get one serial piece, two loads of romantic rubbish, an academic number written by someone who goes to composition classes on Thursday evenings, and just the one piece that may be half-way decent, although even that could be ineptly written for the instrument. As I get older, I find that my feelings for music are becoming more conservative. Whereas only a few years ago, I'd spend six months learning some hideously difficult serial piece, I would think twice about it now. You see, it takes a hell of a time to learn these things, and at the end of it you may only do one or two performances. When you learn a piece, you often get rather attached to it, either to its faults or its virtues. You know you've got to do it, or rather you should do it, because you've been asked. But quite often audiences just don't latch on. I mean it's like food. If you're an Englishman, you accept Italian food, although you know it's different. It's still food, and that you know about. But these days, new music can often be so difficult and so complicated that you can't say to the audience, well, if you hear it *three* times, you'll get a kick out of it, and if I play it better you'll think it's a masterpiece. I mean, it's not on, is it?

'It can also be sometimes rather embarrassing being sent new pieces. You remember I was telling you about trying to find a cottage in the country, and I said that I took a tent down to Dorset and lived in this tent for almost six weeks one summer. Well, apart from trying to find somewhere to live, the other reason was that I had been asked by a very distinguished modern music festival on the Continent if I would play a Guitar Concerto that was being written for them and for me by a well-known musical personality of the avant-garde. I said I would be interested, indeed, I would love to do this piece. I hadn't seen it, but I would endeavour to play it. Well, the piece turned up and was beautifully bound, I remember, in silk. The actual writing, the script, was so elegant, and so full of instructions in Italian how to play it, that I could see it was going to need an immense amount of work if I was going to pull it off— as well as an English/Italian dictionary. So with my tent came my new silk-bound concerto and the old box, and I sat in this tent for days on end trying to work out what the composer wanted to say. If I could find out what he wanted to say, I reckoned, I could sort out how to play the notes. Well, I looked at it and looked at it. I probably spent about 30 or 40 hours looking at it, and eventually I just gave up, because I could not find anything in the music that made any real sense to me. It now became a question of integrity. Could I go and play something I didn't understand and, because I didn't understand it, couldn't really believe in? Or, having worked this far, should I give it the benefit of the doubt? So I spent another week locked up in this tent. I thought I'd have to live and sleep with this damn thing. But, after another week, I realized that never, never in a month of Sundays would I begin to understand what this composer was getting at. So I sent the festival a telegram saying that I was terribly sorry, but my artistic integrity refused to allow me to continue with this piece. Well, they said, they were going to sue me for breach of contract, have my career ruined internationally, expose me as a charlatan and Christ knows what. Actually, I was rather looking forward to going to Court; I would have loved to know how a Court of Law would define artistic integrity. I thought that this case, if it ever became case law, would probably make me more famous than any ability I may have as a guitar player. Bream's First Law!

'Still, I suppose if the audience gets something from a new work, even if I don't, then the whole exercise may just have some merit. It's when the audience gets nothing, or next to nothing, that the music or myself are failing to communicate. Of course, new works often fail on their first performances, and only later are recognized as interesting or even masterpieces of their time. So one mustn't be too discouraged if a work doesn't take off immediately. On the other hand I don't think one should feel that one has a continuing obligation to perform it; because there's always a few up and coming guitar players who will want to strike out in an original and adventurous way, and may even be performing eventually to a more sophisticated public, musically speaking. The important thing is to encourage composers whose music you admire to write for you, and then involve them in the early performances, so that the interpretative factor is as near authentic as you can get it.

'Just as I'm trying to do here at Dartington with Maxwell Davies's new piece. It's not really a question of adjusting the notes if some phrases are unplayable. Some composers simply don't understand the guitar's technical limitations, even when they write what they think is idiomatic music that only needs perhaps a modest ammount of adjustment. Richard Rodney Bennett, for example, writes very well for the guitar, but it's very difficult to alter or adjust his music, and I think he finds it so too. I mean, somehow it's so easy to make his music sound vulgar by leaving out or adding one note, or by suggesting another note which may be easier to handle. It is just that the music is so finely yet firmly conceived within its scheme of composition, that there is very little flexibility left for adjustment, whether simplification or augmentation.

'Now I always think of Richard Rodney Bennett as the Alfred Hitchcock of the composing world. When I recorded his Concerto, he knew that the marvellous pianist Lamar Crowson was going to play the celeste part on the recording, just as he had done in the first performance. So Richard wrote a fiendish part for the celeste because he knew Lamar was a wonderful keyboard player. But, come the recording, Lamar was suddenly taken ill, and Richard—who, incidentally, is no slouch on the ivories—had to play it himself. He looked very, very serious when he was doing it; he'd just flown back from New York, and was feeling a little bit jiggered by jet-lag. I think he found some of the leaps and arabesques a bit hectic. He did it magnificently, but there was a touch of the old rebound tucked in there somewhere.

'The Concerto itself is very much a chamber concerto, with the guitar part by no means always dominant in the conventional sense. It's not a concerto in the nineteenth-century style, much more in the spirit of an eighteenth-century Concerto Grosso. Now, with Bennett, he's not a composer you can suggest things to. He gives you the feeling that he knows exactly what he's doing, and he doesn't take too kindly to any suggested alteration. Once he's done it, that's that. But I'll tell you a little secret. In the middle movement of the concerto, there's a modest little flourish that I make, which isn't in the score. I haven't exactly changed the notes, but I use a pattern of notes he's written and make an arpeggio of it. When I did it, I knew he didn't disapprove, but I also knew he didn't quite approve. Another instance of the practical musician, if you like. He knew that it gave me great pleasure to have that tiny indulgence, and he let it go without a word. There is something French about that. The French have no musical hang-ups. They know there's a job to be done; orchestration and understanding musical textures is a thing that the French have always been good at. It's like their cooking. I mean, they are not so good at roast beef, Yorkshire Pudding and Vaughan Williams; but the French really know how to bring out the best of what is there. They are musically disciplined from an early age. The English prefer to be good amateurs by comparison. Not so much now, but in earlier days; and I can even think of a few English composers who are still with us who almost rejoice in the idea of being jolly good amateurs! It's the same with cricket, you know. The whole thing ideally has to be amateur in approach to be *really* cricket, you know; the idea of professionalism seems to upset some of the upper crust in this country.

'I suppose one of my biggest regrets, as far as contemporary or near contemporary composers is concerned, is that I never managed to persuade either Stravinsky or Shostakovich to write for me. I'd always thought that the guitar would have been a good instrument for Stravinsky, as indeed it might have been for Shostakovich, because the guitar sound has within its vibration some particles, some traces of a very ancient world. I feel at times it has a Grecian quality, a quality Maurice Ravel would have relished. And for composers who indulged in or were inspired by neo-classicism in the twenties and thirties, the guitar would have been an ideal vehicle for them.

'It was very hard to try and get into contact with Stravinsky. I managed eventually, but by then he was about 80 years old. He was tiny and looked like an old raven. But despite being very old and a bit crumpled, he had within him an immense vitality. There was about him such a feeling of energy, particularly in his eyes and his extraordinary-shaped mouth, which—because it had a sort of passive quality—lent even more intensity to his eyes. His eyes were enquiring and alight and aware, and they wanted to know everything. I found meeting him rather an awful experience I mean 'Awe-full' in the eighteenth-century use of the word. I was very nervous. I just felt he knew everything. I played him a few tunes on the lute, and after I had finished playing an impressive fantasia by John Dowland, his only comment was: "Do you know Milano?" I said I did. He then said "Everybody knows the *city* of Milano, but nobody seems to know the fantasias of Francesco di Milano these days." No flies on him.

'Shostakovich was an even bigger problem to get to see. He was at the Edinburgh Festival, many years ago. Do you know, there were bodyguards and several layers of KGB you had to get through. But I was insistent. I couldn't get through to him on the telephone, and I couldn't find anybody to give me an introduction, so I just turned up at his hotel. I wrote him letters saying that I just wanted to play to him some pieces he wouldn't have heard in Russia, some modern pieces on the guitar and some old lute music. Eventually, I was admitted. I remember he had a very angular, rather ravaged face, but it was immensely sensitive. He was like so many Russians; genetically very powerful, but his expressions were refined. He was rather nervous; a worried sort of chap; inward; introspective. His outward gestures were in no way indicative, it seemed to me, of what he felt. It was as though they were a screen. He obviously felt so passionately and deeply about music, and yet his outward demeanour was so low-keyed. He allowed me to play for him, so I played him, amongst other pieces, the "Melancholy Galliard" by

Dowland and he said "Strange, that sounds like Schubert to me." Isn't that extraordinary? Is it because of the political climate during the last fifty years that it appears we've lost that free interchange of cultural variety that must have been so important in previous centuries? Perhaps that was the reason I felt that Shostakovich ought to hear some old English lute music, as well as a bit of modern guitar music. It's not going to make him write different symphonies, but I felt it was nice to be able to give a distinguished visitor a feeling of the local colour and display some of the cultural goodies that would never get to him through official channels.

'I'm not strong on politics at all; in fact, politics don't interest me very much. But in my lifetime the *real* tragedy has been this complete cut-off from half of what is, after all, our common European heritage. It's the greatest tragedy since the Second World War; not the atom bomb, although that was one hell of a tragedy too. But this is a real and continuing cultural tragedy with no end in sight. Nothing to do with killing people, but the fact that Europe has been severed has had a debilitating effect on us all, at least those of us who value certain aspects of a civilization other than a gross concern for materialistic economics. Both Eastern and Western Europe need each other like man and wife. They are essential and complementary. And particularly so for us English, because we are the last western outpost, geographically speaking, of European civilization. So when somebody like Shostakovich came to England, I felt I wanted to give him a feeling, a small expression of what this island is all about. I mean, he comes here, he's shuffled about from one concert to another, one reception after another smothered with bodyguards, interpreters and civil dignitaries—I should imagine, bored out of his mind, poor chap, and I wonder where the *real* value lies in that sort of exercise. Whereas somebody who turns up to play a few local tunes in a hotel room might be getting a little closer to the cultural point. At least it might be a bit more entertaining. I eventually asked him to write a piece for the guitar. I knew it wouldn't come off, but there's nothing like a try, is there?

'Of course, I can see now, looking back, that I never collared some of the finest composers early enough. A composer I much admire, and I've mentioned this before, is the Swiss composer, Frank Martin. I even went round and spent some time with him at his house near Amsterdam. Eventually, I plucked up enough courage to commission a piece and he was most eager to do it. But he was already 80 or thereabouts, which is leaving it a bit late in the day. Not long after, he came to a recital I was giving in Lucerne. It was a morning concert, and afterwards we took a stroll down by the lake to discuss the new piece, he in French and myself in English. Yet we understood each other perfectly. That was the last time I saw him. He died a few months later. I also wrote to Hindemith, but he wrote back saying that he didn't write music to order anymore. I even tried more recently to cajole Lutuslowski, but he said, well, I'm 65 now, and I've got a lot of things I want to write, and a guitar piece isn't top of the list.

'I left with the distinct impression that he—Walton—thought I'd been trying to pull a fast one. . . .'

'I'm also a great believer in getting composers once they've written their first piece, to write another; because once they've been through the whole business of exploring the tonal and technical possibilities of the guitar, it's all there for them to use again. The problem is I'm not a person who can push myself; that's not my temperament. And that's a pity in some respects. Some people are very determined; "I'm going to get that fellah to do it," you hear them say. And they work on it, every day on the telephone, by letter, unannounced visits and so forth. A constant nagging until they get what they want. But it's important for me to go on encouraging an increasing collection of contemporary compositions for a younger generation of players, who don't as yet have my sort of clout within the musical world. Oh Christ, yet another responsibility! I got short shrift not too long ago from old Willie Walton. He wrote five superb Bagatelles for me back in the early seventies, but somehow he's convinced himself that I don't play them often enough. I've been begging him, almost, to do me another piece, so on his last visit to London I presented myself at his hotel to be given a stern but gentle lecture about my responsibilities. I felt a bit like a naughty little schoolboy who'd been playing truant, and although I acquitted myself well, I left with the distinct impression that he thought I'd been trying to pull a fast one.'

Bream's concert at Dartington, the opening event of the season, was predictably a success. He played a Sor Fantasía, two pieces by Albéniz, a Bach Prelude and Fugue, the mammoth Henze Sonata and, from memory, the premiere of the Maxwell Davies piece. Although his ear was troubling him greatly, it was a typical Bream evening. A balanced selection of eighteenth- and nineteenth-century, Spanish and contemporary music, each played with intense concentration, hardly a smile, hardly a flicker of acknowledgement to the audience, little chat, just passionate music making. A few apologetic bows at the end, a brief encore, a standing ovation from a packed house, and the immaculate, balding head waiter paddled off like a disconsolate penguin to his dressing room behind the stage for the last part of the evening's ritual, the fans and the autographs.

To one autograph-hunter he says, 'It's amazing that they design record jackets so you can't write on them.'

'I run this little local festival in North Devon. Of course, it would be a terrific catch for us if you'd consider coming to play . . .'.

'Oh I agree, it would.'

'Who should I contact about it?'

'Well, the thing is that . . .'

'Your agent? . . .'

'Well, I don't *really* have an agent, and usually, in August I like to take a breather. Although it was no breather giving this concert, let me tell you. Let me think about it.'

'Even if you can't next year, the year after, perhaps?'

'I'll think about it.'

Another fan jostles his way in: 'I'm coming from Prague.'

'Oh are you?'

'And to hear your student, Brabitz.'

'Rabbits?'

'Brabitz. Did he not study with you?'

'No.'

'Last year?'

'Well perhaps he did, but I rarely, if ever teach, you see. And I didn't teach last year. Anyway, I hope Rabbits gives a good concert though. Great seeing you, all the best.'

Bream sees a familiar face: 'Hello Annie. You turned up to hear the old dog.'

'Sure, it was super.'

'Oh thanks, was it really?'

'How long are you going to be here?'

'Well I'm going off tomorrow but I'm coming back to go through the new piece one last time with Max. He was very discreet about my performance tonight; he didn't say very much, but probably thought a lot. Fabulous to see you; bye, bye.'

Another fan: 'Could I just interrupt for a minute? I would like to ask you a very good favour. I have a guitar teacher friend who thinks you are very successful, and . . .'

Later, Maxwell Davies and John Amis entertained Bream at an after concert drinks party. Bream spoke to the composer:

'You see, the beauty yet the difficulty for the player is that with the guitar the means of producing the sound is so simple, so primitive. The contact is so very very direct. There are no mechanical contrivances between you and it. It's not like a grand piano which just sits there, and with the aid of a bunch of levers, springs and hammers, the sound is finally produced. You and the guitar are one; the sound is drawn, gently coerced from it. It's part of you in a very delicate and balanced way. It is an informal

instrument, and guitar music is generally an "effect", a personal
point of view! The guitar can perform intellectual music, certainly,
but whatever you do intellectually with the guitar, if it's well
written, it more often comes out sounding naturally spontaneous,
and that can be in a sense, non-intellectual.'

'It's a hard instrument to make sound natural. At least, if it's not
going to sound Spanish.'

'Could be. It is, after all, an instrument of feeling rather than the
intellect. But when a fine intellect uses it, such as Britten, or Henze
or Frank Martin or yourself, then the instrument is transformed.
The sensuality of its sound can be shaped or modelled, as in a piece
of sculpture, so that it takes on other dimensions of expression,
from so many different angles. The guitar is also an instrument of
suggestion; it is not an instrument of declamatory statement. But
it can evoke the sound texture of an orchestra, evoke the spirit of
night, suggest the rugged character of the Orkney Islands—merely
by the way you play it. The instrument becomes a part of you. And
that oneness is terribly important, at least to me.

'Do you know a young composer called George Benjamin?'

'George Benjamin?'

'Yes, quite young, and a lot of promise. He might write a piece
for you.'

'Nothing to do with Arthur Benjamin?'

'No, no nothing at all.'

'Have you met him?'

'No, but I've heard a couple of pieces by him, which are really
quite striking.'

'What sort of pieces? Not a bloody noise.'

'No, not bangs and crackles.'

'I must look out for his music. What about Taverner? Do you
like his stuff?'

'Yes, quite. But I think it's very brave to have commissioned a
piece from Harry Birtwhistle, for instance.'

'I think it is too. But I'm fond of Harry, and I think he has
something personal and original to say in his music. I rang him up
the other day to find out what sort of piece he had in mind. He
didn't say much, except to tell me he was bored and felt a bit
constricted by the low E string on the guitar. So I suggested that he
think of it as D double sharp, then he'd have a whole new ball
game at his disposal. Harry does write the odd tune every now and
then. He's had to. Just to confuse us. Michael Berkeley, Lennox's
son, is also writing me a piece for next year's Edinburgh Festival.
I think that may be interesting.'

'What I would really like to do now is write a chamber concerto
for the guitar.'

'Well, that's a lovely idea. The real problem, however, would be
getting groups good enough to do it. You might in New York, or
London, but the difficulty always with contemporary concertos is
finding people who understand the decibel limitations of the guitar.
I've found the best way to do some of the existing concertos is to
have no conductor at all, because then all the instrumentalists have

to listen so hard for their cues. But you've got to have really good musicians to do that. After all, if the musicians in the band can hear you clearly, that must be the most natural balance you could ever attain.'

'Perhaps, now that we have got such good brass players; that might be an interesting combination.'

'But nearly all of them become alcoholics. At least, the ones I used to know.'

'Alcoholics? One hopes not. I would hate to see some of those young brass players go the same way.'

'The woodwind sound is good too with plucked strings. The problem is with those bloody long necked, wire-strung, fiddles; they kick up such a racket. So, how about 32 sonatas for solo guitar? How about that now? No problems with conductors, rehearsals or overtime rates.'

'I hear Michael Tippett is writing a piece for you.'

'That's right. Perhaps he'll write something impossibly difficult to play, or even very hard to comprehend. But you can be sure it'll be interesting and could be very beautiful. He's in very good nick at the moment. But what I really would love at this moment is a match. Not a cricket match, but something to light a tube of joy with. Nobody smoke? How shall I survive?'

On the way back from Dartington we called at the house of Michael Tippett, who also lives in Bream's home county of Dorset. The last time he wrote for the guitar it was used as an orchestral instrument in his opera *King Priam.* He was also inspired to write three songs with guitar accompaniment—in a sense a spin-off from the original opera—initially intended for performance by Peter Pears and Julian Bream. Peter Pears had a number of reservations about the suitability of the guitar, in terms of its resonance in several passages of one of the songs.

'He said it wasn't very clever, operatically,' according to Tippett, 'To have a guitar accompanying Achilles's war-cry.'

Bream, who is intent on encouraging Tippett to write a new work for him, asked, 'Do you mean the guitar can't accommodate the dynamic of that song?'

'That's right. No one could really expect it to do so. It just hasn't got the sonority—doesn't make enough noise. So that part, which I transcribed actually from the orchestral setting, just doesn't come off quite as it should. I suppose you might call that a composer's mistake.'

'Yes. But you know, for example, if it had been written slightly differently the guitar could have sounded more resonant.'

'But do you know I took a lot of trouble to find out where the fingers go on the fingerboard so as to make it playable.'

'Actually, now I come to think of it, Michael, I once drew out a composer's guide to guitar fingering. I think Willie Walton still has it. I drew out the six strings, crossed them with the frets, and wherever they crossed I put the name of each note. Then I indicated the amount the four fingers of the left hand could stretch, you see,

the number of positions, and then I also put in where the harmonics were. The beauty of this plan was that when you composed for guitar you could just have it near you and see the possibilities—exactly, at a glance.'

'I used something similar to that, particularly for a song that Achilles sings in France.'

'Actually that is very well written.'

'I can remember on that occasion in Aldeburgh—Peter was rather strange as a matter of fact.'

'You mean when we did the first performance, at Great Glenham House.'

'Yes, and do you know Peter didn't want me to come to the rehearsal at all. I'm never really fussy about these things, but I did want to warn you both that as the concert was being recorded for the radio there might be some problems of balance—and there obviously were. If you use the full dynamic of a tenor voice in a recital hall the relationship between the guitar and the voice—in terms of their weights of sound—can cause difficulties. But with the sophistication of a microphone balance the whole disparity could have been corrected, and I would have been willing to come; but for some strange reason I wasn't allowed to.'

'But perhaps Peter might have been a little embarrassed if you had done, because it's so difficult to radically change a performance an hour or so away from the event. But even so a lot of the guitar writing of the other songs I thought very good.'

'You see it's that the words are simply spoken in the other songs, and all the vocal line is related to the size of the guitar's voice. I'd started learning something by then. In fact I took a hell of a lot of trouble over those pieces, but I have to admit that I got bored working out where every finger and every note is supposed to go. It's almost as bad as the different time zones across this planet, having to work it all out. I mean I'm conducting this summer in the States—West Coast—starting with five days' rest in Murray Island near Hawaii to recuperate.'

'But that's bloody crazy, Michael. I mean, fancy giving yourself five extra hours of jet-lag. If I was going to California and I wanted to rest on the way I'd doss down in Bermuda—which is half-way there—for a few days and then go on. It's five hours time change between Honolulu and San Francisco, another four hours between New York and San Francisco and it's another five hours London/New York or New York/London.'

'Not exactly. To be accurate it's not five hours, it's a five-hour flight. But it is either two hours or three hours different.'

'Well the date-line is just West—or is it East?—of Honolulu,' says Bream returning to principles. 'So it has to be . . . let's see.'

'While you're working on that, what about a glass of white wine?'

'Well, with this ear thing it's not supposed to be very good. But I'll try one. Uno per la strada.'

Thanks largely to Bream, the survival of the guitar is now assured. Between 1950 and 1980, over 300 LPs of classical guitar playing have been issued; Bream has contributed over 30, and his example has inspired dozens more. In England alone, almost 50 notable composers have written for the guitar in the last 20 years; apart from those already mentioned, these include Thea Musgrave, Elisabeth Lutyens, Humphrey Searle, David Bedford, Wilfred Mellers, Wilfred Josephs, Sebastian Forbes, Gordon Cross, Phyllis Tate, John Duarte, Tom Eastwood, Denis Apivor and John Macabe. Over 100 classical guitarists are listed in the current (1982) Gramophone catalogue of recorded music, including in their repertoires the music of over 150 composers—Purcell, Couperin, Frescobaldi, Scarlatti, Vivaldi, Diabelli, Paganini, Pujol, Barrios, Poulenc, Petrassi, Tansman, quite apart from the others Bream has described. It would be untrue to attribute this explosion of contemporary interest in the classical guitar solely to Julian Bream, but there can be little doubt that his example as a performer, his choice of repertoire, his willingness to spend much of his life on the road proselytizing, has had a profound influence on the development and future of the guitar.

6 'Blow me up bigger.'

New York in November is the scene of the beginning of Bream's annual tour of the United States: the East Coast one year, the West Coast the next. At the 5 o'clock inspection of the lighting facilities, now at one of the most sophisticated halls in the United States, Bream is speaking to his New York recording boss. Also present are the Stage Manager of the Avery Fisher Hall at the Lincoln Centre, and—later—Harold Shaw, Bream's New York/United States agent since 1957.

'It's a beautiful hall.'

'Small . . .?'

'But lovely . . .'

'Just right for . . .'

'Oh perfect . . .'

'You're allowed to pee on Thursdays,' says the recording man.

'What here?'

'No, at the Ambassador College in Pasadena where you're going in a couple of weeks . . . It has strong religious affiliations, and is owned by some Christian fundamentalist group.'

'Short back and sides; everybody looks terribly well scrubbed there...'

'Like Disneyworld . . .'

'I suppose it is . . .'

'Nobody ever has acne . . .'

'Amazing . . . Do they ever have trombone recitals here?'

'They do in Carnegie Hall.'

'Do they? I've never been to a solo trombone evening.'

'Do you have any idea how long your first half will be?'

'I should think about 35 to 40 minutes.'

'OK.'

Bream turns to the stage manager. 'Now for the concert, what sort of house lighting do you have?'

'This is what we normally would have for a concert.'

'Well, I just feel that there's a little too much light . . .'

'This happens because the light on the ceiling here bounces off, and there's no way to correct this except giving you a *special* lighting.'

'Now what happens if you took those side lights away; could you do that?'

'Well, actually, I can't without eliminating the internal sound recording system, which is all on one circuit; there's one other thing we could do . . .'

'Well let's try that, whatever it is, because this is too spread and too bright. The problem really is that in a very large hall such as this, you have got to visually bring the audience to *you*, so that they can focus on *you*; and if the light spillage is too much, the focus is dissipated and we're all screwed up.'

The stage lights suddenly change. 'Ah, that's good; that's very pretty; that's very nice. Now, how is it in terms of lighting *me*? Is there enough light on *me*?'

'Well, there's a different charge for this lighting.'

'Is this not "on the house", this lighting?'

'No. There's an extra charge for this lighting, as opposed to the first lighting that you had.'

'An extra charge?'

'Yes, because we take these bridges down and we go up and focus the lights, and there's more work in the lights than just sitting around.'

'But I mean this is perfect, and you haven't got any other work to do.'

'And . . . but we just did our other work before you came in, because Mr Curtin (the house manager) said you would probably like "special" lighting.'

'I see. And how much will that cost?'

'About 150 dollars.'

'Well, we'll have to put the ticket prices up, won't we? Do we pay city tax on that too?'

'Yes, but you don't. All I know is that Mr Curtin would figure it out, if, that is, you *did* want this lighting as opposed to what you saw at the beginning. But I have to let you know that there *is* a charge.'

'In New York, people go to your funeral to see if you're really dead or just chickening out of a contract.'

101

Harold Shaw appears: 'Problems?'

'Nothing unusual. Just extra charges. Nothing that would interest you.'

'The one thing an artist doesn't want is an agent who is not interested in their career, and if you don't show it . . .'

'They're off.'

'Someone else will come along with a little flattery and cause a lot of trouble; because you people are motivated by . . .'

'Well, we're pretty selfish . . .'

'Achievers; you're all achievers, and achievers are people who are motivated a great deal by recognition, as well as interest in the product.'

'That's the thing. The whole essence here in America is based on production. And if you're not careful, you'll be run into the ground, simply because you're exploited. Like *any* merchandise; when they've had enough of you, they'll just chuck you away. That can be very hard, and that's why it's very difficult for a lot of young artists to really make a career here. Not initially perhaps, but in a maturing and evolving sense. Once you're blown up like that photograph of me outside the concert hall, once you're blown up that big, it's very difficult to continue for the next 40 years. Do you blow me up bigger, or what? I mean, is it a question of how big the blow-up can be? Or do we just blow the whole fucking lot up sky high?

Well, we have to plan ahead about two years at a time. This whole business is in advance. The sad thing is that you reach a

point where the artist has no freedom in his life, because he's committed for years; to be at *x* point on *x* day, and you just have to be there.

'Monday is always a weak night in terms of box office sales.'

'Well, what actually happens when you snuff it?'

'You get a lot of people very angry.'

'You don't get many people at the funeral with tears? You don't sing *Lachrimae*? . . .'

'No, but they do come and see if you're really dead, or if you're just chickening out on the contract. It's not uncommon in New York for people to go to the funeral just to make quite sure you've actually been called.'

'I think I've only ever missed one concert on the road in my life, because of bad planning on my part or an act of God! It was an important concert actually, in Washington D.C. I had played the previous night in Hartford, Connecticut, and the following day I was scheduled to fly on to Washington. It's not very far, so I thought I was quite safe. I got up about 8 o'clock in the morning and I saw that the ground was covered by a little light snow. But, as the snow was getting marginally heavier by 9 o'clock, I rang up the airport just to check on my flight; and to my amazement they said all flights were cancelled for the day. The airport was socked in, as they call it. That's an interesting expression, isn't it? Very American. *Socked in*. So I said to myself, well, there's only one thing for it, I must get down to New York by train, or bus, and take a plane from there.

'I made some enquiries at the hotel, and they said oh, there's a

Greyhound bus station close by; they gave me the times, and I took the 10.25 Greyhound bus, together with my suitcase, my lute and guitar for New York. For some extraordinary reason, the bus was full of mothers with children and old men, known these days as "senior citizens". Soon after leaving the bus station it began snowing quite hard, but it seemed to me that this great big General Motors bus was obviously going to steam through everything; we're bound to get there.

'Before long, however, the going began getting a bit rough. Cars were ski-ing about, and although the bus kept churning along, suddenly, as we crossed the state line from Connecticut into New York the snow got really thick. At least on the roads in Connecticut, the snow ploughs had been out, but in New York State, not a damn thing. So the bus came grinding to a halt at about 12 o'clock in the morning, and there we stayed. Can you imagine? It was unbelievable.

'By now there was a blizzard, and all the kids began screaming. They were cold, fed up and hungry and nothing seemed to be happening. Hour after hour after hour went by. Eventually, it got dark. Still, nothing seemed to be happening and we were faced with the prospect of an overnight stay in a freezing cold bus; not my idea of a luxurious exercise, especially as the bus driver would only turn on the heat from the engine once every two hours. Next morning, everything outside was completely white, and quite frankly I was very hungry by this time. I hadn't eaten for 24 hours. In fact, everyone was starving; the lavatories were jammed up, and the smell in the bus was abominable. So I thought, well, I was now so hungry I would have to get out and get some grub, anything, find a farm or something; after all, we *were* in the country.

'The trouble was I only had some light leather shoes: as soon as I got on the road, I was sliding everywhere. I just couldn't get a grip anywhere, just couldn't move. I kept falling over, which was somehow rather humiliating. So I had to get back onto the bus, a bit crestfallen. But when I looked down the bus, it seemed to me that everyone had now resigned themselves to die. Nobody was going to leave, or try anything to save themselves. They were just expecting providence to come by, and drop in a food parcel from heaven, or at least from a friendly helicopter. But I was getting so bloody hungry, and I now had a faint but real smell of death in the bus; they *were* all waiting to die, or at best waiting for someone to come along and stop them dying. It was so awful I had to get out. I just had to leave. If I'm going to die, I thought, I might as well do it in Scott of the Antarctic fashion and do a Captain Oates by walking off into the snow saying I might be some while.

'I didn't stick to the road this time, but took a track into a nearby forest. I must have walked about three quarters of a mile, when I saw a car that seemed to be moving a bit on a small side road. It was slithering about like some neurotic horizontal yo-yo, so I knocked on his window, opened the back door and jumped in. I didn't even ask; I just said take me anywhere near civilization. And he said, well, that's where he was trying to head for. After about a mile and a half, we came across one of those unappetizing American institutions—a Harry's Diner. It was very crowded, but eventually I did get something to eat.

'My mind then went back to all those screaming kids in the bus. I collared a young man who had a good pair of shoulders, and asked him if he would help me bring back some supplies to the stranded bus some two miles away. This he agreed to do. Harry's diner provided us with two gigantic cartons of milk, each holding five gallons, six enormous packages of cut cotton-wool bread, and the biggest wodge of American plastic cheese you have ever seen in your life. As the weight of the milk was decidedly heavy, we opted not to use the track we'd come on because we would have fallen over in no time. Instead, we had to wade through drifts of virgin snow; when we did tumble over—and we did, frequently—at least we had a cushion of snow to fall on.

'At long last we got back to the bus exhausted, and then we did our Jesus and the Fish and Loaves act for the dead and dying. By 2 pm, twenty-six hours after we had come to a halt, a snow plough did arrive and the bus got going again. But that wasn't the end. On our way to Manhattan, the bus slid off the road at least half a dozen times, and we were ordered out and asked very politely to push, which we dutifully did. Can you believe this ludicrous situation? To have to push this bloody great bus? Not exactly very good for the hands, as you can imagine. But we did manage to get it moving and we did arrive eventually in New York City by about 7 pm that evening. I was in a hell of a state, cold, hungry and miserable. There was no traffic and no taxis, because no one in the city could move because of all the snow. I then staggered about ten blocks with my large suitcase, my lute and my guitar to a friend's apartment where I drank half of a bottle of vodka and collapsed on the floor for the night. Naturally, I had missed my concert in Washington.'

'I really do think that one should always try to be at one's best,' Bream told me before the New York concert. 'Obviously you can't always be, because you're not a machine; but if I'm going to be at my best, I'd much rather be at my best in New York than anywhere. In the United States, competition is the very dynamic of the country. If you live in New York, for example, it's a competition every day just to exist. It's the survival of the fittest, which is a very practical outlook maybe, though not necessarily a very happy-making one.

'I'll tell you something about New York. When I first came here in 1957, I felt that it was so strange, so foreign; a very hard city. I thought the people that I met were largely superficial and often phoney, and because of the sheer competitive spirit quite often heartless and graceless towards each other. I also thought the skyscrapers, as exciting as they were, had an arrogance about them that was quite overbearing, and as for the slums, well, they made the slums of Battersea look almost palatial by comparison. In those days of course I was very much a conditioned European and a bit of an idealist too. As I've grown older and possibly less sensitive

Julian Bream

'The performer is the fountain-head of a great many materials and human services.'

I've begun to really enjoy New York, and I now positively look forward to my visits here. And another thing, over the years I've had a couple of lovely girl friends in New York. They have transformed the whole place for me, and I could even go as far to add that New York could be the most romantic city in the world.

'And another interesting thing is that whereas nearly every other city in the world that I visit regularly has got worse, and worse, New York has stayed more or less the same. America was the first country where I really built a large following, a good many years before Europe. This is where my career really took off. On my second visit, I did a concert for The Guitar Society, run then as now by a delightful old Russian, who has been in New York now for about 50 years, I suppose, Vladimir Bobri. Bobri has been an important influence in the resurgence of interest for the guitar in

Harold Shaw and Julian Bream—'fastidious, smiling, socially acceptable and professionally charming.'

America, mostly through the marvellous magazine which he edits, called *The Guitar Review*. It's one of the most beautiful magazines I think one could wish to see, a real labour of love. Particularly the art work. And The Guitar Society has become very much the backbone of my audience.'

Harold Shaw, Bream's American agent, breezed in, a jolly articulate, fastidious, smiling man, socially acceptable and professionally charming. 'The facts are,' he announces, 'that we are off about 20 per cent on *everything* this year. But because of the economic recession we've had two windows open at the box office since about 5.30—for late bookings—and had continual selling, which is a very good sign.'

'How many people does the hall hold?' asks Bream.

'About 3,000,' Shaw replies. 'And the interesting thing is that, up until today, all the tickets sold were in the 15 dollar price range—the top tickets—and the cheaper tickets had not sold. So it's a kind of a social comment isn't it; you either have it or you don't.'

'What is the price range of tickets? 15 dollars down to what?' asks Bream.

'I think 7.50 dollars,' says Shaw.

'So they're still quite expensive,' adds Bream.

'7.50 dollars—about £3 or £4—is not expensive for New York,' Shaw pronounces flatly.

'How many people are we expecting tonight?' asks Bream.

'I think between 2,000 and 2,500,' says Shaw. 'Just about that. But it will not look that way because every seat in this hall is completely visible; not like the Carnegie Hall where the upstairs can be completely empty, but because you can't really see upstairs and because the downstairs is full, you imagine the whole house is sold out. Between 2,000 and 2,500 is a fairly substantial audience for a concert artist, depending on whether it's a Saturday night or a Monday night; Monday, tonight, is always a weak night in terms of box office sales, but sometimes you have to take a hall when you can get it. We had originally booked Town Hall, which is where you generally play, but I'm told there are substantial changes being made in terms of the stage area, which has changed the acoustics and made the hall less resonant. That being so I thought it would be better to change the venue for tonight's concert.'

'So in the middle of the season we decided to come here—really quite late—but it's going to work out quite well I think.'

Bream padded off into an ante-room to do a little prac. and calm his nerves. 'In the mid-fifties', Shaw told me, 'I had the habit of wandering through record shops after work, just picking up anything that took my fancy. I happened to chance upon a lute album and a guitar album one day by Julian, and took them home and thought they were marvellous. I called up Westminster, the record company, and got Julian's home address and wrote him a letter. I got no answer at all, so a month or so later I wrote another letter, and again no answer. So I called up Westminster again and asked if I had the right address. Yes, said the lady, that is the right address. Well, that's funny, I said, I've written twice and he doesn't even answer. Our stationery isn't that peculiar. Then, some while later, a fellow named Dick Dyer-Bennett was at the Troubadour Club in London playing guitar, and Dick told me that there was a fabulous young English guy who played guitar, and I really ought to check him out. And I asked who it was and he told me "Julian Bream". "Oh forget it," I said; "I've written him three or four times and he doesn't even answer." "Well," said Dick, "anyone interested in sixteenth- and seventeenth-century music probably doesn't read his mail." So I called a friend who I knew knew Julian and said was it true that Julian never read his mail? Oh sure, said my friend. I'm sure he's got the letters somewhere. I once was in his house and opened up a vast drawer out fell a stack of letters. "Is that all mail?" I said. "Oh yes" he said. "And you haven't opened them?" "Oh no," he said. "Well, about twice a year I go

out the back and shake them around and see if there's any money in them; the rest I just burn." '

Bream came back into his room, looking distinctly ill at ease in white tie and tails, quite unlike his dapper head-waiter's uniform of dinner jacket and smart white cotton shirt. 'Do you know,' he said, 'I sent my dinner jacket to the cleaners, way back in July. Throughout the summer months, I like to wear a white jacket. So I thought, well, I'll have it cleaned, and it'll be fine for the next tour in the States. But when it came back from the cleaners, I didn't bother to check it out. I just put it in the wardrobe. And only when I was packing for this tour and pulled out my black dinner jacket, did I notice that it was so shiny from rubbing on the back of the guitar, that I could actually use it as a shaving mirror. It looked terrible. So I thought, what am I going to do? I can't wear a white jacket in November. But then I saw my old tails, and quickly stuffed them in the suitcase. Haven't worn them for about 10 years. But actually they're quite comfortable. Ah well, here we go again for another evening of spine tingling excitement.

'New York has become very important to me for another reason; it's the place where I have my guitar strings made, by a very nice lady called Mrs Augustine. Her husband in fact was the first person ever to produce nylon strings specifically for the guitar, and when he died she just carried on the business. One is actually at the mercy in this racket of so many factors and so many people; put another way, the performer is the final expression, the fountain

'About twice a year, I shake the letters about and see if there's any money in them. The rest I just burn.'

Rose Augustine—'. . . illegal to run a business in a private house, so we hid the machine in the basement in case the police came.'

head of a great many materials and human services. There is first the man who plants the tree, the forester who looks after it and may perhaps, if he lives long enough, even fell it. There is the guy who cuts it into workable planks, and the chaps who make the glue and French polish, there's the metal artisan who makes the machine heads and the fret-wire, the instrument maker who fashions all these component parts into a harmonious unity. And there is the lady in New York who makes the strings. She is just one strand— but an important one—of a remarkably complex and many faceted chain: the mind just boggles, when you think about it.

'To have good strings is, of course, absolutely vital. But all conscientious guitar players have known that over the years the calibration of the treble strings has got sloppier and sloppier; quality control has really gone downhill. The other day I was rung up by a public relations officer of a large company that produces some of the monofilament material for guitar strings, who said "we've just discovered that one of our prime markets is in guitar strings." I think they thought it was in tennis racquet strings, scrubbing brushes or stockings. But suddenly, after all these years, they had hit on the guitar market as being very lucrative. "So I'd love to come and see you," the PR man said, "because I want to do a special article in an important trade magazine, featuring yourself and the product that we supply." I said I was very busy, but I'd try and fit it in.

'That night I had to change the first string on my guitar; it was clapped out and I had a concert the following evening. Blow me if I didn't go through 15 first strings—my entire supply—and everyone was false. I ended up re-fitting the worn out string—at least it was in tune, even if it was worn out. So when this PR chap rang back, I said I just couldn't support or have anything to do with a company that had produced such crap.

'Each of the six strings for the guitar is mechanically made in one way or another. But because of the *way* they are made by machines controlled by human individuals, batches of strings can vary greatly. Once I get a good string, I'm very loth to part with it until it's completely clapped out. The bass three strings, the lower three strings that is, wear out much more quickly than the top three strings. This is because the top three strings are made from a monofilament plastic which is very durable, or can be if the molecular structure is in phase; whereas the bottom strings have what is called a nylon floss core, which is overlaid with a fine wire metal covering, to give it the correct weight, gauge and tensile strength. These will perhaps last for no more than three or four concerts, but when a bass string loses its life, its resonance, its ring, during a performance for instance, I can often resuscitate it by loosening off to no pitch at all, and then pulling it back up again to pitch—you can sometimes see me doing this sort of nonsense in a concert.

'Further, I find that my left hand often squeaks on the bass strings as I move my fingers up and down the fingerboard. But by burnishing the strings a little bit, you can get rid of the worst of this distressing noise, and Mrs Augustine has found that by making my bass strings with just a small amount of burnishing, she can minimize what is called string whistle. If you cut too deep, you lose the plating. And often, polishing done mechanically can kill the vibrance of the tone, it goes kind of cloudy. So the idea is to burnish off as little metal as possible and yet retain that physical smoothness. Grinding lenses is pretty much the same thing. It *can* be done mechanically, but to do it by hand is the ideal.

'Extraordinarily enough, every guitar could have its own ideal gauge of strings. Lightly built instruments, and in particular the guitars that I use, are extremely sensitive to the slightest differentiation in string gauge, even to a half-thousandth of an inch. You wouldn't think that would make much difference, but I can assure you it does. That's why I always carry my micrometer with me, so that—as I've said—if I have to replace a string on my guitar, I can check its thickness. Sometimes I go through six different new strings until I find one that is just right, which can be very frustrating especially if you've only taken six new strings with you and none of them prove to be any good. When I find a top string for example that's good and stays in tune, I'll stay with it as long as I can. But I throw away any number of strings which are either out of tune or the wrong gauge or both.

'By out of tune, I mean that when stopped it won't play the same note as the natural harmonic that can be produced at that point on the string. Depending on how much pressure you put on the string with your left hand finger, and the angle of that pressure, you can alter the pitch of some notes by almost a whole semitone. You can of course always compensate for small discrepancies within the string, but it can make life rather complicated to have to do that.

'Strings don't often break in performance, at least the top three strings don't, but occasionally the bass strings do. In the old days, when everyone played on gut strings, it was not unknown to break several strings in an evening's performance. But with nylon strings, you're infinitely more secure. Or at least, you used to be. When nylon strings first came out, in 1946, the actual quality of the strings was marvellous. But now, because the same material is used for toothbrushes and tennis racquets, not to mention stockings, fishing line, and sailing gear, it seems the quality is no longer the same—or is Anno Domini playing a trick on me!'

'My husband Albert was an instrument maker,' Mrs Rose Augustine told me. 'And, during the War, there was a shortage of good quality gut and silk for the strings of the instruments he was making. Gut came mostly from the Mediterranean, silk from the Far East, and none was available from those countries. So all the strings my husband put on his instruments just kept breaking. Albert was getting desperate, that's all. And he was down in Canal Street one day, in Greenwich Village, where there is an area which sells surplus war materials. You can buy the nose of a bomber, for instance. I'm not kidding; I've seen them. Plastics. Anything that the factories disqualified because they were defective. And one day be bought some nylon—nylon by the way, was rationed in those days—and tried out some long lengths for strings. And everyone said, OK, but they made the guitar sound nasal. Most players wouldn't tolerate that. He went to guitar string companies, and they wouldn't manufacture it for him so he went to the Dupont company which specialized in nylon products, and my husband said "I can make guitar strings out of this material." But the Dupont company said to him "do you think we're idiots? We know that this material is suitable; we know its characteristics. We've been way ahead of you. But we also have been to all the string manufacturers, and they have told us they couldn't work with the nylon, that it was impossible to work with." But my husband said he could prove that nylon was the material of the future, at least as far as guitar strings were concerned. An appointment was set up, I remember, in my living-room. Three men came from the Dupont company, one was a field manager, one was a technician and one was an accountant. None of them were guitar players. My husband brought out three instruments—one with gut and silk strings, one with nylon strings and one whose strings were nylon—but coloured to make them look like gut. The men from Dupont listened as he played each instrument, and they then picked out the one with gut-coloured strings—in fact made of nylon—as being the instrument they thought had the best "guitar" sound. So that proved it, and from that point on we had every help we could get from the Dupont company.

'The disconsolate, immaculate, balding head waiter . . .' and the standing ovation.

'Then my husband met Segovia. Segovia had wanted my husband to build a new guitar for him, and he was staying in a hotel on West 57th Street, facing the Park. We went up there and my husband was to measure the fingerboard for Segovia and he saw that Segovia had a nylon string on his guitar. Segovia said that some Colonel in the U.S. Army had given it to him and he now wished he could get a second and a third. So from that point the business started. At first, of course, we couldn't get a machine which could manufacture these new strings. We eventually found an old and broken German machine in 1945 which we tried to adapt; basically it was a standard design, but that part of Germany which had made it had ended up in East Germany. The machine was a mess and we had to rebuild it completely.

'It was crooked, so he had to realign the transmission rod. At first there was tremendous friction, and we couldn't make it function at all. Then of course it was illegal to run a business in a private house, but we couldn't afford to rent a big warehouse. So we had to hide the machine in the basement and have a system of warning bells in case the police came. Nowadays, our guitar strings go all over; today we're sending off a huge shipment to California.'

'They're big on the guitar in California,' adds Bream.

'Here's a shipment to Belgium,' she continues. 'Another to Italy, another to Canada; another to Australia, Mexico, Germany, Sweden, Korea.'

'Korea—that's incredible,' remarks Bream, 'guitars going great out there too?'

The concert had gone tolerably well. Bream had played the Second Sonata in C by Sor, a Bach Partita, Henze's *Royal Winter Music* and *Four Pieces* by Tárrega, together with the *Valses Poéticas* by

*'My left hand was sluggish . . .
no inner rhythm . . . the
instrument uncertain. . . .
Another evening of spine-
tingling excitement.'*

Granados. It had been a long concert, with just under two thousand
in the audience. 'The first ten rows were just stuffed with guitar
players,' Bream said afterwards in the dressing room, 'all sort of
watching me avidly, some even through binoculars. But there was
an extraordinary warmth here, didn't you think? I always love
playing in New York, probably more than anywhere, because of
that warmth. They really make you play; they bring out the best in
you. If you're on form here, you really do your best; if you're not
on form, they're gracious about it. They don't give you a kick in the
pants. Tonight, I'm afraid, was not my best. I was very displeased
about the articulation of my arpeggios; they just weren't flowing.
An arpeggio is a very simple thing in a way, just an arabesque on

a chord. But it has an inner rhythm and is not merely a bunch of notes, to strum across the strings. And tonight I found it very difficult to get that inner rhythm. I was a bit disappointed because I had practised very hard for this concert; I've been doing six to seven hours a day for three days. Maybe I slightly overdid it.

'My left hand was sluggish, a bit tired; and the top string on the instrument was a little bit played out. I dared not change it, however, because I might have had to go through another fifteen strings, which would have cleared me out. A good top string is vital in a hall like that; if any string gives presence to the guitar in a big hall, it's the top string. You can make it sing through. So I was rather sad that the top string had lost its life; and the second string wasn't all that much better. The third string I had changed the night before, which is a very risky thing to do, and that wasn't such a good string either. It's the thickest monofilament string on the instrument, and if it's a bit too thick, it loses a certain sustaining quality. Tonight's string was perfectly in tune, but the sound was too thick, a bit tubby. Normally I would have used a set of bass strings for this concert that would have been well played in. But because of all the practice work I'd done, the bass strings had already begun to lose their life, so I had to change them the night before the concert. Somehow the whole instrument was uncertain, not at ease, perhaps as a result. It certainly wasn't it's usual pugnacious self. Added to that my middle-ear nonsense was giving me hell. So I started off tonight on a slightly—I wouldn't say wrong—but uneasy note.

A fan asks, 'Why didn't you play in Town Hall, as you usually do?'

'Because I'm told they've ruined a beautiful hall. Just ruined it.'

'I could take you out to dinner with my old royalties. It would be a good dinner. We could probably afford peanuts.'

'That's true. I've heard the urinals have broken, and because they won't fix them, the sewage smells.'

'Sounds and smells terrible.'

'The worst thing is that I hear they've put big black draperies all over everything, and all it does is absorb the smell, and naturally kill the sound.'

Another wonders, 'Did you receive the guitar sonata I sent you?'

'Yes; I've looked at it,' says Bream 'but I've been away a great deal. I want to study it, because it looks very well written.'

The composer's wife speaks up: 'He wrote a cello sonata for me at about the same time.'

'Did he really? Well, I hope that sounds as good as the guitar sonata looks. Very nice to meet you.'

Another fan: 'I bought a record the other day entitled *Julian Bream, Live Concert*, and it said on the back "Copyright 1980, recorded in Vienna". So I inferred from this that it was done in 1980. So I phoned the record company who said, "no, no, no, this is very old material and my inference was wrong. This music was recorded a long time ago," but the cassettes were manufactured in the eighties, hence the new copyright. So I thought at least you should know about it. I don't know if you are being paid royalties. Is it pirated material?'

'Possibly not quite. I get about a 100th of 1 per cent. The Westminster company who made the original tapes some twenty-five years ago went bust; and because of that, several of us who were signed to them actually went bust with them. I suppose from the royalty I get, per year, from these old recordings I could take you out to dinner with them. But it would have to be at Horn and Hardedts.'

'Gee, thanks. Give me a call sometime.'

A newcomer asks: 'Why did you stop playing at one point and go over and talk to someone in the front row? Was he recording you?'

'Oh no. He was following the score, and obviously turning over the pages as we went along. But he'd got a different score from me, a different edition, and his turns are different. Now I've got a powerful visual memory for music, and I know when I should turn the pages. And it completely threw me, him turning the pages when I knew he shouldn't be. So I had to ask him to stop, which he very kindly did.'

A Japanese fan: 'I come from Tokyo to see you.'

'Sorry, old chap, got to be going now.'

'But could you not spare me five minutes. I very senior student of guitar.'

'Well, you see old chap it's a bit late now and . . . tell you what, why don't you come and see me in England? Next time you're passing. OK?'

Two months later, the Japanese student turned up unannounced at Bream's house in Dorset. On seeing him come up the drive, Bream hid behind the drawing-room curtains. After fifteen minutes had been expended on the door-bell, Bream observed the student walking forlornly off the premises. A sigh of relief was exhaled.

7 'Without a map.'

'Now the most important thing to note about being on tour with The Julian Bream Consort in Belgium, is that out of, how many cars . . .?' I asked the leader of that ensemble.

'Four . . .'

'Four cars travelling between Ghent and Antwerp . . .'

'From London . . .'

'Not one of them has a damn map.'

'Not one of them has a map, yes, that's right.'

'Isn't that something?'

'Ah, but on a beautiful moonlit night like this, who needs a map? Look up there's the Plough, and the Pole star. What better map could you have? I wonder if Michael Tippett could be up there, on the edge of all that, trying to photograph God?'

'Before the war,' Bream told me, 'most people abroad thought we were a rather unmusical nation. And a glance at the names of artists appearing on the London concert platform throughout any season between the two great wars could almost testify to that fact. And was it not the old Krauts who referred to England as a *Land ohne Musik*? Since the war, and maybe in some way because of it, the musical environment in this country has changed completely. From a "land without music" we have become almost paradoxically a land with a surfeit of music, and a cursory glance at the South Bank music calendar says it all.

'When I began my career some thirty odd years ago the old adage was still in currency, though for many of us younger musicians, we knew it was complete rot. There were the composers William Walton, Benjamin Britten, Michael Tippett, who at their best were supreme in their different ways. And performers too—Dennis Brain, Peter Pears, Clifford Curzon, The Griller and Amadeus String Quartets—all superb artists. But still, on the Continent the old prejudice lurked, particularly in France, and to some extent in Germany.

'As I look back I often wonder whether it wasn't a wish on my part to dissolve some of this nonsense that encouraged me to think about forming an old music consort towards the end of the fifties. In earlier times, the Elizabethan composers of the sixteenth and early seventeenth centuries were on a par with anything that was happening in Europe at that time; indeed, in many ways they were more inventive and adventurous. So when I eventually founded my little early music group and called it "The Julian Bream Consort", it very soon caused quite a stir, because similar groups just didn't

'There's always something there which you can't take for granted. . . . You feel that he isn't really touchable.'

exist, at least not on the Continent. Admittedly, in Germany or in France you might have found the odd mixed band of early instruments. But my sextet was unusual in that the music written for it was scored for a remarkable bunch of instruments, and with the same integrity towards instrumental character and colour as Mozart would have used in any of his *Divertimenti* for mixed band a couple of hundred years later.

'Eventually, we had a marvellous success throughout Europe and America, but in the mid-sixties I disbanded the group, which I regretted in many ways. The truth was that my solo career had developed and was absorbing more and more of my time and energy. I couldn't do both. About eight years ago I reformed the group, and we have continued to give concerts, somewhat spasmodically, ever since. Nowadays, we only meet once a year, because not only I, but some of the others are usually rushing about on the road most of the time. But each year we try and do a cluster of concerts, and for these I book my chaps way ahead of time for a couple of weeks. They don't do anything else, only my concerts, solidly. We just live together, do a load of concerts, and that's it. We don't meet again until next year. We rehearse for a couple of days beforehand, just to get into the swing of things, and off we go.'

Bream's Broken Consort consists at present of Catherine Mackintosh, treble viol, Jane Ryan, bass viol, David Sandeman, renaissance flute, James Tyler, cittern and mandora, Robert Spencer, lute and pandora, with Julian Bream on the lute. On their 1981 autumn tour, which took them from London to Bolton in Lancashire, thence to Edinburgh (for the Festival), on to Lucerne, Ossiach, back via Ghent, Antwerp, Aalst and Brussels, the Consort was joined by the tenor, Robert Tear. Characteristically, Bream had made all the tour arrangements himself; characteristically, nothing worked out quite as smoothly or efficiently as Bream fondly believed it would.

'After two days' rehearsal at Jane Ryan's house in London,' Bream explained, 'two days solid—well, not quite solid; a touch of the linctus and nose-bags occasionally, you know—most of us decided to take a train up to Bolton. But when I arrived at the platform, I suddenly found myself involved in a terrible argument with the guard. I just asked, "Does this train go straight through to Manchester?" "What are you asking? Does it stop? What do you mean?" he replied. "Well, does it stop before Manchester?" I asked again. "Why didn't you ask me that in the first place, then I could have given you an answer," he said. "But I didn't want to know the first stop, but only whether it stopped before Manchester," I replied. Whereupon he marched off and wouldn't give me an answer. Charming, I thought, a bloody good start this. Must have been something in the way I asked him, I suppose.

'Anyway, we all get on the train, Bob Tear and myself in the first class, and the rest in steerage. And Catherine Mackintosh, universally known as Cat, comes into my scruffy old first class compartment, notices that we had a much nicer compartment than hers, and after I'd introduced her to Bob Tear, whom she had never met before, the first thing she does is put her leg up on the cushion and start painting her toe nails. A fabulous introduction to a Consort tour, don't you think? But when we get to Manchester, thanks to the new modernization of British Rail, we have to take a connecting bus from Manchester Piccadilly to Manchester Victoria in order to

'The old musicke racket'—at Queen's Hall, Edinburgh Festival, 1981.

'Fingers like a bunch of bananas – to get some players to do a good old decent A major chord would sound awful.'

catch a "connecting train" on to Bolton. So we have to lug all those instruments on to a bus, at least ten of them, a little tiny bus with no luggage compartment. We just fall into this bus, instruments everywhere being trampled on, and then take a train through one of the most depressing and desolate industrial parts of England to Bolton. We do the concert, which went very well, and then the organizers wanted to give us a party. And do you know where they took us? You'd never guess. To Bolton Wanderers' Football Club, where we were entertained right royally.'

'I think my love for the old musicke racket really all started way back at the beginning of 1949. I'd been at the Royal College as a full-time student for about a year; I was engaged to do the odd concert—perhaps one a month, but I also did the occasional bit of radio work to help towards the rent. As I may have mentioned earlier, it was not until 1951 that I gave my first important London concert at the Wigmore Hall. Amazingly enough it was almost full, although I sold most of the tickets myself to my old mates at the Royal College. I used to go round with a bag full of tickets cajoling everyone I saw there. I even got a couple of girls to do the same, and we really cased the joint to get all these kids along. Although things were tough I never quite despaired, because I always loved playing. And I knew that some day, somehow, I was going to make it through, although I sensed, instinctively, it might be a long, long grind. I had a bedsitter in South Kensington; I could eat, just about. I had no other requirements. I used to give the odd lesson to make a few bob. But I had my instrument, and all I really wanted to do was to play; that's what I loved doing, and still do.

'Gradually, the BBC began to offer me more and more work, especially playing incidental music for historical plays from the sixteenth and seventeenth centuries. Shakespeare, Beaumont and Fletcher, that kind of stuff. So I used to go off to the British Museum looking for appropriate music. In those days, you weren't allowed to take photocopies of the old manuscripts kept in the Museum, as you can now, so I worked away in the Reading Room for days on end. And there I came across these endless manuscripts and printed books of lute music. There was a wonderful book, I remember, of over four hundred pieces called *Thesaurus Harmonicus*, by Besard, all printed out in lute tablature—an old style of writing out music, which if you don't know is as meaningful to the layman as Egyptian hieroglyphics could be to a Hottentot. Then there was the Robert Dowland's *Variety of Lute Lessons*, and of course the John Dowland *Lachrimae*, and all hiding away in the British Museum. So I used to spend days transcribing these pieces from lute tablature into the more familiar staff notation, although even to look through the works took a hell of a long time. I spent weeks there. But I'd take what I'd copied back to my bedsit, and run through the pieces in the evening on the guitar. For a kid of seventeen or eighteen years old, you can't imagine how exciting that all was.

'As a boy I'd always been interested in Elizabethan history, so looking back now it seems quite natural that I should be drawn to the lute, which after all is said and done was the princely instrument of those times. The emergence of BBC's Third Programme after the War, and the parallel growth of interest in early music—and for most people early music in those days only began with Monteverdi— meant there was an increasing demand for a lute player, either in ensemble playing, or in solo work, or more often to accompany a singer. Yet nobody played the instrument. I say nobody. There was Diana Poulton, who played certainly, although I don't think she would have considered herself a great solo lutenist. And Desmond Dupré in a modest way was just beginning to get weaving. But, as with the guitar, there were no lute teachers. I was again faced with the same problem. No teachers. In fact, worse than that, no instruments! So eventually I had an old German six-stringed guitar/lute adapted; I had five more strings added, making a total of eleven, which was historically correct. This adjustment was made by Tom Goff, the famous harpsichord maker, who actually built my first *real* lute some two years later, and this I played for about twelve years. It was a beautiful musical instrument. I've still got it, in fact. As for my technique, I just had to learn it myself. I sort of adapted it from my guitar technique. Home-made, really. And as there were no other real players of the instrument, I suppose I quickly became the best boy in the girl's school, if you see what I mean.

'After the pluckery comes the cluckery.'

'I must admit, however, that there was another reason I became very involved in the lute. When you think that, between 1585 and 1620, from England alone there are more than three thousand pieces written for the lute that have come down to us today—and that's not counting music that has been lost or destroyed in the intervening years—that's absolutely staggering; plus hundreds of the most beautiful songs with lute accompaniment, and even more for lute in consort with other instruments, and that's not including either the thousands of pieces for the various keyboard instruments, or the hundreds of madrigals, or the extraordinary volume of literature for the viol consort or even the mountain of beautiful church music. I felt instinctively that this was a musical period in these islands rich in beauty, inventiveness and vitality. And it seemed to me I had a possibility to help revitalize some of this music. I had a mission almost; to present this music in a way that was not of the museum, but of *now*, although still retaining the music's essential spirit. But I felt I just couldn't play it in a modern way, or in an old way; I would just have to learn some of the old performing techniques, the old methods of ornamentation and blend it in with something I instinctively felt, in fact start from scratch. The only person, at that time, I could get to help me was Bob Thurston-Dart, the Professor of Music at Cambridge. He was a marvellous musicologist, and had done a tremendous amount of research into this period. He was also a practising musician, a *real* performer, which tempered his remarkable scholarship in a good and practical way. I learned a hell of a lot from him. He was my mentor in early music. Sadly, he died a few years later, very young.

'But it was also through him that I first came across one of the biggest problems with old music. After a short while of helping me, he suddenly attacked my style of playing, saying it was not the sound which Dowland himself, who was apparently the greatest lute player of all, would have made. Thurston-Dart said that the lute was an intimate, inward instrument, not suited to the concert hall, and thus should be played with the finger tips and not the nails, as I did. By playing it with the nails, he said, I made the lute seem brash. Also I should pluck nearer to the bridge, and avoid the considerable changes of dynamic and tone that were already becoming characteristics of my guitar playing.

'His criticism, of course, came from the point of view of considerable scholarship. But there were also the nut-cracker purists who said that my string-length was too long, the strings were too thick, and my lute too heavy, and that I shouldn't have used metal frets on the finger board. Only tied gut could give you the proper sounds. I ask you! I mean, here I was playing music that almost no one had heard for nearly three hundred years, and suddenly out of the woodwork came all these clever-dicks who knew so much more than I did. At least Bob Dart helped and encouraged me, and even wrote a long and appreciative introduction to my gramophone recordings of lute music when they came out in the early sixties. I will admit, however, that over the years my lute playing has changed, as indeed has the instrument which I now use. It could be said that I am moving slowly towards a more historically correct set-up. Who knows? One day I may even play a feather-weight dinky cardboard lute, with the strings so light that it will feel as if the right hand fingers are poking a cobweb. Perhaps. But I suspect not! Not quite.

'For me, the lute has become a much more personal instrument than the guitar. I identify myself with it in a strange sort of way, and I often get much more musical satisfaction playing the lute rather than the guitar. If I want to express myself in a purely spontaneous way, the guitar is the instrument I would choose, because it gives me much greater accessibility to what I am feeling at any given moment. But the lute responds to feelings which have little to do with the present or its problems, but which have to do with my innermost feelings, my *real* feelings that are not overlaid by present subjective experiences. Obviously I enjoy playing both instruments, in different ways. I have periods when I hardly touch the lute, although that almost never happens with the guitar. The lute has a fine, aristocratic spirit, from another age. It was an age that itself had tremendous spirit, guts and balls, but above all *faith*. I'm sure it's that spirit I respond to, that essential Englishness, being aristocratic, not in the genetic sense, but in the sense of cherishing the cultivated things in life, fine poetry, fine paintings, fine literature, even fine wine. A wholesome and enobling life, in fact, spent in the service of music, and to some extent society. That may sound pompous, and it is; but I can't resist the temptation to say it.'

To make Julian Bream's lute, Goff had X-rayed a lute known as the Tieffenbrucker in the Victoria and Albert Museum. Since Bream had asked for a lute that could be used in concert halls, Goff built an instrument that was slightly larger than the Tieffenbrucker, although proportionately an exact copy. It was set up as Bream required.

In fact, Bream was not quite alone in his advocacy of Renaissance and sixteenth-century lute music. Segovia had already transcribed a couple of pieces by Dowland for the guitar including the 'Melancholy Galliard' and 'My Lady Hunsdon's Puffe'. Alirio Diaz, another fine Spanish guitarist, frequently included a Fantasia by the sixteenth-century Spanish composer, Alonso Mudarra, originally written for the cousin of the guitar and the lute called the vihuela. And in the thirties Emilio Pujol, Tárrega's pupil, played entire recitals of sixteenth-century vihuela music including works by Milán, Pisador, Valderrábono and Narváez on a reproduction vihuela. Indeed, Pujol went on to publish many works by the vihuelistas, and initiate a growing awareness of the treasures of Spanish sixteenth-century music that had remained hidden for over three hundred years.

The vihuela—its name related to the Portuguese word for guitar, 'violão'—had six courses, that is six pairs of strings, each pair tuned in unison. The tuning of its strings was not dissimilar from the modern classical guitar, which made transcription of music written for the vihuela relatively simple, and also suggests that its historical connections with the guitar as we know it are closer than those with the lute. As only one sixteenth-century vihuela still remains in existence—now in the Musée Jacquemart-Andre in Paris, although many doubt its authenticity—it is difficult to be certain of the range of tone-colour and dynamic that would have been expected from such an instrument. As it was hour-glass-shaped, like the modern guitar, and not pear-shaped, like the lute, it would have been heavier than the lute; although since it was made of similar materials—cypress, as opposed to the rosewood from which the present-day guitar is made—it might have lacked the rich tones, particularly in the bass, to which modern ears are now accustomed.

Vihuela music was essentially contrapuntal, much like music written for the lute; it was the music of the Spanish and Portuguese Courts, and it flourished there between 1520 and 1580, the time of Philip II and the Spanish Armada. It was written down in 'tablature', not dissimilar from that used for the lute, but quite different from contemporary musical script known as writing on the stave, and often more or less a private language between devotees of a particular instrument or even a particular court.

Although the fundamentals of tablature remained in common, there were wide variations relating to tempo, phrasing and dynamics. Even the exact tuning of the strings seems to have been left to individual players. The great vihuelist, Milán, advised players to tune the first string *tan alto quanto la pueda suffrir*, as high as possible—just before it breaks.

Segovia never attempted to play vihuela music on the instrument for which it was written, preferring his guitar transcriptions. None-theless, he did awaken a twentieth-century audience to an aware-ness that the repertoire of music that could be played on the modern guitar was much wider than *Nights in the Gardens of Spain* or adaptations of Bach Preludes and Fugues. Vihuela music, even on the guitar, somehow recreated the courtly, sophisticated, elegant world of a lost age. And although Pujol's advocacy of the vihuela as an instrument failed ultimately to establish it as a rival to the guitar in popularity, anyone following in the footsteps of Tárrega, Pujol and Segovia—such as Julian Bream—could not have failed to become aware of the tradition of which the vihuela was a short-lived but crucial part.

'The other thing about the vihuela,' Bream told me, 'is that it was obviously a softer instrument than the contemporary guitar, but not that much softer than my lute. So it's certainly an instrument I could only play in small halls. Now the baroque guitar is also an instrument of great softness, but it has a resonant kind of ring to it because it hasn't got much bass to it; in fact it's a treble instrument really, not the sort of instrument you can play in any concert hall. You have to be careful to choose a place that can lend something to its resonance.'

Another important link in the story is the work of the musicol-ogist, leader of the modern 'rediscovery' of the recorder, Arnold Dolmetsch. He too had begun his voyage of discovery in the British Museum. 'In 1889,' he wrote later,

> I found an immense collection of English instrumental music of the sixteenth and seventeenth centuries. I resolved to play these pieces which had so fascinated me. Fortunately, I felt from the first that this music would only be effective if played upon the instruments for which it was written. Viols, Lutes, Virginals and Clavichords had not yet become the prey of collectors. I had no great difficulty in procuring some. Having failed to find anybody who could put these instruments in sufficiently good playing order to satisfy my requirements, I remembered that I was a craftsman, and I soon rigged up a workshop in the attic of my house and began to work.

Soon other enthusiasts and musicians began to realize the potential of these instruments and their music. In 1920, the scholar E. H. Fellowes published four volumes of Dowland's songs as well as a few songs from *A Musicall Banquet*. And in 1926, the composer Peter Warlock, a friend of Delius and William Walton, produced a book entitled *The English Ayre* which provided a comprehensive introduction to the repertoire of Elizabethan lute songs. The following year, he persuaded the Oxford University Press to publish his edition of Dowland's *Lachrimae or Seven Tears*, and this was the edition Segovia used for his guitar transcriptions. In 1928, Warlock published a further anthology of fifteen lute solos called *The Lute Music of Dowland*, and the first recordings of lute music appeared as long ago as 1927 when the lutenists Diana Poulton and John Goss sang and played Dowland's 'Flow not so fast ye fountains'. As Bream has said, Mrs Poulton was not the greatest lute player the world had ever heard, but she has devoted a lifetime of study to become the leading authority on the work of John Dowland. In her biography of Dowland published in 1972, she remarks how, in 1951, the young Bream 'astonished everyone with the brilliance of his musicianship and his complete technical mastery of the lute'.

'The problem was,' Bream told me jauntily as he drove down the road from Ostende to Ghent at the head of his four-car Broken Consort convoy, 'the problem was that in the late forties and early fifties the lute was not considered to be a very versatile instrument. The lute, particularly the Renaissance instrument which I wanted to play, had a very specialized and highly defined repertoire of music; which meant that those who wanted to listen had to narrow their sights, as it were, to enjoy these sounds of far greater refinement than those of the more robust guitar. It's also quite hard to make an unpleasant sound on the guitar; almost impossible, in fact. But on the lute, you're wide open to all sorts of little buzzes and rattles. Infuriating, in fact.

'I would be the first to admit that my performances were not historic reconstructions, in any sense of those words. It was obviously import-ant to find out what the performing practices were at the time the music was written. Most players played without nails, for instance; they played with gut strings, very light and delicate. I knew you just couldn't pick up the lute and play it like a guitar, although that's what some people say I still do; that I play the guitar like a lute, and the lute like a guitar. In fact, I had and have an ideal of sound in my head, a sort of dream of what the sound of a lute could be. Not what it was or is, but what I think it could be. Now that sound is forever evolving in my imagination, which is why, for instance, I often go to hear recitals by other lute players; they might have done some research on the right hand technique or the left hand ornaments that I can learn from. Who knows?

'The great problem with the performance of early music in the second half of the twentieth century is one of balance and proportion. Musical styles and taste are forever changing; nothing stands still. Which keeps us all on the hop. Good thing too. For me, the performance of any piece of early music is largely intuitive, mixed though it may be with a bit of scholarship. Looking back over many centuries of music, the problem seems to me how to remain innocent after experience. Finally, I suppose, I don't believe that to be possible. So some degree of frig-up may be necessary. But it's the sincerity and the heart behind the friggery that is for me the vital clue. I like to play the lute full-bloodedly, with passion, as well as with delicacy and, I hope, refinement, because I'm sure that Dowland's playing was very expressive and instantly from the heart. He was human after all, like the rest of us; fell in love; got hurt by other people; was hungry, tired, jealous, and at times insecure. You cannot imagine that he was without feelings as we know them, and experience them today however sophisticated his music.'

In 1956, another lute player, Ian Harwood, also an instrument maker, founded the Lute Society which was strongly and publicly critical of what they thought of as Bream's guitar-based lute technique. But it was Bream, with his international prowess as a performer on both instruments, who propelled the lute into the forefront of the concert-going public's imagination. In 1956, he began recording for the Westminster Company a whole range of Dowland's lute music which included not only those works already familiar through Segovia's performances on the guitar, but new extended pieces such as the *Forlorn Hope Fancy*, the famous G major Fantasia, *Semper Dowland Semper Dolens*, the 'King of Denmark's Galliard' and that no less remarkable Fantasia, *Farewell*. 'Above all,' Bream told me, 'I wanted to show that Elizabethan music could be entertaining, as well as doleful and melancholy. In a word, it could be fun—even hilarious. By this time I had developed a passion for the whole Elizabethan world. I don't know whether it was the passion for the composers or passion for the lute as an instrument, or a passion for the entire Elizabethan scene, politically, socially, poetically, theatrically. But obviously music reflected these different facets of Elizabethan life for me in a very vivid way.

'They had one hell of a life, but I have a feeling it must have been pretty grim too. Yet at least it was vivid, real, though I suspect the pain threshold must have been pretty high. On the other hand, do we want to listen to sixteenth- and seventeenth-century lute music every day of the week? Personally, not me. There is probably something to be said for the lute not becoming too popular, in the guitar sense of the word. The music at its best is aristocratic, discreet, not exactly prime material for the Madison Avenue treatment. There are now quite a number of good lute players around, and a couple of really outstanding ones, and I'm very happy about that. It wouldn't be unnatural for me to feel, in a sort of fatherly way, that I've spawned a number of lute players. Admirable, maybe, but for me that's not so important. And I'm not being modest when I say that I don't get any special satisfaction from that. Especially as I have to tell you that quite a number of old music groups nowadays are part of what I call the "old music racket". Many of the players in these ensembles have at best a modicum of ability and there are others who—if they played a regular standard musical instrument—would just about have enough ability to get in the dole queue. You may think I'm being pretty hard but if you asked some of those players to get up and play a good plain decent chord of A minor, I can tell you that in some cases it would sound bloody awful.'

'Initially, I enjoyed tremendously my solo lute playing but after a while, it got a bit lonely playing the lute all on my own. So I had the idea to recreate an instrumental group that was frequently used in the latter part of the sixteenth and early seventeenth century largely as a dance band, providing popular music of the day for the theatre or the equivalent of the local hop. It was for this combination of instruments that Thomas Morley had published in 1599 a very famous collection of pieces called the "First Book of Consort Lessons", and thirteen years later Philip Rosseter followed suit with another remarkable set of similar pieces for the same group. The group of instruments was called a "broken consort".

'There are several theories as to why it's called "broken", but I always like to think it was because the group breaks across several families of instruments. You've got the treble viol and bass viol, two bowed instruments; you've got a low tenor-sounding flute which is, naturally, blown; then there is the pandora and cittern, which are a pair of wire-strung plucked instruments. And finally the lute, which is a gut-strung, plucked instrument. The lute in one guise is the harmonic go-between between the viols and the flute. Because of the style of broken consort music, the divisions or variations between the instruments are often very brilliant and showy. So the lute, with its characteristic clarity and harmonic base, underpins the group as a whole. The most salient features of the Morley and the Rosseter pieces, however, are the incredibly elaborate lute divisions—miles of fantastic cascading scale passages. These are immense fun to play, but boy they can really stretch the old technique to the utmost, not only in order to play the notes fast enough but just to make enough row on the instrument to cut through all the other racket that's going on.

'Just when you might think there's a bit too much cluckery going on in the pluckery, you then have the lovely ethereal, sustained music from the flute and viols. But things can get a bit rocky from time to time in the ensemble too. It's inevitable when you've got four different families of instruments in one sextet. The problem arises because they all initially "speak" differently at the inception of a note, in other words some get off the mark quicker than others. The "chang" section, that is the pandora and cittern, because they are plucked, and are strung with quickly-activated wire strings, are generally first off the mark. followed by the lute, and the viols are pretty close behind, but the poor old flute, which is a large wooden keyless job, takes a hell of a long time to "speak", because of the large column of air required in order to fill such a large pipe. So the player has to think slightly ahead, which believe me is not easy. There can be endless problems of articulation and ensemble in this group, but not only that: problems of intonation are particularly hairy, which keeps us all on our toes.

'But they're a great bunch, my crew, not only are they marvellous people to work and tour with, but they can put up with a raving fuss-pot like myself, which says something for their tolerance and plenty for their application. They are all 100 per cent professional right down to their finger ends, so our music-making is not just stimulating; there are many moments which seem to me just endless pleasure. And that pleasure is more evident today than it's ever been, although I formed the original consort as long ago as 1960 as a launching pad largely to fulfil my love for all this beautiful music.'

"Julian never plays what's on the page," Bob Spencer, the only

David Sandeman playing renaissance flute: 'what you might call a normal musician.'

surviving member of the original 1960 Consort, told me. "He usually says he does to the audience, but if he suddenly has an idea, and he is always open to stimulus, he simply adjusts the music at will. Other people in the early music field tend to play in a safer way and in what they think of as a more authentic way, but Julian takes the most incredible risks. We all have to be on our toes constantly. After all, in Elizabethan times most performers were composers. A lot of them would only have played their own music, and probably wouldn't have written an awful lot of it down. Today, the situation is quite different in that most performers, I mean probably 99 per cent of performers, are not composers, which is a totally different way of looking at music, a very uncreative way of looking at music really, just repeating what somebody has already said. The Purists try to repeat exactly the same intonation and expression that they think the Elizabethan composer wanted, whereas Julian will do quite wild things on occasions, whether he thinks they are authentic or not.

"But he always brings great life to whatever he does," Robert Tear added, "and somehow always manages to combine spirit with style. Working with him is often very extraordinary because I can feel instinctively what he's going to do, and he can also feel instinctively what I might do. And this is a very unusual situation between two musicians, especially between a singer and accompanist, where both the accompanist and the singer are absolutely equal, so every performance is completely different because just as those marvellous sixteenth-century poets seemed to pluck the words out of the air, when we do our songs I feel as though the music is also being just plucked out of the air.

"None the less, on tour, even at his most gregarious, Julian is incredibly self-contained. Although he's giving all the time, you still feel that he isn't really touchable. There's always something there which you can't ever take for granted. I mean, he doesn't miss a thing. His mind is so full of details. If you walk into a new place, for example, I can guarantee that he will remember all the details of the place, from the foundation stone to the colour of the walls. Most people would take a vague sort of, you know, 'what a lovely kind of place' attitude. But not Julian. That's what his music-making is like; it's all there. He gives it out, and yet he keeps it back."

'We're having a whale of a time,' says Bream. 'Just hellish good fun. My fingers are like a bunch of bananas, so tonight's concert in Aalst may well be an ear-plug job. Now have you talked to David Sandeman? He's what you might call a normal musician. He plays mostly classical and romantic music as a flautist in the Royal Philharmonic Orchestra. In many ways, he's the most sane and professional of us all. He seems always to be aware of phrasing and—like all woodwind players—of intonation. And although in a sense he will come out of Beethoven's Seventh Symphony straight into a sixteenth-century Peter Phillips pavan, probably with only an hour's grace in between, he very quickly slots in and seems to me to do wonders with a bit of old hollow wood, without any keys. He's got his own system of fingering which he's developed in order to make the sound quality as full as possible, but not least to keep the instrument in relative pitch with what's going on. He's also an amiable, retiring man, as most woodwind players tend to be.

'Cat Mackintosh is equally at home and secure in the idiom. Cat does a lot of early and baroque music in other groups (about ten other groups, would you believe) and is stylistically so firm; that is a great help to me. I come in straight off this bloody Henze *cum* Maxwell Davies treadmill and into Thomas Morley, and maybe I need time to readjust. But, on hearing her play a phrase or two, I know exactly what I have to do.

'Bob Tear is our trump card. I purposely wait until the second half of the concert to bring Bob on. After the audience have had the gamut of instrumental scrapery and pluckery, suddenly you get the wonderful words—the poetry, and Bob's inimitable voice—and it's as though the whole concert has started over again. And the magic begins to emerge again. But he's a great asset *within* the group, and not least as a referee when the rest of us are arguing like mad and getting a bit hot under the collar and, as is often the case, getting nowhere very fast.'

'From the very earliest days of the consort until fairly recently I have used a violin for the top line instead of the treble viol which is the instrument designated in both the Morley and Rosseter collections. It may have been a bit daring to do so, but at the time there was already enough evidence from historical research into that period to suggest that violins were being gradually introduced into the consort bands, and that for lighter, more functional types of dance music, its gay, strident sound was sometimes preferred.

'Twenty-five years ago there were certainly a couple of respectable viol consorts around, but to my ears the sound and intonation were pretty uninspiring, and the articulation, or what there was of it, woolly, not to say wobbly. To sum up, and with no disrespect, they sounded to my ears like some old puffed-out harmonium. What we really required for our consort was a Fritz Kreisler of the treble viol—no such luck. So the violin it had to be, and we were fortunate in having had over the years two very fine players. The first was Olive Zorian, a very sensitive, aristocratic player, and after her untimely death, Kenneth Sillito, a fantastic pro, marvellous musician, and a hell of a nice guy.

'As Ken was becoming more and more involved with his string quartet, and I felt reluctant to make more inroads on his time, I found myself having to re-think the old treble part again. I asked some of the other members of the consort if they knew a treble viol player around who was any good, and to my surprise they said, "Well of course there's Cat Mackintosh who's a marvellous player."

'Strangely, I didn't think any more about it until one night travelling back late in my car after a concert I happened to switch on the radio and out came the most stunning treble viol playing—marvellous sound and perfectly in tune. The music was beautifully shaped, and the ornamentation deftly executed. I was so impressed that I parked the car in a lay-by and listened through to the end of the programme when the announcer said that the treble viol was played by Catherine Mackintosh. That was it. When I arrived home I sat down and wrote a letter to this Miss Mackintosh to ask her if she would like to join us for a tiny cluster of concerts the following season. She replied and said she would give it a twirl, though I don't think that was quite the expression she used. Marvellously, from the very first rehearsal with her these old pieces began to take on a new dimension, partly because the viol has its own inimitable way of "breathing", thereby creating a natural, unfussed musical line. The sound is also very transparent, which enables the inner voices of the other instruments to reveal their personality too. But above all it's Cat's unerring sense of style, and her ability to breathe life even into the simplest little phrase, that makes her contribution to our group so very special—indeed, so enjoyable.

'Jane Ryan who has played the bass viol for us for the past ten years is an old friend and colleague; in fact we were both students together at the Royal College in the late 1940s. At that time she was a budding cellist, whilst I myself hadn't in those days even contemplated playing the lute. But it was when I was reforming the group in the early seventies, after I'd heard that our original bass player Joy Hall (a marvellously good chamber musician) had given up playing the viol, that I asked Jane if she would join us. Isn't

Catherine Mackintosh, treble viol; Jane Ryan, bass viol. 'The first thing Cat did was put her leg up on a cushion and start painting her toe-nails.'

there a saying that the heart of a good cocktail is the gin? And in the same way I feel that the basis of a good ensemble is the bass—everything relies and in fact rides on that. To this end Jane gives us superb support. That's why I always sit next to Jane: I can feel Jane but I can always look at Cat—that's an ideal combination, believe me. She has also a marvellous temperament for chamber music, quite unflappable. Yet she is sensitive, and aware of what's going on around her, which makes her contribution so valuable.

'As you can see, it's the girls who control the top and bottom of our consort and it's the blokes who largely provide the filling in the sandwich. Therefore there is not too much room for manoeuvre; we have to watch our *Ps* and *Qs*, and there's no getting out of line.

Bob Spencer, tuning his pandora, unofficial tour manager. 'Tonight's concert (in Aalst) may well be an ear-plug job.'

Even so, and within the parameters that are laid down by the ladies, we three pluckers generally have a very good time. Although I myself have literally millions of notes, I have also got my left eye trained on the "chang" section, my right eye on Cat, my right ear on the bass line, and the left ear on the overall sound. So you could say I earn my bread in this group—even if on occasion it's a bit crumby.

'Both Robert Spencer who plays the wire-strung pandora and James Tyler who plays the cittern are musicians of great versatility, they not only provide the rhythmic impetus for the consort, but also the harmonic texture. Their accuracy of ensemble is imperative for the general cohesion of the group, and a great deal of painstaking rehearsal is necessary on this account. But their versatility is also a great asset. Bob, who along with myself is the only original member of the consort, is in his own right a good lutenist, and can sing very charmingly too. He is also the most fantastically organized person I've ever come across, and in every way too. His performances are scrupulously prepared, his copious researches into early music sources are avidly pursued and catalogued, and the organization of his professional career is quite astonishing. When we're all travelling together Bob's always two moves ahead of the game: so much so in fact that we all rely on him to find our way around airports and custom houses, or to find the best seats on a train, or if we are on the road the best route to take. On one small leg of the last tour Bob went independently of the rest of us, and my God did we know it. We all felt left and stranded, as though nobody loved us any more, and our travel arrangements were naturally a disaster of confusion.

'James Tyler is by far the most versatile member of the consort, and incredibly so, because at short notice he could probably deputize for Bob, myself, Jane, David or even Cat, and could play a solo in between-whiles on the pandora, cittern, lute or even the baroque guitar. He is also, like Bob, a considerable musicologist, and they both bring fresh ideas for expanding the repertoire of the group. His solo numbers on whatever instrument he happens to be playing are always done with great panache and gusto. He brings an immediacy to his music-making which I find personally very engaging. And not only that: his personality on stage is very disarming, yet immensely professional, which is a great asset. It also gives great pleasure to us all.

'James Tyler joined us in the early seventies. In the Mark I version of the consort his part was played by the late Desmond Dupré. Though not as versatile as Jim, he was nevertheless an accomplished musician. His great love, I think, was the bass viol, but he was also a good lutenist, and although he never took the cittern very seriously he did his part very well within the consort. He also had the driest sense of humour of anybody I ever met, and at times, when things might be going a bit haywire, he could let drop a remark with the perfect timing of a court jester which would have us all in stitches in no time flat.

'My fondest recollection of Desmond was in 1963. We were engaged to play for Baden-Baden Radio and the producer—an antiseptic, dried-out old-music racketeer if ever I'd met one—took an instant dislike to our music-making, and was at no pains to conceal it. The glitter of David's metal flute sent him into paroxysms of misery, and it didn't help matters when I suggested that we could spray it with plastic wood for the occasion, if it was any help. When the recording was over the producer came into the studio armed with a viola da gamba that he'd recently had made, and to our amazement proceeded to play it. The sound was so thin and lifeless that it would even make a hurdy-gurdy blush. After he had finished playing with an air of evident self-satisfaction Desmond asked if he could have a go on the instrument. After a preliminary tune-up Desmond launched into the most romantic and sentimental version of Saint Saëns's "The Swan" that you could ever wish (or abhor) to hear. The vibrato was a tone wide, and he was sliding up and down the strings with such romantic intensity that the gut frets began to disintegrate. After thirty seconds, the girls started to whimper and act up as if they were crying. About fifty seconds in I began to throw a few coins on to the floor as if into a hat; Bob and David soon followed suit. With the clatter of coins, the wailing of the ladies, and not least that of the poor viola da gamba, near pandemonium was about to break out. The producer, who by this time looked to be in the final stages of neurotic delirium grabbed the instrument from Desmond and scarpered from the studio in a complete outrage. What was amazing was that Desmond performed

Pushing the Volvo, fixing on the jump leads, and 'doing something useful for a change.'

this whole operation with a dead-pan face. He certainly made his point on behalf of all of us. We were never asked back to Baden-Baden.'

'Who left the bloody lights on in the car?' boomed Bream at midnight in a deserted Antwerp street. 'Nothing works; the servo system has packed up; the battery dead beyond the grave.' Earlier, after the concert, we'd walked miles around Antwerp trying to get something to eat. For some reason, nowhere was open. Bream had got really desperate, and ended up with Bob Tear in a Macdonalds Hamburger Bar and eaten about five beefburgers. Tear had rambled on about Buddhism until the moment had come to switch on the ignition and head for the hotel. Nothing. So there we were, pushing this big Volvo, weighing something like two tons; all five of us were pushing, and getting nowhere. Finally, a little man appeared, who turned out to be head of the police public relations department.

He'd been at the concert keeping an eye on things, and now here he was with his little private Eurocar hatchback. He radioed for help on his walkie-talkie, and within seconds an entire police patrol arrived with much wailing of sirens and screeching of brakes. And then another patrol arrived, and a couple of minutes later a third, this one with jump leads. So we got the engine going again, and one of the policemen offered to escort us back to the hotel, which he did, directing us the wrong way up one-way streets, going through red lights, backing up all the wrong alleys. We eventually got back to the hotel, and thanked the police officer profusely. 'Wasn't it nice to do something useful for a change,' he said with some satisfaction. 'Wasn't it just,' thought Bream.

8 'We're in this together.'

'Concert halls? They can be death. Sudden, and not very pleasant. I dread the prospect, when I don't know what I'm in for.' Every day on the road, especially the day of a concert, follows a precise time-table, a ritual almost. Most important perhaps is the visit Bream pays to the hall at 5pm to check the stage lighting, about which he is most particular, and the height of the seat on which he is to sit during the recital. The 5pm visit to the concert hall in Ljubliana, for a short tour of Yugoslavia, was not altogether satisfactory.

'This is my idea of a nightmare.... I don't see why you can't move that screen. It will have to go.... Lights? I want those over here. Yes, and we don't need that light, or that. And certainly not that. Oh, Christ, this is impossible. Good, now can we move these? Can he go up there and move that one down here? ...'

'Are you sure you want the curtains open?' asks the concert promoter.

'Well, it isn't going to make that much difference. It looks pretty awful with or without the curtains. Is it possible to take that screen away?'

'No, maestro, they've got two loudspeakers at the back.'

'I see, so we're stuck with it.' Bream claps his hands loudly. 'I see, no reverberation. None at all. Good, fine. Where is the *salle des artistes*? This is about the most beautiful place you could imagine me wanting to play in, isn't it?'

'You'd be amazed,' Bream told me in the "Salle des Artistes", 'just how much the concert halls of the world vary, not just in size or acoustics, but in the criteria which people think are acceptable for a concert hall. And you'd be amazed what audiences seem prepared to put up with, let alone musicians such as myself. Take the Festival Hall in London, for example. It's a pretty joyless acoustic, at least for me. None of those South Bank halls do anything for me really; in fact, I haven't played on the South Bank for years simply because the halls are so austere visually, and so dry acoustically. They're clear, admittedly, but there's no warmth in the sound, no ring, no bloom. I can't say that I get any real pleasure from playing there. The Festival Hall belongs to a fashion in sound which demanded clinical clarity, which demands to hear the sixth horn part in a Brahms symphony. It all stemmed from the hi-fi craze in the fifties; well, for me that's now old-fashioned. I believe people now actually like and appreciate a bit of warmth and reverberation. So I've only

Checking the hall—'I only wanted two lights and there are 55 up there.'

ever played in the Festival Hall three times, and not in the Queen Elizabeth Hall for as long as I can remember.

'Brussels? The *Palais des Beaux Arts*? Another disaster. It's so dead that the guitar sound only travels half-way back in the hall. The Queen Elizabeth Hall in Vancouver is another one; as dead as a dodo. You see, what is very important with the guitar, as with all plucked sound for that matter, is what happens to the sound the moment the instrument has been plucked. The biggest impact on a plucked instrument is the inception of the note; then it dies on you gradually thereafter. It dies on some instruments very elegantly and very beautifully, but—because of its very character—doesn't sustain. So you need a hall which gives a reverberance to that original inception, so that you can phrase a melodic line, or any line for that matter, and so shape it. It's the shaping of the diminuendos that matters. Now a concert hall can help you do this by gently resuscitating the sound as you play, by giving that sound what I call a bloom. Not only does this mean that your music is actually filling the hall, because when you can *feel* that resuscitation it is in fact hitting the back and sides of the hall and on its journey back filling the hall. In some halls there's a lot of air space to fill. The Sydney Opera House is a case in point. The interior is certainly impressive, the acoustics for general purposes commendable, but for a solo guitar it's a washout. They've got a ventilation system which seems to me pretty dotty. You get the hot air rising from the lower level, with the cold air ventilation above that. So you get a kind of eddying effect in the air, because the hot air wants to move up, while the cold air wants to come down. Miracle you aren't sucked through the roof together with the sound, it seems to me. The exterior architectural design on the other hand is one of the most beautiful things I've seen. Is it not the only truly original piece of architecture to go up anywhere since the war? Full marks. But only seven out of ten for the interior.

'Now the Maltings at Snape in Suffolk, Benjamin Britten's hall, is a wonderful place. The woodcladding and steel bracing in the roof together with the unrendered and rough brickwork round the sides make for a warm and vibrant acoustic, though the bass resonances tend to swim a bit, particularly when the hall is empty, which for a concert you hope it isn't. Of course, when there is such a vibrant acoustic, I have to be careful to take the tempi just a little slower. You see, I always try to adjust my playing to the acoustics of a hall. Normally, this is an intuitive affair, but at Snape I consciously say to myself before walking on to the planks "now take it easy".

'The most perfect small hall I know just happens to be in London, the Wigmore Hall. It seats about 560, and because it is so small, and I have a really good following in London I could probably fill it several nights a week with the same programme. This lovely old hall is perfection in every way for the lute or the guitar, or it was—before the London Transport authorities decided some years ago to run the new Victoria Line tube train right underneath it. Even so, that's a minor blemish compared to everything else it has to offer. Also I like the idea of playing in a small and intimate hall that is situated in the middle of a vast sprawling metropolis like London. There is very little that is small and intimate about London. The buildings, shops, buses, thoroughfares and the like can be huge. The density of population enormous; the traffic horrendous; the noise, filth and the bustle unspeakable, and the individual person? He's just one of millions in the rat race. But if that person enjoys music and chamber music in particular, to walk off the pavement and enter the Wigmore Hall, and sit down quietly with the expectancy of a lovely programme in the offing—well that's a wonderful treat, an experience that I have enjoyed many times myself. But it is more than a treat—in London it is positively a solace.

'On my English tours I often play two concerts at the "Wiggers", and then I might take the same programme down to the Fairfields Hall at Croydon in South London. It's quite a long way from the centre of town, but if there are enough keen guitar players who really want to hear me play, they can always take a train down there. Fairfields is another very good hall; it's big, but it has really good sound. Also I like the idea of playing outside the centre of a city. A lot of people live in South London; they are quite a different audience; so why shouldn't they have a concert? Why should it always have to be in the fashionable West End of London. Anyway, I find the people who run that hall are always so helpful, and rather delighted you've come. Sometimes in other, more impersonal, places it's take-it or leave-it and/or sod off.

'In the United States, Town Hall, New York has it over all the others, except perhaps Jordan Hall in Boston. Both are magnificent acoustically. On the Continent, the Concertgebouw in Amsterdam is an excellent hall for me; it's large, holding over two thousand, I think, but it has the most superb acoustic. And not only is the sound good, the atmosphere is so warm and enchanting; but then the Dutch can lay that on if they want to! I wish I could take that hall on tour with me everywhere. You can play so quietly there, almost inaudibly, and still the sound seems to travel. It has the effect of increasing your whole dynamic range. And, talking about dynamic range, I am often asked why it is that I never use amplification for a solo recital in a large hall. It's not that I'm against the use of amplification in principle, in fact I have used it on occasion for concertos with orchestra where I've felt it would be an advantage to boost the guitar sound. This seems to me an intelligent thing to do, particularly in the Villa-Lobos Concerto where the orchestral writing is so thickly textured. But in the case of a solo recital people have come to hear *you*. They've come to hear the *actual* sound that *you* make. Most people, ninety per cent of the time, hear canned sound, either at a pop concert or from gramophone records, television sets or through the wallpaper. So when the real sound is being provided, it is vital that the acoustics are good and that the sound in its wholesomeness and subtleness can be heard. Anything less than that is an abuse of the very privilege I have of being up there, of being an artist, as well as an indiscretion towards all those people who have paid hard cash for their tickets.

'It is because of this, because of my concern that a recital wherever it may be should be so set-up that the music experience has every chance to be at its optimum that I take such care with lighting and the exact placing of my chair. I gave a recital recently in Genoa, in a small opera house, and all the lighting was fixed for the opera they were due to give the following night. I asked the lighting guy if he would adjust a couple of lights slightly, and he wouldn't. Well, I got a little bit tense about that, because I thought well, bugger it, I'm giving the concert here tonight. The opera is tomorrow night, and tonight's the night for me. I only wanted two lights, and there were about fifty five lights up there. He had only got to go up and adjust a couple for me, and after the concert run up a few more stairs and put them back. But he just wouldn't do it. Finally I just had to raise the roof a bit; I can tell you, under those pre-concert conditions it's not too difficult to get steamed up in order to raise the roof, because by this time you are getting anxious about the concert and the least you ask of your helpers, which includes the lighting man, is a bit of co-operation. After all, he's paid to do lights, and I'm paid to play the guitar. We're in this together, I thought. Christ.

'Another difficulty in our magnificent day and age is trying to get a bit of silence. You cannot buy it. You cannot procure it, you either have it or you don't and I can tell you that in most cities throughout the western industrialized countries it's in very short supply. This is largely because of wheels, ball bearings and the combustion engine, but also because the human race, it appears, must always be on the go. It seems they've largely lost the inheritance or ability to pipe down and be still.

'Just to digress for a moment, in the 1973 fuel crisis I happened to be on tour in Germany and Switzerland. It was a "car tour" and because of the crisis there was a total ban on Sunday driving. This was particularly inconvenient for me as a couple of the concerts fell on a Sunday, and twice within 14 days I had to drive over 600 miles in a day with a speed restriction of 60 m.p.h. in order to arrive at my destination before midnight on the Saturday. Not exactly a joy ride, but an interesting experience, because on the Sunday morning when I awoke there was complete silence everywhere. Then gradually as the city awoke and people began to circulate on foot I was aware for the first time, certainly in a large city, of the sound that people *actually* make when walking and talking. The sound of a lot of people jabbering away in the street isn't exactly music to my ears, but it did create a feeling that cities *can* be human after all. Also I had to make my way to the concert by public transport— by way of an old tram. There I was in my penguin suit all poshed up struggling on to a crowded tram with my lute and guitar together with some of my audience, and a few chaps not so poshed up on their way to clocking in for the night shift. But as we trundled off down the street there was a very convivial feeling in that crowded little tram. People it seems from quite different social backgrounds were chatting together like mad, and a few of my audience were chatting with me, and a couple of them actually carried my instruments all the way to the stage door of the concert hall. Somehow I will never quite forget that day; there was something unpressured and civilized about it, and I'll tell you another thing— the air was a darn sight cleaner. So for my book, no Sunday motoring for ever!

'But going back to that occasion, I remember the hall that I played in very well. It was an old building with an incredible amount of elaborate decoration. The interior of the hall could only be summed up as "Rococo run riot"—a gem of a place for sound, but with only one draw back: the lighting.

'Now, in old halls you have a number of problems with the lights such as the old resistors on the dimmers, they can make quite a hum, and in a lively hall that hum acoustically can build up to a hell of a bloody row. On this particular occasion it was so loud that I opted for being blinded by having the lights blazing flat out, just for some peace. In modern halls, on the other hand, it's the air-conditioning that often makes the racket. You really can't win. I'm continually having terrible trouble with the air-conditioning. Yet, when you mention it to people who work in the hall, they say what are you talking about? They can't hear anything, simply because they hear it all the time. They're air-conditioned. There have been occasions when I've found it absolutely impossible to tune up the guitar because the hum of the air-conditioning unit was out of tune with the relative

'Queen Elizabeth Hall in Vancouver? Dead as a dodo. The Festival Hall in London? A disaster, at least for me. Here in Turin? Fabulous.'

pitch of the guitar. It can drive you barmy having to play in those conditions.

'I have even had to give a concert in pitch darkness once because, in order to turn off the air-conditioning, all the lights had to be turned off too as they were all on one circuit. I said, well, if that's the case, I'll have to play in the dark. A bearing had gone in one of the fans of the air-conditioning system apparently, and it was making a terrible grinding noise. Well, I couldn't begin to give a concert with a noise like that, so I played completely in the dark. A marvellous experience, actually. Naturally, my performances were different. There were moments in the faster moving pieces where I was a tiny bit unsure, and the rhythm lost a little of its inner pulse. But in the slower, more reflective music, it was extraordinary. The audience could just concentrate on the music. It is rare that you listen to music in total darkness, even at home with a gramophone record. But for some music at least, it's the perfect condition.'

'Of course, sometimes you play in halls that are so mad, you have only yourself to blame. Some years ago, I did a tour of India. I had already played in a number of capital cities, with the concerts being sponsored by the British Council. But, as I said earlier, I sometimes prefer playing in smaller centres, away from the predictable touring circuit. So when, in the middle of the tour, the British Council asked me whether I would go right up into Assam and give a concert at the University of Guharti, or Chapati or something, to the students, I immediately agreed. As it happened, they'd never had a concert of Western music there before, so I thought this could be rather an interesting expedition. The British Council said they hadn't much money, so I said, well, look, I don't want that much money because I'm more interested in going to Assam anyway. I'd like the air fare, but what I would *really* like is a large bottle of Scotch whisky, because in those days there was a real drink problem in India and prohibition was the order of the day. If you really wanted to get a drink in India, and you were lucky enough to be a foreigner, you were required to get an alcoholics card, and so naturally, when I first arrived in India, I got off the plane and made my way quickly to the desk at the airport which dealt with alcoholics' cards. I was allowed one bottle of whisky a week, but it was divided up into 27ths. A *chattopeg* was a small whisky, that is three 27ths; and a *barropeg* was a large whisky, which apparently was five 27ths. If, like me, you like to have two or three large whiskies a day, you got through your week's allocation pretty quick.

'And so towards the end of this Indian tour, I had been getting a bit fed up with drinking soda water, which is why part of the deal for this last concert in Guharti *had* to be a bottle of whisky. I knew of course that this British Council fellow could have been run in for giving me the whisky, but I said if they want me to do the concert, they will *have* to find me a bottle of Scotch. He said he'd see what he could do.

'So I got on a little plane, and we flew up to Assam, up into the beautiful hills. And since, as I mentioned, this was the first concert ever given by a Western musician, I was met at the airport by a motorcade of people in other cars and motorbikes, all blaring their horns as I was taken to the only hotel in town. By the time I got to the hotel, I suppose it must have been about two o'clock in the afternoon, so I got out the old box and started a bit of prac. And because I was playing that same day, which is a rare occurrence for me as you know, I didn't bother to go down to the hall, which was an even rarer occurrence. By coincidence, however, at five o'clock there was a knock at the door, and an Indian gentleman appeared with a bottle wrapped in newspaper, saying "this is for you, Sahib." I think he must have thought it was a pre-concert warm-up and the poor old fellow can't get on the stage unless he has had his bottle of Scotch. So there it was, this precious bottle, which I then had to hide in my hotel room.

'The concert was due to start at eight o'clock, and the man who was going to pick me up said I should arrive at the concert about twenty minutes before the show was supposed to start. But as I approached the hall, I heard some very loud rock music. I thought, that's strange, perhaps they've got a rock concert on before me. I said to the promoter, "Can you tell me, have we got a rock band here, or what's going on?" He said, "No, that's the public address system in the hall. We thought it was a good idea to play the audience a little music to settle them down." Can you imagine? The blare of these loudspeakers playing this very loud rock music? The idea that I had to go on and play the guitar right after this horrifying sound! I said to the man, look, let's get this music off. By now, I was really worried, so I thought I'd better check my chair and the lighting. But as I went on stage, I saw the most extraordinary gathering of people; there were hundreds and hundreds of women and children, many with babes in arms.

'I then began to give my usual recital, or at least tried to, but in the middle of a Bach suite, all the babies started crying. I just didn't know what to do. The pandemonium was awful. Very soon it got so hot, the promoter put on a whole row of cool-air fans, and they were making a hell of a noise; one fan even developed a squeak. And very soon it got so humid that the guitar kept going out of tune. Somehow I managed to finish the first half of the concert, but I was in a hell of a state as I came off the stage. I was resting in the artist's room, utterly dejected, when the promoter came round saying "Sahib! What are you doing?" I said, "This is the interval." He said "What interval?" I said "We have a break now." He said, "But in Indian music concerts we don't have this." And I said, "Well, half-way through a concert in the West, we *always* have a break." He said, "Is this half-way through?" I said "About half way." He said "Oh, but Sahib, Indian concerts go on for many, many hours." And I said "But Western concerts never last much longer than an hour and a half." He said, "Oh, Sahib, you must play longer than that, because if not, I'll have a riot on my hands!"

'I didn't know what to do. He was a very nice guy, which made it all more embarrassing, so in the second half of the concert I felt I was playing for my life, and his too. To make matters worse, because Indian audiences are not used to applauding each performance in a programme at the end of a piece there would just be the odd little bang or clap and that would be it. I thought, there's nothing for it, I'll just have to play every damn piece I can remember; just keep going until I stop. Which I did; I played everything I knew. There were kids screaming, people moving about, people going home, other people coming in. I didn't dare look up; as I finished one piece and started into another, I didn't even wait for the normal applause—because there wasn't any. I just kept going on and on, until I ran out of pieces. When I eventually got off the stage, dripping buckets of perspiration and shagged out of my mind, I put the box in it case and waited. But nobody came, absolutely nobody. I thought, well, where's the promoter gone? After about twenty minutes, the door opened and the promoter came in with a wad of notes about two foot high, all filthy one and three rupee notes. He dumped the pile on the guitar case, and said, "There you are, Sahib, it's all yours, I've just collected it from the audience." So I quickly stuffed the guitar case with the notes and left it at that. I can tell you, after all that, when I got back to the hotel I polished off most of that bottle of whisky! Talk about being prepared; I wasn't a boy scout in my youth for nothing.'

'The real problem for a guitarist is that when he feels he can attract a large audience in any given city, naturally the local promoter will want to put on a concert in a hall that will hold the most people. But then the difficulties begin; not only do I feel I should scale my fee according to the hall, I have to risk playing in surroundings that could be totally unsuited to the guitar in order to satisfy the local promoter and his needs, although perhaps the word should be greeds. Some of the halls in Italy, for instance, hold only six hundred people; but I can also fill the Concertgebouw in Amsterdam which holds over two thousand. The fee for the Amsterdam concert will obviously be more, because I don't see why the local promoter should make more money than I do. Because the first promoter I ever had in Amsterdam was not willing to pay a fee which I thought was commensurate with the dimensions of the hall, I arranged that he should pay my normal chamber music fee as a guarantee, plus 60 per cent of whatever money we took above that, less his expenses. He agreed, of course, because there was little or no risk involved for him. I made considerably more money, as it turned out, than the original fee I had asked for, and this is an arrangement I prefer wherever it is possible—it is at least fair, and nobody's being duped.

'In America, I play mostly for an outright fee. It always sounds a fantastic lot when you look at the figures, but for one thing I have to pay my agent 20 per cent, I pay all my publicity expenses, all the leaflets, all my travelling expenses, my living expenses, and I pay Uncle Sam 30 per cent withholding tax on the gross. And in some cases you pay a state tax as well. Now if you just do a few calculations, even if you made £5,000 a concert, Jesus, you don't end up with very much.

'You always know if the impresario is doing a good job in terms of promoting the concert when you first come into town. You can see the posters, the size of them, and how many there are, and where they are. If they're put in a good place, and there are enough of them, you know the promoter is doing his best. I've had the same impresario in New York whom I've worked with for the last 25 years. He handles all the sub-contracts with other promoters in other cities around the States. A lot of work comes from the University campuses; they usually have the wherewithal for a good concert series. Fine concert halls, and a non-aggressive commercial approach to the business of promoting concerts. These University promotions are in many ways the backbone to any projected tour in America for most artists, particularly those artists that have yet to establish themselves.

'In the Socialist countries, behind the Iron Curtain, the State Impresariat run the show. Generally speaking the state organizations are pretty inefficient, simply because everything is very centralized and the bureaucracy horrendous. Not that I've ever played there, but I've heard many people say that the Russian organization in Moscow is an absolute nightmare, it's so inefficient. I think people mean well in these big organizations; it's just that the machinery either gets clogged up or at times there's no machinery at all. In Yugoslavia, it works pretty well; I mean, I wasn't actually paid for my concert in Zagreb, just some money to cover extra costs and things like that. But I know I'll get paid eventually. I remember once having a concert in Prague, however, at a Prague Spring Festival. Everything was agreed, until we tried to get some confirmation about when I was supposed to get there. We could get absolutely no reply at all. We tried telephoning them, but it was absolutely impossible to get an answer. So finally, contract or no contract, I just didn't go. It was the only concert in my life I have reneged on.

'Sometimes—in the west—a concert is underwritten by the City Council or by a private firm, in which case, there is usually enough money available to cover a possible loss should it occur. But the balance *I* have to strike is further complicated by the fact that my audience is often very young. Psychologically, young people don't like shelling out lots of money for a concert ticket. They will, of course, if it's for a pop concert, or some fabulous film, some weird double-X extravaganza. Young people are important to me, not only because of their open yet attentive enthusiasm but because, if you've got young people interested in what you're doing, then you've got a good and continuing audience for many years to come. For this reason alone, I find it very important not to overprice the tickets.

'I'm beginning to try and overcome this problem, in spite of the fact that the economics of giving concerts are getting more and more nightmarish—the costs of renting the hall, the heating, the printing of publicity, newspaper advertisements, these are always going up and up nowadays. I know that the promoters must recoup their costs, otherwise they would go out of business. But the music I play, and in a sense the artistic experience I try to impart, becomes much reduced in the wrong ambience. It's not just the *size* of an auditorium; there are some halls where the sound and the general acoustic is perfect, even though they can seat over three thousand. But for chamber music, which my recitals are, such a vast space is an anachronism. The temptation, the thrill to have great success, and to have a big audience, is very gratifying but it has never been the prime consideration for me. That is why I really hate promoters who try to take advantage of me.

'I remember one terrible incident in South America, on my first major tour there. I was really looking forward to my visit because, as you know, in latin countries the guitar is extremely popular and very much part of the folklore background. So I had arranged a tour whereby I played about one concert a week. The reason for this was that I wanted enough time to visit a number of places purely as a tourist. I gave a concert in Rio, in Brazil, one in Buenos Aires, one in Mexico City, one in Santiago de Chile, and one in Bogotá in Colombia. As I had never been there before, I arranged for my New York agent to handle everything. He in turn sub-let my

OPPOSITE
'Oh Sahib, you must play longer than that otherwise I'll have a riot on my hands.'

services to another agent in South America, who organized the whole tour in the various countries. The agent suggested I give two concerts in one of the cities but I said I didn't want to do this because it would have meant I would have had to prepare two different programmes; quite a lot of extra work for just one occasion. So I told the agent that my visit was only meant to be a promotional tour, to get myself introduced, as it were. If I was a success, I would come back and do a proper tour later. By the way, because there was and is such inflation in those countries—it makes British inflation look very pale by comparison—I arranged that my fees should be paid in US dollars. Everything was agreed, except that the agent kept insisting on two concerts. I said, no, I wouldn't do that; and he wrote back and said if you don't do it, there will be a scandal!

'Well, I thought, I'm not going to be forced into any damned thing. Either I play my one concert in this city or I don't play at all. So when I eventually arrived there, the agent met me at the airport, and said everything was OK, but he suggested I ought to see the British Council representative about the second concert. So I rang the British Council man up on my arrival at the hotel, and he too said that it was very sad that I refused to play a second concert because the organizer of that second concert is politically a very powerful woman, and her series of concerts is the most famous series in the country. It has even been advertised that you are going to play.

'So I told this chap that I was very sorry, but I had not been told it was being advertised, and my agent had always known I was only going to do one concert. Then the British Council man explained; what in fact had happened was that, as soon as the agent knew you were coming, he had booked his own concert into the hall, and then sold you to this woman. Therefore, he's in a very difficult position; because this lady is in a very powerful position—it could even ruin him. And the resulting circumstances could be very unpleasant for you too if you refuse to undertake this second concert. "Lynching in the streets," I thought? Well, I said, I'm just not going to do it on principle. They know exactly why I won't and that's that.

'Next day, I had a phone call from the lady, all very smarmy. She said of course you will do the concert for us. I said, of course I'm not going to do the concert for anyone. Then she started to turn nasty. She said, well, I'm going to cause a scandal. I'm going to take a whole page in the newspaper and make an announcement that you refuse to do the concert. And what's more, because it has been advertised, I'm going to sue you. I said, well, look, this is nothing to do with me. I told the agent I was only doing one concert, and if you go on treating me like this, it will get around. It is difficult enough to get artists to come to this country, and if you are going to blackmail foreign visitors like this and sue them for something which is not their fault, I think you will find that very few artists will *ever* play for your society again. She said, well, the newspapers will go to press at four o'clock today and if you can change your mind, I will be delighted. If you don't, a full page will be taken and I will start legal proceedings. I thought, well, if that's what she's going to do, that's what she is going to do—why the hell did I ever come here in the first place?

'About three o'clock I had a telephone call from the Ambassador. He said, if you don't do that concert, it may cause a diplomatic incident! He said he'd already written to the Foreign Office and warned them that this might happen. "I do implore you", he said, "to make an effort, because at the moment the political situation between Great Britain and this country is quite delicate. So I want you to think about this seriously." But I *had* thought about it seriously. I hated having my arm twisted, and I particularly resented pressure being put upon me by the Diplomatic Service.

'Eventually, I thought, I know what I will do. If they are *so* passionate that I should play this concert I *will* give two concerts, and I'll play the same programme twice; but for the second concert—for the charming lady—they will have to pay my full US fee, which meant they would have to pay 150 per cent more than they were already paying me. What is more, I would demand a certified US dollar cheque in my hands before I would do the concert. So I rang up the lady and said do come round to the hotel, because I would like to see you. This was just two hours before my first concert. The lady came, all smiles, with her secretary, and we sat down in the foyer of the hotel. She said, oh I'm so glad you have thought about it. I said, well, I'll tell you something. I *have* thought about it, and I want to say that I think you've treated me very unjustly, and my feeling is never to come back to this country again. In fact, possibly to leave now. But if it's going to cause embarrassment to your concert society if I do not play, I will agree to do so provided you pay me my full US fee with a certified cheque in my hands before I go on. Her charming smile changed to stone.

'She said, I don't think we can do that because I am only the president of this organization; I have a committee and *they* vote the finances. I said, well, I know how these democratic institutions can be made to be flexible in this part of the world. I'll give *you* a deadline. I'll give you until eleven o'clock tomorrow morning. If you *really* want me to do this concert, you will have to pay what I consider my proper fee for it. Whereupon she stormed out of the hotel.

'Sure enough, next morning at eleven o'clock the telephone rang. It was her secretary to say that it was all agreed. So I went along to the hall a couple of days later, I met the secretary and checked on the chair and all the lights as I normally do, and then I went back to the hotel to have some grub. I then got a cab to the concert hall, found my way to the artist's room, sat down, and tuned up the guitar. There was a vast crowd outside, but no one inside to greet me. I just seemed to have been forgotten. In due course, the secretary turned up and unceremoniously presented the cheque and left. So there I am, waiting, with nobody to tell me when to go on. There was a lady who had a little bar near the artist's room, and I had to ask *her* for directions to the stage. She pointed. I went on, there was much applause, I bowed, sat down and performed the first part of the programme. It seemed to be going quite well, so come the interval I went backstage to my room, and still there was nobody. Then some doorman said it was time to go on for the second half, so I went on, did the rest of the concert, came to the end, a great success to judge from the applause, a couple of encores, and back once again to the artist's room. Someone from the British Council turned up and said thank you very much and then left, and that was it. I tell you, I was waiting for a bomb or something to explode. Eventually I just left, grabbed a taxi and went back to my hotel. Next morning, first thing, I went to the bank, cashed the cheque and got the first plane out. I left almost as unceremoniously as I'd arrived.'

'I suppose basically I hate the whole idea of money, though it is useful stuff to have around—particularly if you have enough of it. To play is for me a *pleasure*, and I just don't see why money should have anything to do with it. Naturally I've got to live like anybody else. For many years, when I started, I was very poor; I had no money at all. I would still be happy, being poor or relatively so, provided I'd got a roof over my head and I could play my music. I've always been lucky, however. I've always somehow had *enough* money. Though there have been a few people in my life who have tried to lighten my burden.

'Mind you, I've never been extravagant. I've always had a nice place to live; I've had my books, pictures, my music and a nice guitar, and that's all I have ever really wanted. I don't let any deal get past me, if I can help it, and if money comes my way, great, I'm not going to give it back: because money can be put to good use, I don't mean on the stock exchange but more importantly for myself. I find money can give me a certain amount of freedom and flexibility within my professional life. For example I haven't got to take every concert engagement that is offered to me. I can pick and choose. I can plan my own programme, and play what *I* want to play. I never have to take on any hack TV film or recording work. I can commission new music, and I can take the time off to learn new works too, and if I want to I can be independent of commercial considerations, if I consider a certain project worthwhile, and in the circumstances *has* to be done. Nor will I play for peanuts, unless there is a very special reason and then I might even play for nothing.

'Some artists I know feel that their whole reputation in the profession is based on what they can get as a concert fee. But that doesn't bother me one bit. The important point is that the music itself must never have to fight an environment which has been dictated to you by financial considerations. The ambience, the atmosphere that I need to give a good recital, is vital, and nothing must be allowed to disturb it if I can possibly avoid it. In a recital of guitar music, and even more so in a recital of lute music, if you haven't got complete control over the ambient conditions in a hall, you can never achieve the rapt intimacy you need to make the utmost contact with the audience.

'The use of tape-recorders or cameras during a concert, for

instance, drives me to distraction. If the tape somehow isn't rolling properly onto the cassette, it makes a hiss, and that sort of mechanical noise can absolutely break the spell, the magic I've been trying to weave. There have been occasions when I've seen a machine in the audience, and I've beckoned to the person who has got the machine to bring it to me. Naturally they become very self-conscious, because it's rather like asking a young boy who has been caught scrumping to take the apples out of his shirt. Sheepishly, sometimes, he or she will come forward. Perhaps they think I'm going to advise them on how to set the machine up to get the perfect balance. But when they offer me their tape machine, I put it on the stage and say "Thank you. Let's leave it there for the remainder of the performance." And they think "This may be good! Do you mean leave it on?" "No," I say. "We'll leave it off."

'Once, in Germany, I remember there was a man in the front row with a very big machine; he had the microphone in his hand, and he was thrusting it as far forward as he could. I looked at him, and shook my head. It didn't have any effect. So at the end of the piece, I went right to the apron of the stage and said "no recording." And he said "all right." I got back to my seat and started the next piece, and damn me if he didn't start the machine all over again with the microphone again thrust as far forward as he could. I looked at him again, and again shook my head. Again, no effect. So once again, at the end of the piece, I went back to the front of the apron of the stage and I said: "Now look, this is not allowed; this is an infringement of international copyright law for a start, and also I don't like it. So would you be very kind and stop the machine?" He said "fine." So I started again, and blow me, he started up his machine again!

'I just didn't know what to do, because I felt I had been very reasonable with him. I thought the best thing to do was finish the piece, and then go off stage, and stay off stage and wait. I felt that the audience would either tell him to leave, or someone would take the machine away from him. Well, there was an uneasy silence for about ten minutes until I heard a tremendous crash, followed by some applause. I thought, my God, someone else is going to continue the concert. So I returned to the stage, only to see this poor chap's tape machine in bits all over the floor. What had happened apparently was that someone had come down from the balcony, got hold of this man's machine, walked back upstairs, and thrown it from the balcony. It was really very sad to see this poor chap picking up all the bits. There was tape everywhere, and plastic components all over the floor. Rough justice, maybe, but practical justice as far as the audience was concerned.

'Likewise photographers. I mean, one flash bulb can simply kill off the whole musical spell that you may have been trying to create for an hour. If it's not the flash, then it's the shutter noise of a camera. I get really thrown when people insist on taking photographs. I try to be reasonable. Naturally, the local photographers want to get a picture of you playing in their hall, particularly the local press. But there are ways of doing it; either they come

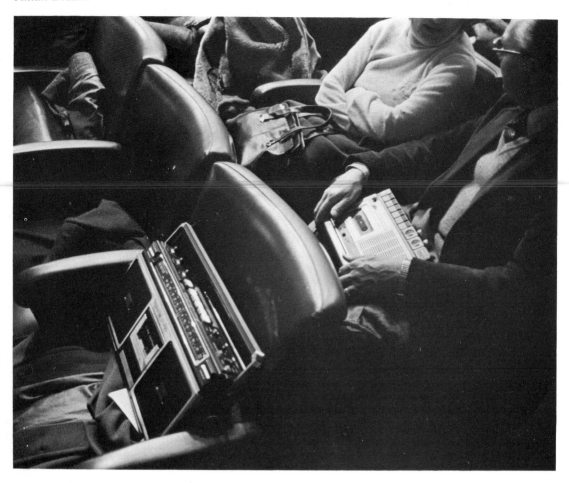

'Concert-going is a ritual. You don't go to church in a pair of dungarees do you? Nowadays you take your tape-recorder.'

backstage before the concert and take their happy snaps in the artist's room; or I have, on occasions, offered to go back onto the platform right at the end of the concert for a quick snap so that the concert itself is not interfered with.

'There have been times when, suddenly, particularly near the beginning of a recital when you're trying to build up this intimate rapport with an audience, someone has gone and let off a flash. Normally I can lay on a fairly good look of annoyance at the drop of a hat, as you know; the message gets across and they don't push their luck. But not so very long ago, in California actually, a photographer actually marched noisily down the central gangway of the hall just as I had begun playing my first piece. He came right up to the edge of the stage and, only two foot away, focused his camera straight at me. I was simply amazed. I mean, I looked up with an expression of abject, agonized annoyance and really glowered at him, hoping that he would not want a hideous picture by which to remember me. But, of course, that didn't help my interpretation of the music. I was now having to play entirely from muscular memory, as it were; I didn't want to stop; that would have been a disaster. but I wanted to get rid of him as soon as possible. I decided to try and stare him out.

'At first, he moved back a little bit, but then he proceeded to focus his camera again. So I stared back at him with even more intensity, and he moved back a little farther. Once again he began adjusting his camera, so I absolutely glared at him with all the glare I could muster. He got the message, or so it seemed, and moved back even farther. But each time he moved back, he just re-focused his lens. Finally, I gave him the utmost look of abject, agonized annoyance I could summon up—Christ, I must have looked awful. But it worked. I can see him now backing away, right out of the auditorium, and eventually just falling over in the foyer! Remember that old expression; if looks could kill. Well, mine is the face that has flattened a thousand photographers.'

9 'Minimizing the squeak.'

'Making records is very much a regular part of my life on the road, except, as you will see, this part takes place *down* the road, a mile or so from my home. For a guy who hates microphones I've made an awful lot of gramophone records, and even after all these years they can be a terrible bore. For many musicians, much of their professional work is done in studios—television studios, radio studios or recording studios. It's a day-in-day-out job carried out with nonchalance and ease, yet somehow the whole thing always seems to me finally a bit artificial, even phoney. It is artificial in the sense that you are trying to grab and hoard something which ideally should be left alone. A musical sound, and indeed a performance, is something which happens and then disappears into thin air, literally. To try and capture it abuses the very nature of that phenomenon, it seems to me.

'Obviously I can see the advantages of gramophone records, particularly for enthusiasts who love to hear the same piece of music over and over again, or for people who can never manage to get to recitals or concerts, or who perhaps live in a part of the world rarely visited by musicians of high calibre. I can see there is a lot to be said for using these mechanical devices to participate in something that is unique to the time of its duration, but for myself I would much prefer to be free of the worries that the microphone brings. Particularly when a "live" concert is being recorded it is sometimes difficult to project the guitar in a concert hall, and quite often, particularly in the louder passages, you are utilizing the instrument in such a way as to produce the optimum amount of sound from it. And occasionally sound almost at the point of distortion. In a concert hall, however, that optimum sound is distilled in the air; by the time the sound gets to the audience, any modest distortion contained in it is rectified. But a highly sensitive condenser microphone can pick up that distortion, however faint it may be, and when I am making a gramophone record I am always aware of this. It therefore takes me time to relax and settle down at a recording session and it may take an hour or longer sometimes, before I can really begin to *make* music. Once I've got the measure of the microphone and the studio I'm on my way, and hopefully getting something really worthwhile into the can. I cannot say that it's an utterly pleasurable experience, although I must confess I often enjoy the challenge.

'I rarely play my own records, although I will admit I play other people's records and get a great amount of enjoyment from listening to recordings, particularly of chamber music. But is it not finally a cheat, I think to myself? Can one ultimately kid oneself it's the real thing in the same way as one might with canned or frozen peas? The problem is that modern equipment and modern recording techniques are so refined that it has become an even worse cheat because it sounds almost as if it *is* the real thing. Modern technology has brought the real thing into your living room, or so it seems. Are we being kidded that this is so totally the real thing that it makes no odds? I know this may seem a bit old fashioned, even a bit prissy, but I don't think *real* music-making should be imprisoned in this nonchalant, mechanical way. Music is made, and it's gone; it has disappeared, and therein lies much of its real magic. The fact that you can't go back to the beginning again is after all, one of the truly wonderful things about music to my mind. The music has finished, there is silence. You can never know where the music has gone to. If you play a few notes, where do they lodge themselves? In that picture? Up the chimney? *Where* do they go? It's a whole bloody mystery, isn't it? And yet somehow the nature of recording can destroy that mystical element. Now, considering I get a nice little cheque every six months for my record royalties, I'm doing a lousy PR job aren't I.

'Yet, like so many of the conveniences of our modern life, to suddenly be without gramophone records, I suspect, would engender a lot of resentment, sadness, and possibly neurosis for many people. The question, therefore, is how—as an artist—can one best come to terms with the artificiality of the medium of recording yet retain the true essence of performance, which is a uniquely spontaneous affair, and furthermore preserve something of that human interaction which has nurtured the very act of performance for thousands of years? I find the ambience of a modern recording studio for instance, very clinical, visually as well as from the sound point of view. I would go so far as to say that a recording studio, particularly if it is very dry acoustically, can debilitate the very spirit of music. You play a few notes and it sounds like throwing a load of old toothpicks around in a large-sized matchbox. When you're trying to play a phrase of Bach, for example, with all its curves and its arabesques, you look up, to heaven as it were, and what do you see? Horrid angular shapes, nasty colours and cold electric or neon light. In many recording studios, the fashion seems to be having very little reverberation, and it's your unfortunate lot if you're put into a "pop" studio because pop musicians cannot stand acoustically alive conditions. Their studios are dead, acoustically as well as in every other way, because it is now considered the smart thing to do, to re-mix the sound and afterwards add all that echo stuff. It's like all the processed food that we eat, advertised and enriched with alphabetic vitamins. A person who *really* knows about nutrition knows its a load of crap.

'Well, that is all very well. But when you play a plucked instrument, where the impact of the note is immediate and thereafter gradually dies on you, you need the resuscitation which reverberation and reflection can give you so that you are able to shape a phrase properly—remember, we discussed this in relation to concert halls. In a very dry studio, therefore, you finish up with a series of plonks and silences. Now it's all very well for the engineers to say, well, we can put that right afterwards. But I need it *now*, to make my music *now*. Apart from anything else, the tempi you choose are often determined by the amount of reverberation in any given hall or studio. If you have a little or none you don't want to have a lot of silences, so you quicken the tempo a little. It's no good at all taking a quick tempo because the studio is dry, and then having the engineers put on dollops of echo, because it completely screws up the articulation of the music.'

Bream has been making gramophone records for almost thirty years. He has completed, in all, about forty discs, including re-pressing and re-groupings of earlier records, a total of over four hundred different pieces—transcriptions from harpsichord music, piano music, from the vihuela, from the five-course guitar, orchestral music, lute music, music he has commissioned, as well as a complete cross-section of the entire original repertoire for the guitar. 'I've got a couple of gold records around somewhere, and some silvers. I've also got half a dozen Grammy Awards. I won two Edison Awards for records of contemporary music, which I'm rather proud of, especially as they've now discontinued the award, which I think is a pity.'

'Of course, the big problem recording the guitar, and even more so the lute, is the quiet sound of the instrument, which is often so delicate that you need *absolute* silence. But absolute silence is now almost impossible to find in London, Paris or New York. First, there are the various underground transport systems, which can create a nightmare of endless rumble. Then there are the jet aeroplanes and the traffic. Most people don't hear such things, but these modern microphones and the digital system of recording can pick up this background rumble and make it sound like a bloody earthquake, in stereo! Last year, I did a recording in New York, in the RCA building. It is a good studio; it gives some life and bloom to the sound; certainly not a dry old dustbin. But next door is a multi-storey garage which contains a lift—you know, the kind where they take the cars up and down to the various floors. Every time a car went up in this lift, there was a terrible whining noise as the lift went higher and higher, a glissando in a crescendo. There was then a great clonk as the lift came to a halt and finally there was the noise of the car engine starting up and the back wheels skidding off the lift. In terms of musical inspiration, not to say human tolerance, the situation became absurd.

'Things are just as bad in London. Once, I was recording in Kenwood House in North London. All of a sudden, the fog came down, so I decided to take the tube home. The Producer wanted to take the tapes away with him to have a listen, and he too travelled home on the tube. The next morning, when we came to listen to the tapes again, the most extraordinary thing had happened. What we heard was the sound of a tube train accelerating throughout a Bach Sarabande. The tapes had picked up the sound of the train engine through a freak of magnetism and had recorded it. It was back to the drawing board on that occasion.

'Another time I was playing with rather a large orchestra and trying to record a concerto in Walthamstow Town Hall, in East London, and we had a bomb scare. We were immediately ordered out of the hall to foregather on the precincts outside. It was a hot and humid afternoon, but naturally we took our instruments with us while the police checked the place out. It took an hour or so for the police to complete their work, by which time all the stringed instruments, reacting to the warm sun, were thrown completely out of tune. When we were finally let back into the Town Hall, it took us ages to tune up again, and all the original impetus that we had worked towards at the beginning of the session was thwarted and dissipated.

'Again, at another "recording studio" in London—actually, it was a sort of converted scout-hut, somewhere near Finchley in North London—disaster struck. We had chosen the place purposely as it was some way from the jet flight paths. But throughout the evening it rained and rained, and we kept hearing tremendous noises of splattering rain like a miniature Niagara Falls. There was nothing for it but to check the gutters, which we did. Can you imagine, there I am trying to record a delicate piece for the lute by William Byrd, and what am I supposed to do in order to make it possible to carry on recording? Clean out the gutters! Well, the producer climbed up a ladder, forgot I was underneath, and threw all the muck that was in the gutters all over me. I was covered from head to foot with decayed slime and rubbish; not surprisingly, I was uncomfortably damp for the remainder of the session.

'None of this has really endeared me to the idea of recording, and at one time I became so self-conscious about my studio playing that I cancelled one particular tape and took a year off from recording altogether. The artificiality of it all had begun to drag me into despair. The quest for technical perfection, and the wish to eliminate ancillary off-stage noises had gradually worn me down. My performances in the studio were becoming lifeless and self conscious. The phrasing was becoming mannered and there now was a tension in my playing that said nothing about music, but plenty about my inner frustrations. So I decided to chuck it all in for the time being; I took up flying gliders instead.

'At that time I had been living in the country, in Wiltshire, for a couple of years or more, and it crossed my mind more than once that possibly my recording career could be resurrected down here, in some church perhaps or even in a lovely room of some grand country house. At least we would have no jets, tube trains and the rest. Little did I know that less than two miles down the road lay the answer to my prayers. I had heard tell of a beautiful eighteenth-century chapel in the vale of Wardour. So one day I went to have a look at it. I just happened to bring along the old box, in case the acoustical characteristics of the chapel were such that I might be tempted to strum the odd tune. But on entering the chapel, I was bowled over by its beauty and proportions. It seemed like some wondrous jewel set in that old yet curiously domestic vale of Wardour. It seemed a profane act almost to open the guitar case and strike a chord in this wondrous space, but that I did, and in doing so I knew instinctively that you could bung up a microphone anywhere in that building and produce a magical sound. I knew it was so absolutely right for me, and a few days later when my producer, Jimmy Burnett, came down, my original expectations were confirmed—it *was* the perfect place to record the lute and guitar. The only difference, Burnett pointed out, was that instead of jets, tube trains and cars, there were birds singing, the wind in the trees and the Warminster artillery gun range! Were we back to square one? Not quite, happily.

'The chapel is in fact a Jesuit house of worship, and through the kindness of the trustees and the Reverend Father I was soon allowed to use it pretty much as and when I wanted, providing it did not interfere with Mass which was said about twice a week. The interior was unusually interesting because it was originally designed by a much respected Italian architect who flourished towards the end of the eighteenth century. The style is a fascinating mixture of Palladio and Italian-cum-English baroquery. It is not as elaborate as you might find in Venice or Bavaria, but more restrained, rather English in fact. You can almost imagine what the architect must have said to his draughtsmen: "Now boys, don't let's go too far; you know, we mustn't kick over the traces. You know how English people are. Just hold back a bit. Else we'll lose the job." The result was a building of exquisite proportion, an interior that is a veritable feast for the eyes. As for musical sound, for the lute and the guitar; it is perfection. One is obviously slightly upsetting the main reason for the pile to be there in the first place, by cluttering it up with equipment and microphone leads and God knows what. But I've nearly always found that it's the Jesuits or the high Catholics who are the most flexible and reasonable, and seem not to mind too much about the fact that their beautiful house of worship is temporarily turned into a recording studio. It's very interesting that. If you wanted to use a Baptist Chapel, for instance, I mean there could be hell to pay.

'For me, the Chapel is almost too good, I am spoiled, because there is nothing more encouraging than to walk into the dreaded recording session and, as you tune up the guitar, realize that in fact you are making a lovely sound. You soon forget all your reservations about making gramophone records. There are inevitably a few snags. As I mentioned, there is a well known gun range at Warminster ten miles away, and every now and then they decide to send a barrage in our direction. Other times you have a damn great rain storm, and because the Chapel is rather old, the guttering cannot cope with the downpour and the rain just splatters down the side of the building. You can hear it making puddles outside. It might be OK if you were recording the Spring Song by Mendelssohn, or some other rainy piece, but it's not too good for

'To capture a sound abuses the very nature of that phenomenon.'

anything else. Then the oil heating sometimes starts rumbling, we have to turn off the heating and freeze. Then we have an evening chorus of the birds. So what we have to do is time everything; we know roughly when the birds are going to start up, and we time our sessions accordingly. Actually I don't mind the occasional sound of a blackbird on my records. I mean, if people know I record in the countryside, it wouldn't be unusual to hear a blackbird, would it? In fact, it's quite a pleasant sound, probably as beautiful as anything that I can make. But I think I draw the line at gun fire.'

'As important as the Chapel is to me—and you must remember that not only do I make most of my RCA recordings there and my occasional BBC recorded recitals, but I've also done numerous television and film productions from there—the real key to my recording career is held by the skills and immense patience of two lovely, and in their way remarkable men, my producer Jimmy Burnett, and my engineer John Bower. I often wonder whether it is because all three of us have the same initials, or that we are all roughly of the same age, or that we are all equally barmy, that we work so well together. I have worked with Jimmy since 1949, and with John since 1960. You could say we know each other quite well. I've done a few records with other people, but most of my recordings have been done by Jimmy and John, and most of them

have been made down here in the Chapel at Wardour.

'Jimmy has an extraordinary ear for music, and he knows my playing backwards, all manner of sideways and forwards. He has also got immense tact with artists, and no less with me. He knows how to get the very best out of you, in the nicest possible way. For years he was with the BBC, as a sound balancer, so he knows instinctively about the acoustical properties of a given place; where to place the microphones, for instance. When you are recording a guitar, you have got to get the presence of the instrument, that is the nearness of the instrument, but at the same time you need the ring, the magic of the instrument, that is its sense of perspective and distance. It's a tricky balance. The sound has somehow got to be in proportion to what the instrument might sound like in a good concert hall. When I'm making a record of contemporary music, I might have the microphone a little nearer because of the higher dynamic contrasts in the piece; in classical or nineteenth-century romantic music, I might withdraw the microphone a little. Six inches can make a world of difference. And yet, in spite of this infinitely delicate balance, Jimmy insists on using just one microphone, with two heads. The stereo "picture" is tight, but so well focused that I find it difficult to imagine that, as recorded sound, it could be bettered.

'John Bower is an equally amazing engineer. There is nothing he

Jimmy Burnett . . . 'equally barmy. He knows my playing backwards and sidewards.'

does not know, he says, about the latest sophisticated equipment. He can pull a whole tape machine to bits and remedy a fault if required, right down to the latest printed circuit module. And he is marvellous to work with in the editing room. We all get on fabulously, well, at least 95 per cent of the time. For the remaining 5 per cent sparks do occasionally fly, and they're not electrical either. Perhaps this is because I'm a Cancerian—instantaneous indecision; John is Taurus—inflexible about being flexible. I'm not too sure about Jimmy's astrological star, but he's a darn good referee, so I suspect he must be a Capricorn.

'Most of my recording sessions now take place in Wiltshire over a long weekend. John will arrive at my house sometime in the mid-afternoon on a Friday, his battered old Peugeot car stuffed full of tape machines, amplifiers, preamplifiers, Dolby stretchers, loud-speakers, and about five miles of cable not to mention recording tape. He collects the key of the Chapel from me and then unloads and sets up his equipment in a little room to the side of the Chapel. About an hour and a half later, Jimmy turns up at my house and we may look through some of the music we are going to record that evening. John returns, having rigged all the equipment; we all have a cup of tea and a natter, and then push off up to the Chapel and proceed with the evening's work.

'Like the rest of my time on the road, I prefer to keep a fairly strict timetable. We usually record at the Chapel in the evening, preferably after the evening chorus of birds has died down, working through to about midnight, which is a good time for music-making, I think. Then, as we've got a double lot of equipment (with the exception of the main recording machine), we come back to my house and spend the next morning editing the previous night's tapes. As the chaps always stay in my house during the recording sessions, we're all in it together, if you see what I mean. We spend the day editing the tapes we've made the night before, so that when we start the next session that evening, we're absolutely fresh. At least, we've got no backlog of work to do. Also, while Jimmy and John are editing, I am preparing the music for the next session, although I am obviously on hand to choose the material that I want from the various takes of the night before. We put in twelve to fourteen hours work a day. But it's concentrated work, which is what we all like. We work away for two or three days, and, at the end, with a bit of luck we've got a new gramophone record!'

'Of course, no matter how good the recording facilities, they still cannot hide certain other sound problems I have. You have probably noticed that on stage I grunt a lot; my wheezing and grunting can be quite awful, but what can I do? The grunting comes not from effort exactly, though sometimes it does, but from an excess of what I can only call passion for the music, and often the real enjoyment of that passion. It also comes from the fact that the guitar is not by nature a projecting instrument; not like the piano or the violin, for example. The audience has to come to you, or at least meet you half way. So the grunting tends to come from a communicative wish to get a little more out of the instrument than is genuinely there. The grunts are often my own recognition of the limitations of the guitar's sonority, particularly in a large concert hall, and the frustration this builds up inside me because of my wish to project more than the guitar can or should. I have to get rid of the steam somehow, so the grunts may be an escape valve.

'Another difficulty is the squeaks you make sometimes as your fingers travel up and down the fretboard, like the clatter of jacks on the harpsichord. It would be lovely if squeaks were not there, but they nearly always are. Some performers manage to eliminate a lot of the squeak; John Williams, for instance, doesn't squeak very much, partly because I know he takes especial care not to squeak, but also because his left hand release action is meticulously correct. I squeak more than some, possibly because I tend to let myself go in concerts. If I worried about taking my fingers off the string, and then putting them down again on the same string, merely to avoid the squeak, I might lose the musical line. I know that if you keep your fingers on the string while you move to the next position, you risk a squeak. But at least the melodic line is unbroken, and there are ways of minimizing the squeak. That's what I'm working on at the moment. Christ, I sound like the Prime Minister and the problems of the inner cities; you know, "I'm working on it at the moment."

'After a while, though, I don't think some of these sounds matter too much, provided they are not too distracting from the music or distressing for the listener. Sometimes, I even get carried away and start tapping my foot; I suppose that comes from my old jazz band days when it seemed unnatural *not* to tap one's foot. There's a recording I made many, many years ago of a Bach Partita, and in the Fugue you can quite clearly hear me tap-tap-tapping away. Jimmy Burnett said to me, well, I know it's a lovely "take", but we can't use it because we can hear your foot tapping. When I listened to it, I thought in fact the tapping slightly enhanced the music; it gave it a Count Basie-like rhythm section. Jimmy raised his eyebrows for a minute or so, but we kept it in.

'So, thanks to Messrs. Burnett and Bower, as well as the happy chance of having discovered nearby the ideal "recording studio", I've now reconciled myself to the problems of having to make gramophone records, and I've now begun to plan my concert life on the road around these recording sessions. I've mentioned before how I usually need many performance of a work, not only to perfect the techniques involved, but more importantly to allow the music to mature in my imagination so that I can begin to explore some of its more inaccessible depths. So when I plan a tour on the road, I usually choose the music for that tour knowing that some time soon I shall go into the Chapel and commit those pieces to tape. Of course, I hope that they're in good shape technically before I ever play them before an audience. But I do learn about those pieces through the audience's vibes and reaction, and hopefully this improves my understanding of the music.'

'My record company, RCA, has always given me *carte blanche* to record just what I want and how I want. I know I am an extremely lucky person to be given that facility. They may suggest something, but normally speaking they allow me to select the music to be recorded. This all comes from many years of trust, of course, and a certain amount of success. Obviously I know that certain records will not sell as well as others, but when I've done a record which I have really wanted to do, although I have known it was unlikely to be a great commercial success, I will then try to do a more popular album next time. There are certain pieces of music that *have* to be recorded willy nilly, whether it is commercially desirable to do so or not, and I think these big companies have a certain duty to underwrite those pieces just as I have a duty to perform them. Nevertheless, it helps to understand the whims and predicaments of a large corporation such as RCA; to get what one wants in any walk of life is usually a question of understanding and negotiation.

'I now like to plan years ahead, but a few years ago by chance I was listening to a BBC broadcast of a newly formed string quartet. I happened to know all the people who were playing intimately— they were all old friends—and I thought they played together quite wonderfully. There was Hugh Maguire, Iona Brown, Cecil Aronowitz and Terence Weil. So I rang up Hugh and said, look, would you like to do a recording with me of a couple of guitar quartets— which I had had in mind for several years, the Haydn Guitar Quartet and one of the Boccherini string quintets for guitar and string quartet. Hugh said yes, so I quickly booked—or rather Jimmy booked—a little church in London and we made a really lovely recording. It was joy all the way. Sadly, for various reasons, the quartet was disbanded soon after that. I had a premonition that they would break up quite early on, which was why I arranged the recording sessions so quickly. I just felt that, as a string quartet, they could not hold together for long. Their sound and ensemble was almost too ideal, like a brief but beautiful love affair. It transcended time and the practical considerations of continuity. Anyhow, we got them on wax, and so I have, I believe, their only recording, so their sound was not lost forever. Which, if you think about it finally disproved for me my aversion in principle to the gramophone record. Yes, of course it is artificial; of course it is radically altering the very nature of music-making; it is imprisoning something that should be free. And yet, as in this instance, I must admit it has its value.

'What one must never forget, however, is that recording as an artistic medium is quite separate from music-making in the concert hall. Which is one reason why, when I see someone recording one of my concerts with one of those cassette machines or even in some instances those remote control tape decks, I get very worried. I've no idea who's going to hear this, so must I be careful not to overdo the dynamic range of my music because it won't register all its subtleties on that damn tape recorder? This sort of artificial constraint imposed upon me when I'm playing to a live audience, not only breaks the circuit between me and that audience, and thus destroys what I hope will be the magic, the flow and the uniqueness of that occasion, but also represents a complete failure on the part of the person attempting this illicit recording to understand the fundamental differences between the media. There is no way, for instance, in which a gramophone record can convey the physical aspect of a public performance; gestures that I make when I'm playing, which sometimes help to give the audience a feeling of what is happening in the music, can never be captured on a wax disc. If one plays in the concert hall without any facial or bodily expression, it looks to the audience as though the music is running along in the same rather flat, unflamboyant key, that the music is as a matter of fact, even perhaps boring. But if you move along with the music—when you hit a loud chord, say, and give a fairly demonstrative movement to accompany that chord—then you convey to the audience a little bit more of the dynamic character that you are trying to put into that chord.

'A record can also rarely convey that sense of fun you can have when performing with other people, although some years ago I did a live album with John Williams which we recorded partly in the Avery Fisher Hall in New York and partly in Boston. That, in many ways, is one of my favourite recordings to date simply because, miraculously, it really does encapsulate the sense of fun and yet seriousness that we impart in our live performances together.

'Two guitars is an excellent combination, if you're a plucker. John is a very different type of guitarist from me; his playing has a fine, aristocratic quality; quite unique; very classical and beautifully controlled. He is the sort of player that Mozart would have liked; Beethoven perhaps might not have gone overboard, because it is the restraint with which he plays that is so remarkable. He doesn't over-indulge; everything is held in proportion, nothing is overstated. In fact very eighteenth-century. I do not envy him his abilities, as much as I admire them. I don't know why. Sometimes I wish I could play half as neatly as John does. I suppose it is because there is such tension between our different styles that we stimulate each other as much as we do. I don't play a great deal with John, which is sad, because when I do I find I learn a lot by watching and hearing him play. With his extraordinary technique and almost phenomenal control, John could probably play the pants off me, though I suspect not quite. In any case, he doesn't, because I feel sure he is aware of other things, principally that we are making music together. I often feel I am the woman in our duo, the feminine end of the stick. I sort of buzz around him, and bother him, opening up new ideas to which he *has* to address himself. But I don't push him too far because in many ways he's like a rock on which I depend.

'He hates travelling, which is one reason why we don't play together more often. Once, we were on tour in the north of England and got stranded on York railway station. It was pissing with rain and was a dismal morning. The train was late and it was very gloomy on the platform with the rain actually coming through the station roof. John looked up in a melancholy sort of way and said,

Christ this is awful; I can't stand it. I'm going to cancel all my out-of-London concerts next season. And he did. Absolutely amazing, don't you think?

'The other thing about John is that, for myself, I hate the idea of feeling relaxed on stage, in the way that one might in one's own drawing room, playing to a few friends. But I think that is what John prefers. I think he finds that the artifice of giving a concert constricts him. I mean, he always wears a nice outfit, but it's not the sort of outfit that most people wear on the concert platform. I just stick to the old black or white tie, but he says, why should we be dressed up like a couple of penguins? He's right really; why should we? There was a time in the late sixties when John and I used to spend most of the time at rehearsals discussing what we were going to wear, with the result that we got very little serious practice done. We never seriously considered ourselves as a duo anyhow, in the professional meaning of the word. We were just two people coming together to make music; we did try, certainly, to get the ensemble right, but our performances weren't always as perfect they might have been. On the other hand, many of our performances were beautiful and for me unforgettable experiences. That's the wonderful truth about *real* togetherness, as far as I'm concerned.'

"With very little formal education", Peggy Ashcroft, that doyen of the English stage, told me, "Julian has a total instinct for anything artistic. He's dead on, whether it's furniture, or a place or whatever. He's got a smell, a sixth sense, for all sorts of things that you would not think were part of his world at all. He has, for instance, an absolutely true instinct about poetry. The moment he hears a poem, he senses the music that is appropriate and applicable to it. It's enormously stimulating to devise a programme of poetry and music with him because the end result is somehow always more than one might have hoped."

'She has been an old friend for almost twenty-five years,' Bream reminded me, and we have been giving programmes of poetry and music for many many years. Occasionally she kindly invites me to stay in her house when I go up to London. I've always admired Peggy—not just her voice, which I think is extraordinarily beautiful, but her sheer artistry on stage. You would think that just sitting reading a poem would not give her the same opportunities of dramatic interpretation as say the full-blooded performance of a great dramatic role. But you would be wrong. It's the small movements, the smallest expression in her voice as she projects a poem—absolutely fascinating. I love to be on stage with her because I suppose we musicians have all got a bit of the actor in ourselves; we wouldn't be putting across the goods if we hadn't. So sitting next to a great actress can be an object lesson in communication; the movements of her hands, her eyes, her head. Her timing—you finish a piece of music, and the pause between the end of the dying sound of the music and the first word of the poem is remarkable, not to say uncanny. Even the way she walks on the stage. Recently she had an operation on one of her ankles, and

walking for her became quite difficult for a while. But as soon as we got to the wings of the stage, she was like a woman of twenty-five, prancing onto the stage. And I know she is well in advance of the age alloted to us all in the Bible.

'Working with a great singer, particularly one who has experience in opera, can be similarly rewarding. Peter Pears, for instance, is not only a superb musician and a fine singer, but also a fine actor. He also happens to be a charming man with the most beautiful manners of anybody I have ever met, perhaps the most civilized man I know. Our backgrounds, age, and way of life are so very different, yet I think that made us into a duo with a bit of pepper and salt. We had a great success on the Continent as long ago as the mid-fifties, when getting about was a bit more complicated than it is now. We had those old Viscounts and wind-up aeroplanes. It used to take you ages to get anywhere, particularly if the wind was blowing in the wrong direction.

'I have learned such a lot from Peter, about phrasing and—more so—about the subtle art of accompanying. When I was in the army playing rhythm guitar all night in a dance band, people used to say, aren't you absolutely bored out of your tiny cotton-picking mind, knocking six hours off bashing out chords? But I've always liked being in support, and I can find no greater pleasure than being in support of a really fine singer. The truth is that I love the bass end of music, the foundations of it all. Sure, I like to play tunes, and my special delight in this respect is to be able to "float" a melodic line, but this cannot be done unless the bass is properly established, with its own line, articulation and most importantly, inner rhythm. In chamber music, for instance, this is fundamental. But it is no less so in the art of accompanying. The perfect example of this, and its most difficult exercise, resides in those wonderful lute ayres of Dowland, Morley and a host of other similarly gifted Elizabethans.

'Most of their lute songs are set out for four or five voices, or alternatively for solo voice and lute, in which case the lute is responsible for handling the other voices. Even if all the notes are relatively accessible on the instrument, the difficulties of phrasing and sustaining the different contrapuntal lines are pretty formidable. Since the character and emphasis of the phrasing comes largely from the articulation of the words and their relation to musical pitch, it is the singer who must lead, with the lutenist following suit as best he can. From the age of twenty, it has been my greatest good fortune to have met and had a long and much enjoyed partnership with Peter. It was from him that I learned about the art of lute song accompaniment, and from hearing and sometimes discussing the problems of accompaniment with Benjamin Britten. I also learned a great deal from just watching Britten accompany Pears. I tell you, he was no slouch on the ivories. From Britten I learned that with singers you have to be a little ahead of them. Not physically ahead, but you must be aware of them preparing the next note or phrase. You can sometimes see from their breathing or their facial expression just what they want to achieve, so if you're on the ball you can be slightly ahead of the game—not a very reverent way of putting it, but succinct nevertheless.

'It can be a very pleasurable occasion, of course, being on stage with other musicians—with a singer like Peter or Robert Tear—but with conductors it can be risky, you have to watch out. I well remember, in 1954 I did a BBC Promenade Concert at the Albert Hall. I was pretty young—about twenty or so—and had been asked to play the Rodrigo Concerto with the BBC Symphony Orchestra and Sir Malcolm Sargent. I was really very nervous about the whole thing because among other things the Albert Hall is such a huge barn of a place. Anyway, we rehearsed in the morning with Sargent and he went through the piece in dapper style, until the last movement which he took at a hair-raising speed. I just couldn't keep up. So I said to him, Sir Malcolm, could we do the last movement a little slower because I can't keep up with you. He said, huh, can't keep up with me, huh? Well then, he said, let's start from the beginning and we'll take it a little easier, especially for our poor young soloist. Once again, about two thirds of the way through, it was going at such a helluva lick that we broke down and I said, Sir Malcolm, look, this is impossible to play at this speed. And not only is it impossible for me to play at this speed, but it's losing its shape musically. He said, well, not to worry, we'll all get the tempo and shape right on the night. So, at the concert, I went on stage and played the first two movements which went pretty well, and blow me if he didn't take the last movement at an even faster tempo than at the rehearsal. I mean, the whole thing was over in half the time it normally takes. I don't know how I kept going. My fingers were going nineteen to the dozen. What a terrible thing to do to a young musician making his debut at the Proms— really unforgivable.

'But of the musicians I have met or performed with, Peter Pears was the most dedicated of them all, the most dedicated to his Art. To have been so closely associated with him, particularly in my younger, somewhat helter-skelter days, when the pursuit of musical excellence was not quite so central to my life as it is now, was indeed a blessing. I learned not just about breathing, phrasing and such things; Peter had mastered those techniques while I was still in the cradle almost. More importantly I learned about musical discipline, musical priorities, what the business of music-making is really about. I learned that one must be dedicated to something other than making money, other than pleasing a vast public other than hogging the limelight at every conceivable opportunity. In brief, I hope I learned what it could be to be a *real* artist. Sir Peter and Dame Peg can teach us all a thing or two. I mean, compared with them, can I say, we might just be a bunch of wilted daisies.'

10 'Members of the Savage Club.'

'I'm not a political animal, in any shape or form. And, as I mentioned earlier, I don't hold any strong political views. I feel I was lucky to be born in England, and in as much as I hold any political views at all I suppose that within the system that prevails in England I could reasonably call myself a Liberal, though at times I find it difficult to clarify the political outlines of Liberalism as such. Perhaps that is why I like the idea.

'I do believe that government should be at the service of the people and not the people at the service of government. I also believe that a politically inspired social environment that stifles or wittingly destroys the individual spirit for the sake of centralized collectivism cannot be good—it may even be positively very dangerous for the human predicament in the long run.

'I think that individuals who are lucky enough to live within a political system that will tolerate their uniqueness—and in this sense I would call every person unique—are very fortunate indeed. I might even go further and say that in this day and age such a realization might even be treasured. But this realization, this condition of social structure, does demand from the individual a sense of responsibility towards themselves and some way towards society itself. The fact that some political systems do allow the individual room for manoeuvre, allow them some leeway in order that they may fulfil their own unique destiny, does place on the individual within this society an obligation to be aware, to be in a sense accountable socially, materially or morally for their decisions or actions.

'At this point we are transcending politics and moving into ethics, and I'm running into deep water, so for the time being let's leave it at that. But where is the artist in the last quarter of this crazy twentieth century, what is he trying to do, where is he going?

'Some people think that artists should be figure-heads—even cultural and political revolutionaries. Do you know, I couldn't give a damn about all that. I care when people are suffering, but only people that I know or I'm involved with or when I'm in some situation where I can help. I find it very difficult to get upset about people suffering in Tobago or Samoa or some such place. I just can't relate to that personally although I may well feel some objective compassion.

'I also don't believe in cultural boycotts. I went to Greece, for instance, at the latter end of the military dictatorship there. I had several friends in Athens, artists and intellectuals, who were very critical that I had gone there to play while the Generals were still in power. But, as I pointed out to my friends at the time, if you try and impose a boycott on all things Western, it's the ordinary people who suffer, not the middle or upper-classes who've got sufficient clout and money so that, if they want to go to the opera, they can always fly over to La Scala in Milan or Covent Garden in London. It is the *ordinary* person who may happen to love painting or music or whatever and who possibly has no money or cannot get a visa who generally suffers from such boycotts. I went to Chile for the same reason, and to Argentina, because there people seemed literally cut off. I don't believe anybody would really suffer distress if they never hear another note from my guitar; on the other hand to go to these places, play a few tunes, earn a few bob, give a bit of pleasure, meet a few sympathetic souls can't be that bad, can it? If one were really serious, one might almost call it a duty to do so.

'None the less, I won't go to any of those countries simply to wave the Union Jack. Recently, I've been to Yugoslavia and to Rumania, but only because *they* asked me. As it happens, I've never played in the Soviet Union, or in China, but I have to admit that I've never been invited to do so. Had I been, I know I would have had considerable apprehension about accepting, lest there might be political ramifications behind the whole enterprise. I might find myself paraded as a piece of British culture, part of some bloody detente or cultural revolution or export drive. None of that has the slightest interest for me. I really love playing for people, but political systems such as totalitarianism—whether left or right—give me the creeps. I'd much rather play in Workington than play in Moscow, because at least in Workington there would be a natural flow between me and my audience. It would be a straight date—no messing. There might of course be a natural flow between me and my audience in Moscow, but you can bet your bottom dollar that the reason for my being there could well reflect political connotations which I would ultimately find a bit vulgar and certainly not enchanting.

Heathrow, London, is not the most organized airport in the world. It appears full of willing souls unable to communicate more than their willingness, although to do what often remains a mystery. Bream, plus guitar case plus suitcase, finds it more confusing than most.

'I say, I've been given a non-smoker. Do you have a smoker? OK, thanks.'

The ticket clerk addresses the tall, distinguished elderly businessman in a grey suit standing beside Bream: 'Excuse me, but I'm afraid that I will have to alter your seat.'

'But why? Surely *I've* booked this seat.'

'If you don't mind, sir, the club class *is* very empty. Perhaps you could just move back a row?'

'But why?'

'Well, there is this Julian Bream, sir, and he's got to have a seat for his guitar, and so he's changed from the non-smokers into the smokers.'

'Julian who?'

'Julian Bream, sir.'

'Julian Bream, who's he?'

The clerk explains in a whisper: 'An international concert guitarist.'

'Oh well, I wouldn't want to sit next to a chap like that anyway.'

Later on the plane, Bream realizes that he has also been separated from his photographer, Daniel Meadows. The man in the grey suit has obligingly moved back a row. So Bream says to the hostess: "Would it be possible for my friend Daniel to come up to sit with me, because he's taking photographs of me." The hostess replies: "Oh no, that's not allowed; there is no way we can allow that sort of thing." Whereupon, the man in the grey suit says "Well, I find that frightfully hard. I'm going to have a gin and tonic; will you join me?"

'So there we were; the gin and tonics arrived just as we took off, and I was sipping mine one row ahead of his. He said, "What are you doing?" I said, "I'm a concert artist and about to give a concert in Bucharest." '

'Interesting. Are you a member of the Savage Club by any chance?'

'No, what makes you say that?'

'Well, I just wondered. Have you ever heard of a chap called Edward Garby?'

'As a matter of fact, no.'

'Well, he's a marvellous chap, a distinguished sculptor; you know, one of your types.'

'D'you know, I've never heard of him.'

'He's done the most magnificent sculpture of my two-day-old daughter.'

'How did he do that?' The man in the grey suit now has Bream's interest.

'Oh, I asked him to come to the maternity hospital. He measured her up with a pair of callipers, did some drawing, and then went back and did a wonderful sculpture. You people are quite remarkable.'

'Well, I think you are too. May I ask what you do?'

'I'm an international banker.'

'Well, I think you're really remarkable too.'

'Do you really think so?'

'Yes, we'd be nowhere without you lot.'

'Interesting. Do you mind if I come and sit next to you?'

'So he came round, and promptly ordered another gin and tonic. He said, "do excuse me, but I hate flying, and the only way I can bear the whole business at all is to get happy." Then we had another gin and tonic. I'd had almost no breakfast, by the way, and there was only the most ghastly, plastic British Airways meal—just inedible. So as we carried on talking and sipping our G and Ts, this banker fellow began to sound to me a rather sad man; he explained to me how he did his finance, and he then said: "I really admire

people like you, because, do you know, I have to work with people and I hate it. But you are on your own." So I was consoling him about being a banker, and I felt really sorry for him. Eventually he went back and sat on his own, and had five more G and Ts! I couldn't keep pace with him at this stage, and anyway I knew I had to practise at the end of the journey.

'A little later the pilot came down, and I thought I would like to go up to the cockpit. I'd never done that before; this was a Trident 2. Also, the whole business of navigation, particularly in Eastern Europe, fascinated me. I asked "Don't you find that at this time of year the clouds are very beautiful?" and he said, wistfully, "Well, I do get to see a lot of clouds." '

'Do you find the clouds very beautiful at this time of year?' 'Well, I do get to see a lot of them.'

Eventually, Bream arrived in Bucharest. But, as he gets off the plane, such is his state of inebriation that he leaves behind his duty-free on the plane, and so has to go back and collect it. At the airport, he is met by the Cultural Attaché to the British Embassy. At the customs desk, Bream is asked what is in his guitar case. Guitar, he says. *Ah, Jittar*, says the customs man. *Eletronique*? No, said Bream. Acoustica, very expensive, very unique. Romaniloff! *Ah, Jittara*, said the customs man, and gave Bream a receipt with 'Jittara' scrawled all over it. Having then got through passport control, immigration, customs, and a dozen x-ray machines, the plan is that there are to be two cars: the cultural attaché's car and a taxi in the charge of a woman from the State concert organization which has booked Bream as part of the Georges Ernescu 100th Anniversary Festival.

But as Bream stepped out from the airport building into the twilight of Bucharest, there was no car. Indeed, there was no car of any description anywhere in sight. There was an immense dual carriageway stretching away from the airport, but not one car to be seen. Just a few little flags fluttering. No street lights, no sign of human movement on the carriage-way. What's more, the woman from the State concert agency had disappeared. Her car had gone, into the misty blue. One car did eventually make its way slowly through a crowd of people waiting for non-existent buses and taxis. So Bream pulls out a little miniature of Cointreau given him on the aeroplane, and takes a swig. The single little car turned out to be the Embassy's hatchback, so we all piled in, complete with guitar and suitcases, and drive down the ramp of the airport building, and onto the motorway.

'We'd done about a kilometre', Bream remembered, 'when we ran into a road block. Couldn't get through; cars all held up; a total foul-up. But by now we had got wind of the fact that Colonel Gadaffy from Libya was in town, and because of that, all the roads had been closed. You just couldn't travel from the airport into the centre of Bucharest. So here we were stuck in this bloody road block, with an English car, with English diplomatic plates, when suddenly the chap from the Embassy just drove straight through, wiggled in between the cars and went straight on. But as we left the road block, an armed policeman attached himself to the door handle, whistling and shouting at the top of his voice. Our Embassy man, fearless to the last, drove on, and the armed policeman was finally left staggering in the middle of the road. Fifty yards further down the road, however, there was another bunch of soldiers, but they all jumped to attention and saluted. So we headed off, lights ablaze, down the open road, and every street corner we pass, there is an armed guard which stands to attention and salutes. We just sailed along, as if in a Royal Procession, but at break-neck speed.

'It was a marvellous mellow misty, autumnal evening, and quite incredible to be driving through these huge avenues, very wide and tree lined, motoring very fast with headlights full on and not another car to be seen anywhere. Very soon, however, we were being followed by a car with its headlights also full on. I thought, Christ, here we go again, we're in for it now. But we were getting so many salutes from the armed guards at the intersections, that the guy following us must have thought we were part of the Libyan colonel's retinue, and finally he disappeared down a side turning as we approached the centre of Bucharest.

'It was a big hotel, where they had put us, right in the centre of town. We were very late, three hours later than we should have been, and I was getting very anxious because the three hours' practice time that is always so very important to me had disappeared. Worse, our Embassy man was determined to take us out to dinner. There was also a British Film Festival going on in Bucharest at the same time, and the director Jack Gold and the actor John Hurt were in town. The Cultural Attaché was responsible for looking after them as well, and wanted us to join them for dinner. Knowing that Eastern Europe is not the easiest place to get a quick nosh, especially a good one, we decided—in spite of our knackered condition—to accept, simply because I felt it was the only way we were going to get anything to eat at all. So we just had time for a quick turnaround, dump the suitcases, and buzz back into the car.

'Well, by this time I was naturally feeling a little tired. My ear problem had suddenly come back with a vengeance, what with the long flight, the general excitement and the worry that I had not had those three hours to do my practice. My head was really swimming round, although in truth I was feeling quite "happy", having had a fair number of gins on that very long flight. Worse, somehow I got very, very depressed because everybody around me seemed so very English and curt, in an English, official way. I mean, nicely mannered, but very unwarm. What else do you expect from English people in the Diplomatic Service? The conversation was all bubbling along, in a faintly pert, English, polite, dinner-party style; the daughter was talking about the University at Durham, the wife was talking about how it was impossible to get any food and how impossible it was to get English television programmes sent to them through the post on video cassettes, and Jack Gold and John Hurt were being good polite guests and entertaining everyone. There was also an Irish secretary I took a bit of a shine to, indeed would have been happy to take her off into a corner, actually. And then, for reasons which I can't exactly remember, I began to let a bit of rich language fall every now and again, and it rippled around the table like little shock waves. And I also think that my amorous advances towards the pretty Irish lady didn't go down very well with our diplomatic friends. Do you think I was losing my touch?'

I wonder if that is the best way of putting it.

'But she didn't seem to mind, did she?'

'No I don't think *she* minded.'

'And that was it. Everyone was looking at each other and thinking, "Oh my God." You can imagine, things got pretty bad. And then in the middle of all this Jack Gold started arguing with me about Television. He said television was *the* art of the future. I said television was a load of balls; and so it went on. It was one of those arguments that nobody was going to win or lose. Our hostess said to John Hurt, "Now, why don't you get involved in this conversation? You're a big television star." And he said, "Oh no, no one can win. One is fishing, and one is bitten, and I ain't going to be the trout; or the bream, as it happens!" Finally, our hostess very diplomatically said: "Well I think Julian Bream looks very tired—I think we should break the evening up and all go home."

'The following day I ordered breakfast in my room. I wasn't feeling very well, natch, and my old ear problem was really giving me hell. The coffee wouldn't pour properly, so in order to get the coffee into the cup I thought I had better tip it out of the top of the jug. But as I tipped the jug up, a large cockroach fell out of the bottom, which doesn't exactly start the day too well, does it? And then I realized to my horror that I'd left my shaving soap at home. All right, I know it was a Saturday and this was a Socialist country, but you might have thought you could get some shaving cream in a big city like Bucharest. Not a bit of it. There was a huge glass cabinet in the foyer of the hotel just full of toilet requisites,

including some shaving cream, but when I went up to the counter and said, how can I get some of that shaving cream, they said no way until three o'clock. At three we get the key, they said, and then you can have as much as you like. But at three o'clock it was still closed. Ah yes, said the man behind the desk, that's because today we have a wedding party. And suddenly there were hundreds of cars, all screaming around with ribbons, and flowers cellotaped to their bonnets and God knows what, but no shaving cream.

'Well, by this time I was getting worried about finding something to eat; you will remember how important it is for me to have *something* to eat before I play, so we went to the hotel restaurant and sat there for a hell of a long time and got nothing. I was now feeling *so* bad, I really didn't know how I was going to make it on stage. But the woman from the State concert agency arrived and was so effusive about the fact that I was in Bucharest, the whole place was absolutely sold out, nobody could get a ticket, it was a lovely hall, so it became obvious that, come hell or high water, somehow I'd got to pull this concert out of the fire. But I was so nervous, and by now scared, I didn't know really how I was going to do it. Then the local TV news crew arrived because they wanted to "commemorate" the performance as a news item, but I said no microphones and no cameras. I just want to give a concert. But they said, "Do you mind if we take 30 seconds with no sound?" This was 3.45 in the afternoon—the concert was due to begin at 4. Reluctantly, I said OK. But at five to four, they said: "Can we take

30 seconds *with* sound with the lights on?" OK, I said, too tired to think straight anymore, take the first 30 seconds of the concert. Put the lights on as I come on stage and don't turn them off until the end of the first movement, so that they don't destroy the mood of the music. But, I insisted, you can only record the first 30 seconds. They said they would do just that, so I relaxed. So on I go, a wonderful reception, and suddenly there are lights everywhere. It was worse than being in Studio A at the BBC Television Centre; full of technicians, moving about, adjusting mikes., fiddling with hand held lights. And this was the beginning of my very first public concert in Bucharest. Phew, I nearly died. I was feeling really terrible. Anyway, I started playing the Sor *Fantasia* Opus 7, and I had just got to a very difficult variation when a whole lot of extra lights suddenly went on. The whole thing, at a stroke, became a TV show, and that really made me feel suicidal. I followed the Sor with the Bach Sonata in A minor which went amazingly well, and then came the Henze *Royal Winter Music*. Twenty-eight minutes of tortuously difficult music. I was apprehensive about the Henze, as this would be something so strange to their ears because I had gathered that they knew very little contemporary Western music. Unfortunately, I got off to a bad start. The first note of the Sonata is an accented bass note marked treble *forte* and in order to achieve the maximum dramatic impact I hit the string with such a wallop that I instantly knocked it out of tune by a quarter of a tone. I feverishly tried to rectify the string between snatches of rests in the

'I'm just in it for the loot, and the TV, and the audience, and the hell of it.'

music but bugger me if every time I tried to make the adjustment it was either too much or too little. I was in despair, and so much so that for me personally it wrecked the whole of the first movement. The other movements went quite well, but I never regained the poise that enables one to perform this sort of piece at its best.

The audience, bless them, sat in rapt attention throughout, though it did cross my mind that it may have been due to their good manners rather than to the merits of my performance. I felt there were some outstanding moments, none the less; the hall was beautiful acoustically, my nails were just right, and the audience were quite young, attentive, and very enthusiastic; and I did countless encores. But I was beginning to flag when suddenly, a girl came up to me on the stage with some flowers, and I thought, marvellous, this *is* the end of the concert. So I took that as a cue, as though fate had come to my rescue; everybody gave me a great round of applause, I took several more curtain calls, staggered off the stage, and that was the end—and I can tell you I could have really "booked a rest".

'Well, it wasn't to be, because when I went back to my dressing room, a vast hall of a place, it was full of women, members of the orchestra who had arrived for the next concert, the final gala. They were all due to go on in 35 minutes or so, and were all running around, hiding behind each other as they took off their petticoats. I didn't know whether to go in, or stay out or quite where to look. And then a massive crowd of people came in to speak to me. One chap had somehow got hold of part of the manuscript of the Henze Sonata and had transcribed other great chunks of it into his notebook from my performance. Another guy came up with an indescribably fudged photocopy of Britten's *Nocturnal*. Having pulled it out he then said: "Now tell me about this bit here, Mr Bream, where it goes bom, bom de bom, bom, bom, just before the little tune at the very end. "How do you play that? And he was standing there discussing the interpretation of this music, written for me as long ago as 1964 for half an hour or more. I mean, that's rather incredible, isn't it?

'Back to the airport the following morning, and I reckoned I ought to change back some of my local currency, because you are not supposed to take Rumanian money out of the country. So I went over to the currency counter, but the man said, "Oh I can't change your money without any documentation; before I can give you Western money for them, you've got to prove to me how you got them." Well, this was getting all a bit complicated, so I just stuffed the notes back in my pockets. But as I was going through the customs, I was fiddling with my wallet and out fell the loot. I thought, Christ, this is it. There was a sort of mild panic, not helped by the fact that, as usual, I had a ticket for myself and one for the guitar. They'd never heard of this before. "Mr Bream, smoking, Mr Guitar, smoking, but I'll take the drinks for both", I said. The guy behind the ticket desk gave me an old fashioned look as if to say what the hell is going on here? "Mr Guitar, are you Mr Guitar?" he said, pointing at me. That seemed like the last straw.'

But not quite. Bream is sitting peacefully in the airport lounge, sipping a little Slivovits, waiting for the plane to land, when up bounces a reporter. The look in his eye tells Bream that there is to be no escape.

'You are interviewing me on behalf of . . .?'

'It is a very fine Rumanian publication.'

'Oh, I see, fine. It's good to know these things.'

'You are maybe the only great guitarist of your generation that did not study with Segovia, which means for you the absence of such a guide. Have you been influenced by this fact? And you did not study with Segovia by choice, maybe a polemical choice, or because you did not have the possibility? And what differences are there between Julian Bream and his other great colleagues who did study with Segovia, technically in terms of repertory. It is a composed question.'

'I see.'

'It is a whole question with five answers.'

'Yes, I see.'

'Yes?'

'Well, I did have two lessons with Segovia . . . one in 1947, and one, as I remember, in 1948. But it wasn't my good fortune to be a student of his. I think that if I had been my technical facility might have been considerably better. You see, I'm mostly self-taught so it took much longer to develop my technique . . . My technique's home made . . . I have largely taught myself . . . Do you understand?'

'Yes.'

'So it took a long, long time. It was much harder to do it that way. But it's a slow and sometimes tortuous way that suits me, to be alone, to slowly work it all out . . .'

'Why did you not bring the lute? I am told the lute is the instrument of your heart.'

'It speaks to me. It speaks to me with an ease which gives me immense pleasure and satisfaction. I find the guitar is a difficult instrument. In fact bloody hard. It is also at times temperamental. Like a lovely Rumanian woman—the very spirit of contradiction and contrariness.'

'How is it possible to explain your Englishness?'

'What, me?'

'Yes. What can you tell us about the fact that you are English?'

'Well, at least I'm not Chinese. Not that I've got anything against the Chinese. Some of my best friends are . . .'

'Sometimes we know that you renounce . . .'

'Renounce—that's a good word . . .'

'Yes, renounce the concert world, because you are very occupied for the period of the countryside works . . . At the sheep shearing?'

'Sheep shearing . . . yes. I'm good at sheep shearing. But I'll tell you one thing, you have to watch your finger nails.'

'The countryside for you, is it a hobby or something more? And is it true, because there is a legend here that you are . . .'

'A farmer? Well, I don't milk cows these days. But, do you know,

'You renounce the concert world, because you are very occupied for the period of the countryside works . . . at the sheep-shearing?'
'Yes.'

I used to, when I was seven years of age and evacuated to a farm in the last war. It was wonderful training. That's why I have such a strong left hand . . .'

'Are you tired?'

'No, I'm fine, but could we grab some refreshment?'

'What do you want to drink?'

'Could I have a little more Slivovits?'

'Do you think that there is a school of guitar which really satisfies you as to its method of teaching? And, in case of affirmative answer, who are the most important guitar teachers in your mind today?'

'Well, the thing is I haven't taught anybody for a long time. So my knowledge of teaching is very limited; in fact, it's almost non-existent. I never give lessons now. I only teach myself these days. One day I will teach. But at the moment, I don't want to perpetrate my faults upon others.'

'Which are your next recordings?'

'I'm hoping to do a series of four or maybe six records on the history of Spanish music, the guitar, the lute and the vihuela.'

'The vihuela . . .?'

'Yes. I'm having two instruments built. And I'm going to play some Mudarra, some Milán, some Pisador and some Narváez. It's simple music, and yet highly disciplined. But the simplicity makes it very hard to play. You need to have a much better technique to play this old Spanish music than for anything else. It's music without flesh; all bones. You can't fake it.'

'You have played all kinds of music, but we would like to know what type do you love best?'

'A lot depends on how I'm feeling. If I'm feeling flamboyant, I might play some of the Villa-Lobos Studies. They're not great music, but very good pieces. If on the other hand I'm feeling sad and reflective, a chromatic Fantasia by John Dowland would fit the bill a treat. I cannot play music that I have no real affection for. Music, everything, is ever-changing. As I get older, perhaps, I'm getting more conservative. I'm beginning to know what I enjoy, and what I want to play, and that's not necessarily a lot of contemporary music. But I love bringing contemporary Western music here, to the Eastern European countries. It's important, I believe, in spite of the difficulties, that you chaps ought to have some idea of what's going on over the other side of the fence. You don't necessarily have to admire it, but to sit down quietly with an open ear may prove to be a very worthwhile and stimulating experience; and that's really why I've come.'

'And last: If Julian Bream was not a guitarist, would he be a musician anyway? Or something else?'

'I would have to be a musician. I'm locked in. I have no choice.'

11 'Consuming people.'

'I regret change. I realize of course it is often a necessary adjunct
to life. But when I first went to Aldeburgh, for instance, to
Benjamin Britten's festival, it was an intimate and very personal
affair. The old Jubilee Hall. You just couldn't get the numbers in.
And there were some really stunning performances in that little
hall. It had a less than good acoustic, but what made it all work
were the people who performed in it, the people who organized it,
the people who worked for it and the people who came to it. There
was a need for a festival, and so the enthusiasm worked. It was a
manifestation, a realization of what a few remarkable people
wanted. The whole idea of a beautifully appointed hall, such as
they now have in Aldeburgh—or rather Snape—is wonderful, but
it is a wonderful accessory, not a necessity. For me, the more ideal
the circumstances, the less satisfying it can sometimes be. There is
the danger that you are making music for reasons other than the
real joy of making music. Non-musical considerations can suddenly
become paramount. I accept that nothing stands still in this world;
it seems that the human condition cannot cope with standstill.
Either there is so-called progress, or things slowly slide down the
inevitable slippery slope. It happens with all institutions; they
change, and the change can often wreak havoc upon the original
conception. There was a shop in Aldeburgh that used to make the
best sausages in the world. I used to fill the boot of my car to the
brim with these wonderful bangers and then drive like mad down
to Wiltshire and bung them in the deep freeze, which kept me
going for about six months. Last year the butcher stopped making
them. I mean, can I ever go back there again, I ask myself?
Sometimes I think there are fewer and fewer places I really want to
go back to.

'It's ludicrous when you think about it, isn't it? To dress up in
front of all those people and go through all that nervous hee-haw
just in order to play a few tunes. There must be another way to
earn a living, other than going through all that night after night. I
suppose one part of me could go on doing this sort of thing until I
fall into my coffin. But I'm not so sure that's what most of me
wants to do. I sometimes feel I have become trapped in a guitar
mania which I helped to create, and sometimes catch myself feeling
just a little bit peeved, if that's the right word, that there are now
a tremendous number of guitarists about, some of whom play
nearly as well as I do and some, for all I know, a damn sight better.
Throughout the sixties, I remember, there was a tremendous

rekindling of interest in eighteenth-century music. And the guitar, being a plucked instrument and having a very clear, light sound as well as a literature from that era, became associated with that. It was a happy coincidence. And then, due to various social changes, there was a great revival of interest in folk music, or rather modern folk music which is after all more or less composed songs and not traditional folk music—at least not as I have come to know it. And the guitar was very much associated with that. Then there was a revival of interest in swing and jazz. There were also a number of really good jazz guitarists about this time, Wes Montgomery and Joe Pass being particularly outstanding.

'But above all it was the rock and pop scene that really got hold of the guitar and wrung it by its neck and electrified its guts out of all proportion to the original conception of the instrument. Now you may think I am one of those classical players that abhors or rules out completely the electrified version of the guitar as a viable musical instrument. But you must remember I played a primitive version of that instrument myself some thirty years ago, and I can tell you if you are a classical player and can handle an electric guitar it is initially a thrilling experience to play one, in fact it's positively exhilarating. The exhilaration comes largely from the fact that at the flick of a knob you can positively drown out any other colleague that happens to be playing with you, not the most musical or charming of sentiments, but exciting none the less.

'As for the sound—the *musical* sound—I frankly find that to be

'Fewer and fewer places I want to go back to.' Bream at Snape, ground floor, fifth window from the left. Upstairs?

the most boring, lifeless, phoney, vulgar noise that could have ever been contrived by humankind on this planet. Having said that, I think the electric bass guitar is the invention of the century as far as musical instruments go. Now this is a really good sound, and for my ears a *true* bass instrument, and in good hands it has a flexibility that is quite amazing. I feel sure there's a great future for the electric bass guitar, and not least as a modern symphonic instrument.

'But let's get back to the ordinary guitar, and its phenomenal resurgence as *the* popular classical instrument of our time. I have often thought about this, and the only reason for it that I can come up with is this: maybe it's because the instrument cuts across so many different styles of music which have had great booms in popularity throughout the last three decades, and the guitar is so versatile in other fields of music, that the classical instrument has benefited. This created a general revival of interest in the guitar as a whole. I can remember going to Liverpool in the mid-sixties and you could walk up and down the streets and be amazed to hear Beatle-type groups coming out of almost every window. A lot of those young people, moreover, were not just kids from the street; some of them possibly had had a grammar school or university education. When they eventually settled down and got married, some of them may well have maintained their interest in the guitar and took up the classical instrument as a hobby. Since practising the electric guitar is a very anti-social habit, because of its loud, raucous sound the classical instrument became an ideal instrument for the home. The versatility of the instrument, once again, has added to its tremendous increase in popularity.

'In the sixties, I used to get quite a lot of pop freaks in my audience, all that long hair stuff and the clothes. I don't think you would have seen them at a string quartet concert, but they did come to a guitar concert because the guitar had become part of their culture; ironically, an instrument of romance, escape and protest. They would probably come out of curiosity to see this balding, square guy, kitted out in a penguin suit, sitting up there on stage quietly getting on with it, nobody smoking, no dope, clean living, and all that stuff. What's *he* doing, playing the bloody guitar? What's so classical about *that*? And I used to amuse myself watching them, because they were absolutely astounded at the ritual of a classical concert. Everybody sitting neatly in lines; absolute quiet. Can you imagine the quietness for people who'd been probably the evening before to a rock concert? But also as these kids looked around they found they were brushing shoulders with all sorts of "straights" and "squares"—businessmen, intellectuals, office workers, and middle-class ladies all perfumed and dressed up to the nines—they must have wondered sometimes what the hell they were doing there. But they generally stayed to the end of the concert, and as I surveyed the audience from the concert platform there was certainly no evidence of the so-called cultural cum generation gap which was prevalent it seems throughout that decade.

OPPOSITE
'All that nervous hee-haw in order to play a few tunes.'

185

'Yes, there were literally hundreds of these young aspiring guitar players. Sometimes there were so many of them that I wished I'd taken up the ukelele. After all, when you do something which formerly very few people did, it does give you a rather special feeling, even if nobody wants to hear you. You're an individual, at least you're breaking new ground. I always felt that to some extent on the guitar, and that was certainly I suspect a reason I took up the lute; it gave me a feeling once again of being a pioneer. But now there are quite a few lute players, and hundreds of guitar players, and I just wonder sometimes how were all going to earn our bread.

'Of course, if I'd wanted to, one possible route of escape might have been the world of jazz and improvisation. After all, improvisation was always a very important element in music from the fifteenth century right up until the nineteenth century. We've lost that now in classical music, and jazz is the only vehicle which is able to resuscitate the art of improvisation and give it a dynamic and a shape which is musically not only worthwhile, but I believe very important to our time. In one sense of course, I am improvising all the time, but of course it is within very strict parameters. Every time I play a piece, I present myself with another set of problems which I want to solve. I find, in trying to solve these problems, I can reshape and re-invigorate each performance. So often the music seems quite fresh to me, simply because I may have tried to change the quality of sound of a particular note. This means that the note which precedes it and the note that comes after, tend to be a little different also. Music-making for me is a constant voyage of discovery. The way I play a bit of Bach or a bit of Cimarosa is quite different from how I played it five years ago; or at least, so it seems to me. To some people, it might seem a darn sight worse. But it's different; that's the point. With me, it can differ from performance to performance. On any given tour, six concerts on the road for instance, I can give six performances of the same piece which are totally different, in phrasing, colouring, tempo, the lot. Over the years I've become more interested in the shape and form of a piece of music, rather than worry about the subjective effect of each passage or phrase. But now I'm thinking that perhaps I've been overdoing the abstraction bit in my performance, and I want now to concentrate on the finer detail, to re-think the mood. That's a good thing, I believe. The swing of the pendulum!

'I find I am constantly searching for the true spirit of a piece of music. There's a short Fantasia by Roberto Gerhard, for instance; I must have played it probably fifty times, but I've only ever played it as I really wanted to play it just once. Just once I managed to get the mood right from the very first note; the very first note sounded magical. I had got within an ace of it before, but I had never got it as I knew it could be. But on just one occasion, everything seemed to fit into a perfect slot. And it was getting that first note which did the trick. The chord that follows it had a special resonance and I managed to place it in such a way that it enhanced the whole bar. And then the piece, as if miraculously, became a performance to which I could give myself *entirely* without thinking. It was this non-thinking, yet total awareness, which may have been the right approach here. I know I'll never get it like that again for a long time, although I will keep plugging away.

'Improvisation by way of jazz, however, has always had an appeal for me. I've always enjoyed its spontaneity, but I was never a good jazz player. When I was a kid aged eleven I used to play the jazz plectrum guitar, and in the army in my late 'teens when I was stationed at Woolwich in the Royal Artillery, I played regularly in a dance band. For over three years, I played in a big band, sometimes twice a week in the winter; five saxes, six brass, four rhythm. We used to play awful Charing Cross Road arrangements of standard tunes. But we also had a smaller combo within the big band, consisting of piano, clarinet, bass, drums and myself on electric guitar. I played a battered old acoustic plectrum guitar with "F" holes rather like a cello. I didn't own the instrument; it came from the army instrument store. Most of the time, I played just plain acoustic rhythm guitar. But in order to give the brass players' lips a rest, the leader of the band used to yell out "busker", which meant that our little combo had to get into operation pretty smartish. For our little group, I fitted a small pick-up unit onto the acoustic guitar and ran it through to a battered and very ancient Leak amplifier that occasionally went up in smoke. In the small group I played finger-style electric; I never touched a plectrum. As a group, we rarely if ever rehearsed, and if we had a style, then it was based on the then marvellous George Shearing Quintet. All our music was improvised, and on occasion it sounded so, but at our best we were a very tight group. We all knew most of the "standards" backwards, and our only problems were ones of which key to play in. I hated playing in A♭, D♭ and E♭, which was a bit unlucky for me, as many of the standards were originally written in those keys. I always preferred "open" keys. We used to get into a fair old tizzy about this, but on stage there was no time for argument. We were in. If I didn't like the key the pianist had chosen, when it came to a chorus or two from myself, I used to yell across to the pianist and tell him the key I was going to take my break in. But in order to change key, I would have to put in a two or four bar transition intro. which sometimes brought out some fascinating harmonic modulations, particularly if you were attempting something outlandish like getting from the key of A♭ to D major. The real difficulty was trying to get the group back into A♭ at the end of my chorus. The enharmonic chromaticism of the opening of *Tristan und Isolde* wasn't in it, and there was often chaos in the camp. Bream got his harmonic knickers in a twist, and at the end of the number there were hostile looks all round. But what fun. Sometimes when I look back, I kid myself that I might have made the grade as a jazz player, but I know indulging in that would have messed up my classical guitar playing.

'Just occasionally my jazz past catches up with me though. There was a time, not so many years ago, when I was very friendly with two or three people in London who loved jazz. One played the piano, one the clarinet and sometimes we managed to get hold of a bass player. And every two or three weeks we would get together and have a good old blow. And I used to love it, because so much of classical music is rehearsing, practising, and not a little artifice and contrivance really, and it was so lovely just to let go. You had to use your instincts, to let things break apart. All sorts of ideas flowed when we were in the mood and it was a fabulous form of relaxation. So when the violinist Stefan Grappelli asked me to take part in his 70th birthday concert, I thought why not? I had always admired Grappelli greatly, and I thought the whole thing would be a real hoot. Imagine, just sitting playing rhythm guitar next to my old hero George Shearing; not exactly an unmusical experience.

'But then, the more I thought about it, the more I got in a hell of a state. I mean, doing this sort of improvisation in your own room with a bunch of friends and a crate of beer, well, that's one thing. But doing it in public, with all that added pressure, that's not on, not really. And in the Albert Hall too, with all those lights and damn television cameras not to mention millions of microphones. Anyway, I was still wondering what exactly it was they wanted me to do—whether for instance they would want me to play some Spanish music or "Smoke Gets in Your Eyes"—when the organizer rang up and said, oh Grappelli would like you to do something with him as well as a solo piece. Well, by now I was getting very nervous about the whole shebang, but I thought at the very least I must go and see Grappelli.

'Now you have to remember that the great guitar player who had played with Grappelli in the old days was Django Reinhardt, someone I admired above all guitar players, including—you may be surprised to hear—Segovia. I met Grappelli in a little flat in Fulham, in London, and we talked a bit about Django and then he suggested we might do something together for violin and guitar. We eventually decided we would do "Nuages", a famous Django tune. Luckily, it was a number I knew; so that was a good start. So I got the guitar out and played a few notes. He then asked if I knew the chords of "Nuages". I said, well, I thought I could remember them. But, before you could say half-a-sixpence, he went to the piano and played the number through with some chords which were somewhat different from the chords I knew, although very nice they were too. Anyway, I made a note of his chords on a bit of paper and we decided we'd meet and rehearse at two o'clock on the day. But before I left we both thought it would be nice if I joined his swing group for a number. Although I was just a little apprehensive we decided to do an old number of Django's called "Bellville" which he hadn't done for a long time. I then pushed off.

'Come the day of the concert, I was really scared out of my mind. I turned up at two but, of course, he wasn't there. Eventually he turned up and said, What shall we do now? Shall we do "Nuages"? So we started rehearsing, and I did a little rhapsodic introduction, and then he started off playing absolutely superbly. Here was I, doing my best to accompany him, and suddenly he whispered; you do the next eight bars solo. So I did, and he joined in, and we made a little cadenza and the whole thing seemed to have a nice shape about it. Afterwards, we ran through the other Django number, this time with his group, and I even took a couple of choruses; though I must confess they were rather laboured. However, I felt that with a bit of luck I might pull it off. In any case, I was also going to have my own little seven-minute spot in which I would play a short Bach Prelude and "Asturias" by Albéniz. By the end of the rehearsal I felt the pressure building up, especially as I was the only straight musician in the whole line up.

'Although I was not on until the second half of the concert, I decided to get there at the beginning to get myself into the mood of the whole thing, and concentrate on what sort of breaks I was going to do in my jazz solos. I was really steeling myself for the ordeal. I knew Grappelli was going to introduce me; I was going to play the Albéniz, a little Bach Prelude, then the fiddle and guitar number, and finally the jazz number at the end. So I got on stage, and he introduced me. And then he announced that we were going to play "Nuages". I can tell you, I did a double take. I mean, I realized the show had to go on, but I had my fingers poised to play "Asturias". I realize that jazz people can be very loose in their programming, but this was a bit much.

'The Albert Hall was packed; and the TV lights were phenomenal. But I got through "Nuages" pretty well. Until the end, that is, where we had agreed that he played a cadenza for twenty seconds or so, and then I had to come in on the last beat. So there I was, poised, watching, and he just went on and on and on. I thought, well, Jesus, it was like a concerto he was playing—the Bach fiddle Chaconne, or something. There were double stops, treble stops, chromatic and diminished arpeggios all over the instrument. He was fonzing about in all sorts of outlandish keys. At one point I didn't think he was ever going to make it back to G major. By this time the cadenza had been running, I swear, for every second of three minutes. This was the biggest self-applied ego massage I've ever witnessed in public, and when the rhapsodic neurosis finally came to a grinding halt I was embarrassed out of my mind. I just hit a loud chord of G major and collapsed in a heap.

'So now it occurred to me, well, this *must* be my solo spot. But not a bit of it. Grappelli announced that I would now do a number with his group, and before I knew where we were, he glanced across at me, indicating that he wanted a four-bar intro. This I provided. After the initial 32 bar chorus, he glanced over to me again which meant that I should take the first solo, which I did. I wasn't making such a bad fist of it, when Grappelli walked over to me and said "take another". I thought this was pushing it a bit, but there was nothing I could do but comply. By this time my powers of improvisation, such as they were, were beginning to ebb rapidly. All the little riffs and embryonic ideas I had thought over in the dressing room vanished from my fingers, and in the final eight bars of the second solo I was reduced to simple arpeggios on block chords, sounding not unlike Giuliani on an off night. Worse was to come. As I was finishing the second solo, Grappelli walked across to me and muttered "take another". And that I can honestly say was the most embarrassing moment of my life. When I finished and I thought at long last my moment had come to do my solos, Grappelli just said, thank you very much Julian Bream, now we'll get on with the show. So I plodded off stage in complete disarray. Christ, that was a nightmare to end all nightmares. I could have killed him.

'The danger with jazz, so it seems to me, is that the improvised music can sometimes eschew musical discipline, a kind of self-indulgence takes over, often lacking *real* musical ideas, and revealing on occasion a dreary *ad hoc* series of mechanically contrived ideas. But with really great jazzmen, the music has a flow, it is brim-full of ideas—ideas that sometimes begin quite fragmentarily and are then developed, transformed into a remarkable linear activity that is pulsating with the essence of *now*. It is this quality of spontaneity, of excitement, that makes good jazz so appealing to the keen listener. And for the musician that knows a little bit about it it is sometimes near miraculous how the mind, fantasy and fingers are combined at lightning speed, co-ordinating not only the musical structure, but also the progress of the imagination. I find that incredibly exciting.

'But for all that I wouldn't feel musically bereaved if I never heard another jazz number in my life. Strange, isn't it; thinking about it, there is for me a vital element missing from jazz. I can't quite put my finger on it, but I suspect it has something to do with the underlying spirit of the music. It never really plumbs the depths, except those of despair. It has a profane quality compared, say, to a Haydn string quartet or a madrigal by Monteverdi. That is its asset in our modern instant world and therefore, finally, jazz is, at least for me, of fleeting musical significance in the long run. It is also wide open to commercial exploitation and frequently mass-produced, relying on tricks, devices and clichés that are the very opposite of its true nature—its spontaneous musical expression. There is also undoubtedly nowadays a fashionable jazz circuit, and the big bands that were the rage in the thirties and forties are back again in business, which is a welcome revival. Just recently I heard a concert given by the Count Basie band which was a very enjoyable experience. Not only was the evening chock-full of delicious nostalgia, as you would expect, but the musicians and the music swung along with such verve and zest that it was incredible to think that many of the musicians had begun their playing careers whilst I was still a babe in arms. It was an unforgettable evening. It would be a pity if the big business operators drove this revival movement into the ground through overexploitation, which to a smaller degree is happening in the world of the guitar.

'In a number of big cities concert promoters have instigated a guitar series. Now why do they have a guitar series? Well, clearly they think they can make money out of it. They will book half a dozen guitarists, a couple of whom hopefully have international reputations that will draw the audience. The other four guitarists probably don't have the drawing power so they will be playing for comparatively smaller fees. On the face of it there is nothing wrong in this; in fact, there is actually a hidden virtue here. For it is incredibly hard sometimes for a young and highly promising player to get established, to be on a really good platform with a guaranteed audience. He is of course to some extent riding on somebody else's back, but I for one don't mind this one bit, in fact I welcome it, if it helps to further a real gift and is done with a modicum of grace. But the real problem of the series idea is something other. Perhaps it can be summed up quite neatly by saying that if we guitarists had the equivalent of 32 Beethoven Sonatas for the guitar, a guitar series might turn out to be a real musical feast. But we haven't. The literature of the guitar, charming though it is, is actually quite limited as far as music of high quality is concerned. There is not enough good guitar music to make these so-called guitar series stimulating. People get bored with the same old lightweight pieces, and that's not very good for the guitar. But it could be even worse for the continuing career of a really promising young player.

'There are many other factors in our cultural life today that are not dissimilar. Say a gifted young artist does quite an original work of sculpture, for instance. He may with luck find a gallery or dealer who will take him on. The dealer then gets to work on the media and promotes the sculpture. An exhibition is put on. It's a huge success. The critics pontificate in a near-unreadable intellectual jargon. There may be a splurge in the Sunday Sups and immediately the dealer will want more of the same. There will be no asking whether the artist may now want to do something different, to develop, to evolve, to exploit a different style, to do something which could be less acceptable. No. The merchants want him to do more of the same, because their Public Relations department has made the chap into a star overnight. They'll exploit him to the hilt and then, when the public have become sated and the artist has done every possible variation on one original theme—to the extent that it may have stultified his development for life—he is then dropped, killed off. A very similar thing may be happening to the guitar. In the late sixties and early seventies *anybody* who could play the guitar tolerably well could fill the Wigmore Hall. The monthly calendar of concerts in those days could show four or five guitar recitals at a glance, which is incredible when you think that I can remember a time when there was only *one* a year, and that was when Segovia came to town.

'Now the whole position has changed. It is becoming increasingly hard to fill the Wigmore for a guitar recital, even though the performer may have a distinguished reputation; which is a pity because the standard of playing among the younger performers has improved by leaps and bounds over the past few years.

'Publicity, in my experience, doesn't always relate to the quality of the goods on show. In fact, it can quite often be the reverse. I believe that if anything is really good, it doesn't need that much marketing. But of course it takes time. When I was 21 I played the guitar quite well, but I wasn't continually under the glare of lights and the publicity machine; I had time to develop. If I was at the beginning of my profession today, however, and I suddenly stopped playing for six months, in terms of my career that could easily be a disaster. I think the life of a professional musician is going to become difficult and increasingly complex as time goes on, and not least of all for guitarists. And that's paradoxical, because for the first time the guitar is being taught in most of the Conservatoires in Europe and America, and good guitars are being mass-produced at a terrific rate. Even good guitarists. But that is the point. Music is not, nor cannot be, a mass-produced product. It has to be compelling; there must be some magic to it, and the musical impulse must impart the joy of spontaneity. And if I have any contribution still to make, it is at best the constant reaffirmation of that belief.'

12 A life on the road.

'I'll be fifty in a year or so's time. And, after thirty-five years of all this nonsense, you might reasonably ask why I continue to press on. After all I'm tearing about from one concert to another, having to dress up like a penguin, or a waiter, and go on like a hyped-up puppet. You do your bow, sit down, fuss with the chair and tune up—how many thousands of times have I done that? It must be thousands and thousands. There must be easier ways of earning a living. Yet I do earn good money, although I have to give a lot of it away in taxes of all sorts, not to mention paying off my ex-wives. Nowadays I try to limit my activity on the road to forty-odd concerts a year. If I only make half the money that I do and I still wanted to live in the way that I do, then you might think I might be tempted to do more concerts. But in fact I would not do any more concerts. Not one more. I would live a different life. The whole idea of giving concert after concert, city after city, country after country, has to be a ridiculous way of life. There are also all the considerations of the audience, whether or not they're responding to what you're doing; then there's the acoustics of the hall; the travelling conditions; the weather; how you are feeling; how much practice you have managed to fit in; the laundry, your health, finger nails . . . A life on the road, necessary though it is for me, is surely total lunacy.

'Then there is the day-in day-out mechanics of it all. The only way I can overcome the mechanical process I'm caught up in, is to try and re-live each and every performance as if it were my last, to give myself to the music absolutely. Luckily the guitar is an instrument that can express—almost at any given moment—exactly what I feel; it has harmonic, melodic and expressive possibilities which can be unique to the individual player. If you play the oboe, for instance, you have to blow your bloody lungs inside out just to get a sound; if you play the clarinet, you can spend half your time fussing about the reeds; if you play the violin, unless you're very good it can be a bit brash and heady, high and tense, and when practising quite possibly socially unacceptable. But the guitar you can play anytime and anywhere. It's comparatively easy to play when you start off, although it does get more difficult as you go along. But at least it is self-contained; you don't need a piano or any accompaniment, and the box itself is easy and cheap to run. Making the sound is so immediately tactile and so pleasurable; you can feel the strings with both hands. You've got no damned bits of ivory in the way, as you have on a piano; no bits of old horse hair, as on the violin. There is nothing between you and the thing which *is* the sound. Nothing. And, what is more, you hold the box against your gut, so it couldn't be in a better place.

'The guitar is an interior instrument, not a projecting instrument like a trumpet or a violin. So it's an instrument that is largely given to reflection. But it is also very direct. The sound sometimes feels as though it is coming in some extraordinary way through your body, like some immediate natural sensitivity of expression. If you're any good as an artist, therefore, the sound that comes out can indicate pretty faithfully what you feel about the music and, in a more subjective way, what you feel about yourself in relation to it. I find that the intimate, personal nature of the instrument allows me to respond immediately and personally to the music. In fact it becomes an extension of how I feel about life at any given moment.

'It is a warm and evocative instrument, particularly so I think for Northern Europeans or for people who manage to exist in the cold, damp and misty climate of England. It has an exotic quality, romantic, seductive in a female way. On the other hand, the lute is more masculine, more honest really, and does not have the same essentially non-musical connotations. The soft, plangent sound of a lute can certainly evoke the spirit and charm of a bygone age, but lute music—by its largely contrapuntal nature—is much more intellectually conceived than guitar music. Its contrapuntal lines and sound texture do not in themselves necessarily reveal the personality of the music. Thus, once again, it is the performer who has to add *life* to the notes by the sheer force of his own intuitive responses; he has only his instincts and hopefully a firm intellectual grasp to guide him as to what the music is *really* about. These are what I try to put at the service of my performances of early music— indeed of all music. In fact it is these instincts, this intuition, this awareness which is absolutely essential to keep oneself alive throughout one's musical career. In most jobs, that is becoming very difficult to achieve, in our day and age. So much of our lives can be spent either professionally or artistically, in the pursuit of material things. Our careers are shaped around the need to acquire them. But if you become a slave to this end—a slave to production— the magic and the beauty which you may hope to impart could gradually disintegrate and, eventually, dry up.'

"To travel on the road with Julian Bream—and his life *is* being on the road—is like travelling with a caged lion," José Romanillos told me. "He is under such pressure, that it's a miracle if you survive. Most people don't, of course. He consumes people; he consumes novelty. And when the novelty wears out, heaven help him if there's nothing solid behind it. I don't think he means any harm, but his human relationships on the whole are a tangle. It's only the artist in him which keeps him going; the restless energy, and the aggressiveness. But that's what I love about him; he's a man who knows the system and could make a fortune out of it. But he refuses to do so, refuses to sell himself. He gets there, wherever it is he wants to go, but at a terrible cost. He's so demanding of people; it's a rough journey. If you get his respect, you're OK. But if you don't, watch out. You have to be straight with him. If you're not honest with him, he sees through you. If you're a phoney, he doesn't want to know you. And he has to deal with a lot of phoney people."

'I must say that I've been delighted by the resurgence of interest in the guitar over the last thirty years. There are now people who are completely crazy about the guitar, just as people are crazy about collecting stamps, locomotive numbers or cricket. For some it has become a lifetime's devotion. I have that devotion within myself, of course, but by no means totally to the guitar or lute as *such*. It just so happens that I have made my *professional* life on the lute and the guitar; it has given me my reason to live—my life. When I was at the Royal College of Music I studied piano, cello and composition, although I've never used any of that training in later life. So my academic training was nothing to do with guitars; which, upon reflection, has been a good thing, because it has meant that my interest in music has not always depended on the literature of the instruments I play. When I meet people who are passionate about the guitar to the exclusion of every other kind of music, it irritates me profoundly, because guitar music is after all limited in its scope, musically speaking. There is no piece of guitar music that has the formal beauty of a piano sonata by Mozart, or the richly worked out ideas and passion of a late Beethoven string quartet, or for that matter the beautiful mellifluous poetry of a Chopin Ballade. The guitar literature is not something to extol, to cherish. But it is perfectly adequate, if you know how to handle it. For my own purposes, I don't need to perform profound music in order to say what I want to say. On the contrary, I find that simple guitar music is a good vehicle for my musical utterances—such as they are. I know that I can invest unsophisticated, naïve, even corny guitar music with a poetry which can entice the ear, and with it create an experience that is perfectly valid for present-day musical circumstances. I only need a handful of notes, nothing special, and I'm away.

'You see, each time, each performance I consider as if starting from a completely fresh canvas. I will stretch and prime that canvas in my practice room, but only when I go out on stage do I begin to paint. My materials are simple, primitive even, but the process of transforming them is what counts. That is the creative act for me. In this context, the sheer thought of contemplating the complex musical as well as the performance factors of say Beethoven's *Hammerklavier* sonata would drive me bananas. On the other hand, when I'm not performing, the music that gives me most pleasure is chamber music, and preferably without the guitar. In the long winter evenings, after dinner, when I've got a nice wood fire burning, I love to put on a Haydn or Mozart string quartet on the gramophone. It is the most satisfying music I know. Far more than all that guitar stuff.

'So when I come across an audience that are enthusiastic about my playing, to the point of fanaticism, as they are in Japan, for instance, I really begin to worry. I begin to wonder what it is they are so enthusiastic about. The music? Or the guitar? Are they going overboard about the music, or just about a musical instrument? There are thousands of guitar players in Japan, possibly because the sound of a plucked instrument is very near to their own indigenous music and their own cultural background. And to see those old Japos having a go on the old box—and some of them, believe me, are really good players—is an unbelievable sight. They have guitar magazines by the dozen, make guitars by the million and have guitar pluckers by the box-load. They even come over here, to England, and follow me about. Absolutely everywhere. And always asking questions: How long you grow your nails? How many hours do you practise? Do you drink coffee for breakfast? Can you give me any ideas on how to make my trills better? Quite extraordinary. But it is sometimes, I feel, a fanaticism without purpose, without any deeper understanding of the nature of what it is they are getting fanatical about.

'Music is at its best to my mind when it is a revelation of what one might call, for want of a more apt phrase, a religious experience. It does not have to be music of the Church, of course; in fact, quite often it is not. But fine music is for me something very sacred. The spirit of music can reach people who are sensitive enough to receive it in such a way that the experience is a revelation both the spiritual and the mystical. Ideally the performer has a special function, which is to bring the listener to the edge of that experience and to open the doors of this perception in such a way that those who wish to enter can. Of course, in a materialistic age like ours, it is easy to mock devotional feelings such as these; so-called rational minds have always found it easy to pour scorn on this kind of mysticism. But I cannot see anything wrong in ascribing to music these high ideals. After all, what is the point of music that is destructive, that advocates the breaking up of instruments? There is more than enough destruction all around us, I would have thought, to waste it on art. Some people say, well, art is a reflection of society, and if there is such wanton destruction in our civilization, then to have it in music or art is a valid expression of our culture. But I find I cannot agree with that.

'Nor do I think that merely because you believe music to have a mystical or religious function, that this is necessarily elitist. I mean, no one in their *right* mind would *really* listen to a piece of Stockhausen, would they? Most people would not even know who or what Stockhausen was, if the public relations officers had not told us. I wonder what would happen if the English Sunday papers did not have an Arts page? Do you think this would affect the shape and style of things to come?

'But how do you explain all this to your audience? I mean, I don't want to get up on stage at every concert and make a long spiel outlining my aims, philosophy and beliefs, do I? That's why I took up music. It says everything for me in a very honest and eloquent way, and I feel that I've failed as an artist if I don't get some of that across. That's why I'm never very keen to give interviews, because

by and large you're always asked the same rhetorical and mechanical questions. How is it you decided to play the guitar? *Why* play the guitar? *Why* this and *why* that? Why anything, for that matter? I recognize that interviews can have a certain relevance in as much as they help keep your name and what you do in circulation. People will realize that you're in town, that you're still alive and—so I'm told—having your face in the paper probably sells a few extra tickets, although in my case I doubt it. No interview with me I have ever read, with a rare exception, has come anywhere near what I am *really* about, or what it is that I really want to *express* in music or what the hell I'm trying to do.'

"What amazes me is that artists like Julian Bream can endure the life-style they impose upon themselves," Peggy Ashcroft told me. "Because it's all got to be woven out of your own imagination; you've got to spin the web yourself, haven't you? You don't really feed off anyone else. How could one really know such a complicated person as Julian? I wouldn't say he knew what image he has of himself, because he's such a mixture of immense soft-heartedness and yet with a very tough core of self-protection. Off-stage, for instance, he talks in his funny broad Battersea accent, and tells funny jokes and is generally very amusing. But the moment he gets on stage and makes one of those rare announcements, he has a completely different voice. He talks posh. He acquired that, oh, a long time ago. It's a platform piece and has nothing to do with the

'Shit scared, but with a box that's easy and cheap to run.'

real him at all. He's such an odd mixture of the shrewd and the really dotty. I mean, he's extremely careful yet he will take the most appalling risks, especially with his hands. He loves playing cricket, yet he knows that his hands are his fortune. He broke a finger nail mending my car, which absolutely terrified me. And he even slipped in the lane outside my house once and broke a finger. At heart, I think he's an amiable conservative who has found a pace of life which suits him, and yet which he finds unsatisfying. He's condemned himself to a life of aloneness, almost. Most of us work with other people, and from them we gain strength and a sense of renewal. You have the feeling, certainly as an actress, that you don't have to do it all yourself. But this is precisely what Julian is forced to do, to do it all himself. Most people have someone; he has no one."

'The paradox for me is that although I love feeling the audience is with me when I'm on stage, there are times when I really can't stand to be with them, especially before and even sometimes after a concert. I try never to be rude, although I am, on occasion, and I'll always try and mix in if there's a formal reception that has been organized. One part of me, particularly after a day of travelling, would adore to be with people. I love just chatting, preferably over a glass of wine. I have a few special friends in various cities, but I find that to see them breaks the continuity of preparation. I feel sad about that, because there is part of me that is very gregarious. But I know that however much it could be a welcome break, somehow these diversions with other people diffuse my concentration. I would much rather sit down and read a couple of poems than go out and have a beer with close friends. It's that bloody concert that is always at the back of my mind. It's a cross to bear, I don't mind admitting.

'So the hotels I pick on the road, for instance, are always those which can provide this anonymity. I'm not unduly affected by the misery of a plastic modern hotel in a ghastly city on a rainy day. And I sometimes find that when the atmosphere inside and outside my room is ugly and unsympathetic, the music I may make within can have an added beauty as a reaction almost against the ugliness. Anyway, I don't mind ugliness, provided I haven't got to live with it for too long. I was in a hotel quite recently that was bombed by terrorists; they completely smashed in the front of the hotel, which was a bit noisy. I've been in hotels in Rabbitsville, Nebraska, which were simply terrible. I can remember one hotel in Cologne which I'd chosen out of a hotel guide, and it turned out to be a whore house. That was pretty hectic, I can tell you. The business was continuous all night; it was unbelievable what was going on.

'So I don't need sumptuous comfort; that's not really my style. I'm often happiest in rooms that might completely demoralize other people. If I get offended by a picture on the wall, I can always take it down, and quite often I do. The simplicity of my surroundings is, for me, a help; so what I'm doing in relation to that simplicity can have heightened clarity. It can exist happily within itself.

'Even after the concert, although I reckon I could eat my way round Europe, I still prefer to be in a simple restaurant with just a few friends. I find it very difficult to sit down to a large, beautifully cooked meal, which is going to cost a lot of money, if I'm not in the mood to enjoy it. I'd much rather have bangers and mash and a glass of beer in my hotel room. My routine could be thought to be a bit sad and solitary. Even if it is, I wouldn't change it. Even if I thought my life on the road was one of total loneliness, I would still continue, because that's my job. I need that degree of self-imposed self-discipline to do my job, but I also get a bit of self-satisfaction from it too. I wish more of my friends would understand that about me.

'One thing you learn very rapidly in this business is that you are part of a continuing tradition; that the future of the guitar, for instance, is every bit as important as its past. As I've got older, I've tended to sharpen my focus a bit. I'm much too old to specialize, not that I would ever want to do so. That's one of the reasons why I keep a little corner in contemporary music going, because although my great love is early music, it's the contemporary music that, oddly enough, keeps me on my toes with the older music. It gives me another vantage point. Modern music has many problems which you have to solve, other than the technical ones. And those problems are by no means divorced from the problems you have to solve in earlier types of music, indeed they are often closely related. So the great thing is to keep your eyes and ears open and not to get

'Can't stand to be with them, before or after a concert.'

'Most people have someone. He has no one.'

too complacent as you run along the inevitable tracks. So while the Elizabethan music circuit is an enjoyable razzmatazz, there is still so much to learn and more that I could achieve if I felt really ambitious.

'But I find now that I don't want to cast my nets too wide. There's too much to do as it is, and just to try and do what I do, as well as I would want to do it, would take me I reckon a lifetime and a half. So I take good care not to widen my spectrum too much; I think there's a dangerous tendency for people today to do a great variety of things, to do as many things as they can cram in. Ironically, I find that I'm whittling it all down now. I'm beginning, I think, to know what I really want to do, and in order to do just these few things as I really want to do them, I must concentrate all my efforts, because to achieve real excellence will surely take a very, very long time. I want to be recognized for what I am, for what it is I am trying to achieve. I believe that what I have thus far achieved has been done through a lot of hard work, a lot of thinking about music, and a fair amount of suffering. I don't mean physical suffering, but rather the anguish of performance and the singular way in which I've conducted my life in order to attain those goals which are still nowhere within my reach. As I've got older, and I'm no great age really, I've found that my little world is actually going inwards. It is little things which attract me now, intimate things. I'm less expansive than I was. I'm interested in one thing at a time, rather than a lot of compounded things. Perhaps I'm no good at travelling any more, because that is an art in itself, believe me.

'I'm also losing my sense of cultural mission, at least in the sense of wanting to rush all over the globe converting people to the guitar or the lute. Is there not something alien, a bit arrogant even, dragging one's one indigenous culture across all the continents of this planet. After all, other people have their own things to express in their own inimitable way. Transplantation can be, in some cases, an interesting and sometimes enriching procedure, but nothing thrives as rightly and naturally outside its own habitat, and sometimes there is a real danger that it may begin to lose its identity. I once made music with Ali Ackbar Khan, the famous Indian sarod player, when he first came to England in 1962. We actually made a television film together, improvising. I fumbled along, but it was an interesting experiment. And then, early in the following year I went to India for about three months, because I was becoming fascinated by their culture and their music and beginning to be a little disenchanted with my own. I stayed in Calcutta with Ali Ackbar for several weeks; well, I didn't actually stay in his house, but I went pretty much every day, because I was so interested in how somebody could become so great, such a complete master of his instrument. I knew he was a great musician, this man, but I wanted to try and understand how he achieved this greatness. I suppose I was younger in those days and more impressionable, but I went absolutely overboard on Indian music. I found I could listen to it for hours at a time and even today I derive great pleasure from it. But some time ago I heard he had moved out to California, and I went to hear one of his recent performances. His playing of the sarod was as remarkable and as beautiful as ever, but the style of his improvisation had changed, it had become much more westernized. There were all sorts of implied western harmonies, which seemed totally alien to my ears. Of course you may think I'm being conservative, you might even approve of this kind of transplant; but as a musician, with, I hope, some integrity, I found it pretty sad to hear some of the things Ali Ackbar is now doing.'

"He's always striving for perfection," a friend who didn't want to be named told me. "That's why so many people have come unstuck with him. If he wants roses in his garden, they have to be the best roses in the world; the best potatoes, the best lettuce and cabbages, the best ping-pong table. So his intensity frightens people off. He's a man who needs to be stimulated all the time. And stimulated in something worthwhile. He never likes to hear you say that. Not because he's afraid of the truth, but because he knows it already. You can't tell him anything about himself. You can't tell him that he's drinking too much wine; because he knows it already. His awareness of himself is sometimes overwhelming. And that is his problem. That is why he is so terribly lonely. I mean, he has to put up with a lot of bullshit, and he cannot stand it. But he is the official guitarist of this country, isn't he, so he can't really say what's on his mind. Not often, anyway. I think he suffers from

Julian Bream

'Know what I mean?'

being a big star. Not many people realize what is behind the life of a great creative artist like Julian. They have to be so dedicated to keep on top of the job. I'm sure if you were to touch his back before a concert, sparks would come off. He loves the limelight, obviously. But this is not what motivates him."

'It's a lovely instrument, the guitar,' Bream told me. 'There is a lovely proportion about the six-string guitar in the way it's strung and tuned. It seems complete in itself. Of course, you could extend the number of strings, why not? Narciso Yepes has done. You can extend anything, but what is the point? If something is of a beautiful proportion, it seems to me important to leave it alone. But the economics of things are such that we always seem to want more, so I have tried to understand that there comes a point when you cannot get more. You may kid yourself you're getting more; you may even seem to be getting more. But I know now you're not. I don't think I'm a great artist, but I know I'm a good one, that I have got something to say, however modest. And I am happy to be alive and to be able to say it and to say it with some degree of eloquence to people, people you don't know, strangers. I sometimes wish I was a composer; that would be the most magical thing of all. But I'm a lousy composer. I enjoy writing music, but I don't want to play it particularly, and I certainly don't want anybody else to hear it. But I do have to get it out of my system; I have to write a piece every now and then, even if it's only for therapeutic reasons. My life is just doing what I do, continuously. I haven't any ambitions left really, anything that I desperately want to do or change. I just want to play better, to understand a little more about the significance of certain things, and to find out why one puts up with all of this, what it is that spurs one on.

'The basic thing about playing the guitar is the pleasure you get from it. There's nothing wrong with pleasure is there? There are so many awful things going on in this world, every second of every day, that perhaps playing the guitar is one of the more harmless activities. That just about sums it all up. Nothing more complicated than that. If Mr Reagan and Mr Brezhnev, two rather dreary men, played the guitar for a bit of relaxation, and once a year gave a duet concert for the benefit of the United Nations, perhaps the world would be a little more peaceful, a little more enchanting. Know what I mean?'

Miesbach
14 February 1982

DISCOGRAPHY

US catalogue numbers, when distinct, follow UK catalogue numbers in *italic script*. Discs are suitable for stereo or mono reproduction, except when specified.

1955

An Anthology of English Song	Decca LW 5243 (mono)	London, Decca Studios

Peter Pears, tenor; Julian Bream, lute

Thomas Ford	*Fair, sweet, cruel*
Thomas Morley	*Come, sorrow, come*
Philip Rosseter	*When Laura smiles*
John Dowland	*I saw my lady weep*
Thomas Morley	*It was a lover and his lass*
John Dowland	*Awake, sweet love*
Philip Rosseter	*What then is love but mourning?*
John Dowland	*In darkness let me dwell*
Thomas Morley	*Mistress mine well may you fare*

Lute: Thomas Goff 1951

1956

Sor, Turina and Falla

	Westminster XWN 18135 (mono)	Vienna, Mozart-Zaal

Julian Bream, guitar

Fernando Sor	*Estudios, nos. 5, 9 and 12 (ed. Segovia)*
	Minuetto (from op. 22)
	Largo from op. 7
	Rondo from op. 22
	Andante largo from op. 5
Joaquín Turina	*Hommage à Tárrega*
	Fandanguillo
	Andante (Sonata in D)
	Ráfaga
Manuel de Falla	*Homenaje pour le tombeau de Claude Debussy*

Guitar: Hector Quine 1954

Villa-Lobos and Torroba

	Westminster XWN 18137 (mono)	Vienna, Mozart-Zaal

Julian Bream, guitar

Heitor Villa-Lobos	*Five Preludes*
F. Moreno Torroba	*Prelude in E*
	Sonatina in A
	Nocturno
	Burgalesa

Guitar: Hector Quine 1954

1957
A Bach Recital for the Guitar Westminster   Vienna, Mozart-Zaal
                                   XWN 18428 (mono)

Julian Bream, guitar

J. S. Bach *Chaconne (from the D minor Violin Partita)*
          Little Prelude in C minor
          Sarabande (from the E minor Lute Suite)
          Bourrée (from the E minor Lute Suite)
          Prelude and Fugue (from the C minor Lute Suite)
          Prelude, Fugue and Allegro

Guitar: Herman Hauser 1947

Julian Bream plays Dowland Westminster   Vienna, Mozart-Zaal
                                XWN 18429 (mono)

Julian Bream, lute

John Dowland *Queen Elizabeth's Galliard*
             Lachrimae Antiquae Pavan
             Mrs Whites Nothinge
             Mrs Vauxs Gigge
             Farewell (a Fancy)
             Orlando Sleepeth
             Fantasia
             King of Denmark's Galliard
             Melancholy Galliard
             My Lady Hunsdon's Puffe
             Semper Dowland Semper Dolens
             An Unnamed Piece
             Sir Henry Umpton's Funerall
             Forlorne Hope Fancy

Lute: Thomas Goff 1951

1958
A Recital of Lute Songs Decca   London, Decca Studios
                             LXT 5567 (mono); SXL 2191

Peter Pears, tenor; Julian Bream, lute

John Dowland *Five Knacks for Ladies*
Thomas Morley *Thyrsis and Milla*
John Dowland *Sorrow, stay*
Thomas Ford *Come, Phyllis, come*
Thomas Morley *I saw my lady weeping*
             With my love my life was nestled
Frances Pilkington *Rest sweet nymphs*
Thomas Morley *What if my mistress now?*
Anon *Have you seen but a white lily grow?*
Thomas Campian *Come, let us sound with melody*
Anon *Misere my Maker*
Philip Rosseter *What is a day?*
Thomas Campian *Fair of you expect admiring*
             Shall I come, sweet love?
John Dowland *If my complaints*
             What if I never speed?
Philip Rosseter *Whether men do laugh or weep*

Lute: Thomas Goff 1951

Julian Bream

1959
The Art of Julian Bream   RCA   New York, RCA Studios
                                           RB 16239 (mono)   Prod. Peter Dellheim; eng. Lewis
                                           LM 2448   Layton
Julian Bream, guitar

          Girolamo Frescobaldi
               (arr. Segovia) *La Frescobalda*
          Mateo Albéniz
               (arr. Pujol) *Sonata in D*
          Domenico Scarlatti
               (arr. Bream) *Sonata in E minor (L.33)*
               (arr. Segovia) *Sonata in E minor (L.352)*
          Domenico Cimarosa
               (arr. Bream) *Sonata in C# minor*
               (arr. Bream) *Sonata in A*
          Lennox Berkeley *Sonatina, op. 51*
          Joaquín Rodrigo *En los trigales*
          Maurice Ravel
               (arr. Bream) *Pavane Pour Une Infante Défunte*
          Albert Roussel *'Segovia', op. 29*

Guitar: Herman Hauser Jr. 1957

1960
Guitar Concertos   RCA   London, Decca Studios
                                           RB 16252 (mono)   Prod. Michael Bremner
                                           LM 2487 (mono)
Julian Bream, guitar

The Melos Ensemble: Richard Adeny, flute; Gervase de Peyer, clarinet; Neil Saunders, horn; Emanuel
    Hurwitz, violin; Ivor MacMahon, violin; Cecil Aranowitz, viola; Terence Weil, cello; Adrian Beers, double bass

          Mauro Giuliani *Concerto in A, op. 30*
         Malcolm Arnold *Guitar Concerto, op. 67 (directed by the composer)*

Guitar: Edgar Mönch 1959

1961
The Golden Age of English Lute   RB 16281 (mono); SB 2150   London, Decca Studios
  Music   *LDS 2560*   Prod. Ray Minshull
Julian Bream, lute

          Robert Johnson *Two Almaines*
                             Fantasia
          Francis Cutting *Walsingham*
           John Dowland *Mignarda*
          Francis Cutting *Alman*
          Philip Rosseter *Galliard*
          Francis Cutting *Greensleeves*
           John Dowland *Galliard upon a galliard*
          Thomas Morley *Pavan*
           John Johnson *Carmans Whistle*
                Bulman *Pavan*
        Daniel Batchelar *Mounsiers Almaine*
      Anthony Holborne *Pavan*
           John Dowland *Batell galliard*
      Anthony Holborne *Galliard*

Lute: Thomas Goff 1951

1962
An Evening of Elizabethan Music   RCA   London, Decca Studios
                                         RB 6592 (mono)   Prod. Ray Minshull
                                           LD 2656

The Julian Bream Consort: Olive Zorian, violin; David Sandemann, flute; Joy Hall, bass viol; Desmond
    Dupré, cittern, lute; Robert Spencer, voice, pandora, lute; Julian Bream, lute

William Byrd	*Mounsiers Almaine*
	Pavana Bray
	My Lord of Oxenfords Maske
John Johnson	*The Flatt Pavin*
Richard Allison	*The Batchelars Delight*
Anon.	*Kemps Jig*
Peter Phillips	*Pavan*
Thomas Morley	*O Mistresse Mine*
	La Rondinella
	Joyne Hands
John Dowland	*Lachrimae Pavan*
	Fanatasy
Richard Alinson	*De La Tromba Pavan*
Thomas Campian	*It fell on a summer's day*
John Dowland	*Dowlands Adew*
	The Frog Galliard
Anon.	*La Rosignoll*
John Dowland	*Tarletons Resurrection*
	Galliard: Can she excuse?

Lute: Thomas Goff 1951

Popular Classics for Spanish   RCA   London, Kenwood House
    Guitar   RB 6593 (mono)   Prod. James Burnett; eng. Bob
                                         LD 2606   Auger

Julian Bream, guitar

Heitor Villa-Lobos	*Chôros, no. 1*
	Etude no. 11 in E minor
F. Moreno Torroba	*Madroños*
Joaquín Turina	*Hommage à Tárrega*
Heitor Villa-Lobos	*Prelude no. 4 in E minor*
Isaac Albeniz	
(arr. Bream)	*Granada*
(arr. Bream)	*Leyenda*
Manuel de Falla	*Homenaje pour le tombeau de Claude Debussy*
Trad. arr. Llobet	*El Testament d'Amelia*
Joaquín Turina	*Fandanguillo*

Guitars: Robert Bouchet 1957 and 1962

1963
Julian Bream in Concert   RCA   Wellesley Mass.
                                       RB 6646 (mono); SB6646   /New York, Town Hall
                                       LM 2819 (mono)   /London, Wigmore Hall
                                                  Prod. Peter Dellheim, James
                                                      Burnett; eng. Anthony
                                                      Salvatore

Julian Bream

Julian Bream in Concert (*cont.*)

Julian Bream, lute

John Dowland	*Captain Pipers Galliard*	
	Queen Elizabeths Galliard	
	Sir John Langtons Pavan	
	Tarletons Resurrection	
	Lady Cliftons Spirit	
William Byrd	*Pavana Bray*	
	Galliard	
	Pavan	
	My Lord Willoughbys Welcome Home	

(with Peter Pears, tenor)

John Dowland	*Wilt thou, unkind, thus reave me?*
	Sorrow, stay
	The lowest trees have tops
	Time's eldest son, old age
	In darkness let me dwell
	Say, love, if ever thou didst find

Lute: Thomas Goff 1951

Music for Voice and Guitar　　　RCA　　　　　　London, Kenwood House
　　　　　　　　　　　　　　　　SB 0021　　　　　Prod. Christopher Raeburn
　　　　　　　　　　　　　　　　LSC 2718

Peter Pears, tenor; Julian Bream, guitar

Benjamin Britten	*Songs from the Chinese, op. 58*
	Folk Song Arrangements
	(Master Kilby; The shooting of his dear; Sailor Boy; I will give my
	love an apple; The Soldier and the Sailor)
	Second Lute Song from Gloriana
William Walton	*Anon in Love*
Mátyás Seiber	*Four French Folk Songs*
	(Reveillez-vous; J'ai descendu; Le Rossignol; Marguérite, elle est
	malade).
Peter Racine Fricker	*O mistress mine*

Guitar: Robert Bouchet 1960

1964
Julian Bream　　　　　　　　RCA　　　　　　　London, Walthamstow Town
　　　　　　　　　　　　　　　　RB 6635 (mono); SB 6635　　Hall
　　　　　　　　　　　　　　　　LSC 2718　　　　　Prod. James Burnett; eng. Alan
　　　　　　　　　　　　　　　　　　　　　　　　　　　　Stagge

Julian Bream, guitar
The Melos Chamber Orchestra (leader Emanuel Hurwitz), conducted by Colin Davis

　　　　　　　　Joaquín Rodrigo *Concierto de Aranjuez*

The Julian Bream Consort: Olive Zorian, violin; Frances Mason, violin; David Sandeman, flute; Desmond Dupre, bass viol; Joy Hall, bass viol; Robert Spencer, chittarone, tabor; Julian Bream, lute

Benjamin Britten	
(set by Bream)	*The Courtly Dances from* Gloriana
Antonio Vivaldi	*Concerto in D for lute and strings*

Lute: Thomas Goff 1951
Guitars: Manuel Ramírez 1963, Robert Bouchet 1960

J. S. Bach Suites no. 1 and 2	RCA RB 6684 (mono); SB 6684 *LSC 2896*	London, Kenwood House Prod. James Burnett; eng. Bob Auger
Julian Bream, guitar		

J. S. Bach *Lute Suite no. 1 in E minor, BWV 996*
Lute Suite no. 2 in C minor, BWV 997

Guitar: Robert Bouchet 1960

1965 **Baroque Guitar**	RCA RB 6673 (mono); SB 6673 *LSC 2878*	New York, RCA Studios Prod. Peter Dellheim; eng. Bernard Keville
Julian Bream, guitar		

Gaspar Sanz *Pavanas*
Canarios
J. S. Bach *Prelude in D minor, BWV 999*
Fugue in A minor, BWV 1001
Fernando Sor *Fantaisie (largo), op. 7*
Minuet, op. 25
Leopold Weiss *Passacaille*
Fantaisie
Robert de Visée *Suite in D minor*
Leopold Weiss *Tombeau sur la mort de M. le Comte de Logy*

Guitar, Robert Bouchet 1964

1966 **Lute Music from the Royal** **Courts of Europe**	RCA SB 6698 *LSC 2987*	London: the Scout Hut, Hornsey Prod. James Burnett; eng. Sid Doggart
Julian Bream, lute		

Landgrave of Hesse *Pavan*
Simone Molinaro *Salterello*
Ballo detto 'Il Conte Orlando'
Saltarello
Simone Molinaro *Chromatic Pavan*
Peter Phillips *Fantasia*
The galliard to the Chromatic Pavan
John Dowland *A Fancye*
Queen Elizabeths Galliard
Gregory Howett *Fantasia*
Alonso de Mudarra *Fantasia*
Albert Długoraj *Fantasia*
Finale
Villanella I
Villanella
Alfonso Ferrabosco *Pavan*
Hans Newsidler *Mein Herz hat sich mit Lieb' verpflicht*
Hie' folget ein welscher Tannz
Ich klag den Tag
Der juden Tanz
Valentin Backfark *Fantasia*
Jean-Baptiste Besard *Air de Cour*
Branle
Guillemette
Volte

Lute: Thomas Goff 1951

Julian Bream

20th Century Guitar   RCA   England: Wardour Chapel,
                                      SB 6723   Wiltshire
                                      LSC 2964   Prod. James Burnett; eng. J. W.
                                                                 Bower

Julian Bream, guitar

Reginald Smith Brindle *El Polífemo de Oro*
Benjamin Britten *Nocturnal, op. 70*
Frank Martin *Quatre Pièces Brèves*
Hans Werner Henze *Drei Tentos aus Kammermusik 1958*
Heitor Villa-Lobos *Etude no. 5 in C*
Etude no. 7 in E

Guitar: David Rubio 1965

1967
The Dances of Dowland   RCA   England: Wardour Chapel,
                                      SB 6751   Wiltshire
                                      LSC 2987   Prod. James Burnett; eng. J. W.
                                                                 Bower

Julian Bream, lute

John Dowland *The Earl of Essex Galliard*
Lachrimae Antiquae
My Lady Hunsdons Puffe
Lord d'Lisles Galliard
The Frog Galliard
Lachrimae Verae
The Shoemakers Wife
Unnamed piece in the style of an Almain
Sir John Smiths Almaine
Melancholie Galliard
Sir Henry Guilfordes Almaine
Dowlands First Galliard
Mrs Vauxs Gigge
The Earl of Derbys Galliard
Semper Dowland, Semper Dolens

Lute: Thomas Goff 1951

1968
Julian Bream and his Friends   RCA   London, Bishopsgate Institute
                                      SB 6772   Prod. James Burnett; eng. J. W.
                                      LSC 3027   Bower

Julian Bream, guitar
The Cremona String Quartet: Hugh MacGuire, violin; Iona Brown, violin; Cecil Aranowitz, viola; Terence
Weil, cello; and George Malcolm, Harpsichord

Luigi Boccherini *Quartet in E minor for Guitar and String Quartet*
Boccherini (arr. Bream) *Introduction and Fandango for Guitar and Harpsichord*
Joseph Haydn *Quartet in D, op. 2 no. 2, for Guitar, Violin, Viola and Cello*

Guitar: David Rubio 1966

Classic Guitar	RCA SB 6796 *LSC 3070*	England: Wardour Chapel, Wiltshire Prod. James Burnett; eng. J. W. Bower

Julian Bream, guitar

Mauro Giuliani	*Grand Overture, op. 61* *Sonata in C (allegro)*
Anton Diabelli (rev. Bream)	*Sonata in A*
W. A. Mozart (arr. Bream)	*Larghetto and Allegro, K anh.* *229*
Fernando Sor	*Introduction and Allegro, op. 14*

Guitar: David Rubio 1966

1969

Sonatas for Lute and Harpsichord	RCA SB 6812 *LSC 3100*	London, Bishopsgate Institute Prod. James Burnett; eng. J. W. Bower

Julian Bream, lute; George Malcolm, harpsichord

J. S. Bach	*Trio Sonata no. 1 in Eb, BWV 525*
Antonio Vivaldi (ed. Malcolm)	*Sonata in C for Lute and Continuo*
J. S. Bach	*Trio Sonata no. 5 in C, BWV 529*
Antonio Vivaldi (ed. Malcolm)	*Sonata in G minor for Lute and Continuo*

Lute: Thomas Goff 1951

1970

Elizabethan Lute Songs	RCA SB 6835 *LSC 3131*	London, Conway Hall Prod. James Burnett; eng. J. W. Bower

Peter Pears, tenor; Julian Bream, lute

Thomas Morley	*Absence*
Philip Rosseter	*What then is love but mourning?*
John Dowland	*I saw my lady weep*
Philip Rosseter	*If she forsake me*
John Dowland	*Dear, if you change*
Thomas Ford	*Come, Phyllis*
John Dowland	*Stay, time*
Thomas Morley	*It was a lover and his lass*
John Dowland	*Weep you no more*
Philip Rosseter	*When Laura smiles*
Thomas Ford	*Fair, sweet, cruel*
John Dowland	*Shall I sue?* *Sweet, stay awhile*
Thomas Morley	*Who is it?*
John Dowland	*Can she excuse?* *Come, heavy sleep*

Lute: David Rubio 1967

Julian Bream

Romantic Guitar

RCA
SB 6844
LSC 3156

England: Wardour Chapel,
Wiltshire
Prod. James Burnett; eng. J. W.
Bower

Julian Bream, guitar

Niccolò Paganini	
(arr. Bream)	*Grand Sonata in A*
Felix Mendelssohn	
(arr. Bream)	*Song Without Words, op. 10 no. 6*
	Canzonetta (from op. 12)
Franz Schubert	
(arr. Bream)	*Menuetto (from op. 78)*
Francisco Tárrega	*Prelude (Lágrima)*
	Adelita
	Mazurca en sol
	Marieta

Guitar: Manuel Ramírez 1968

1971
Julian Bream plays Villa-Lobos

RCA
SB 6852
LSC 3231

London, EMI Studios/Wardour
Chapel, Wiltshire
Prod. James Burnett; eng. Bob
Gooch/J. W. Bower

Julian Bream, guitar
London Symphony Orchestra, conducted by André Previn

Heitor Villa-Lobos	*Concerto for Guitar and Orchestra*
	Five Preludes for Guitar
	Schottisch-chôro (Suite Populaire Brésilienne)

Guitar: Herman Hauser 1950 and 1936

Together

RCA
SB 6862
LSC 3257

England: Wardour Chapel,
Wiltshire
Prod. James Burnett; eng. J. W.
Bower

Julian Bream, guitar; John Williams, guitar

William Lawes	
(trans. Bream)	*Suite for two Guitars*
Ferdinando Carulli	*Duo in G, op. 34*
Fernando Sor	*L'Encouragement, op. 34*
Isaac Albéniz	
(arr. Pujol)	*Córdoba*
Enrique Granados	
(arr. Pujol)	*Intermezzo* (Goyescas)
Manuel de Falla	
(arr. Pujol, rev. Bream)	*Spanish Dance no. 1 (La Vida Breve)*
Maurice Ravel	
(arr. Bream)	*Pavane pour une Infante défunte*

Guitar: Herman Hauser 1936

1972
The Woods so Wild

RCA
SB 6865
LSC 3331

England: Wardour Chapel,
Wiltshire
Prod. James Burnett; eng. J. W.
Bower

Julian Bream, lute

The Woods so Wild (*cont.*)

William Byrd	*The woods so wild*
Francesco da Milano	*Fantasia*
Frances Cutting	*Packingtons Pound*
Francesco da Milano	*Fantasia*
John Dowland	*Walsingham*
Francesco da Milano	*Fantasia*
Anthony Holborne	*The Fairy Round*
	Heigh Ho Holiday
Francesco da Milano	*Fantasia*
John Dowland	*Go from my window*
Francesco da Milano	*Fantasia*
Frances Cutting	*Greensleeves*
Francesco da Milano	*Fantasia*
John Dowland	*Bonny sweet robin*
Francesco da Milano	*Fantasia*
Anthony Holborne	*Hearts Ease*
Francesco da Milano	*Fantasia*
John Dowland	*Loth to depart*

Lute: David Rubio 1967

1973   RCA   London, EMI Studios/Wardour
Julian Bream '70s   SB 6876   Chapel, Wiltshire
          ARL1 0049   Prod. James Burnett; eng. Bob
          Gooch/J. W. Bower

Julian Bream, guitar; The Melos Ensemble, directed by David Atherton

Richard Rodney Bennett	*Concerto for Guitar and Chamber Orchestra*
Alan Rawsthorne	*Elegy*
William Walton	*Five Bagatelles*
Lennox Berkeley	*Theme and Variations*

Guitar: Hernandez y Aguado 1965

1974   RCA   England: Wardour Chapel,
Together Again   *ARL1 0456*   Wiltshire

Julian Bream, guitar; John Williams, guitar

Prod. James Burnett; eng. J. W. Bower

Ferdinando Carulli	*Serenade, op. 96*
Enrique Granados	
(arr. Llobet)	*Spanish Dance no. 6*
Isaac Albéniz	
(arr. Llobet)	*Bajo la Palmera, op. 232 no. 3*
Enrique Granados	
(arr. Llobet)	*Spanish Dance no. 11*
Mauro Giuliani	*Variazioni Concertanti, op. 130*
Isaac Albéniz	
(arr. Llobet)	*Evocación (Iberia)*

Guitar: José Romanillos 1973

Julian Bream   RCA   England: Wardour Chapel,
Julian Bream, guitar   ARL1 0711   Wiltshire

Prod. James Burnett: eng. J. W. Bower

Mauro Giuliani	*Le Rossiniane, op. 121*
	Le Rossiniane, op. 119
Fernando Sor	*Sonata in C, op. 25*

Guitar: José Romanillos 1973

Julian Bream

Concertos for Lute and   RCA   London, Barking Town
Orchestra   ARL1 1180   Hall/Rosslyn Hill Chapel
                                                         Prod. James Burnett; eng. Bob
                                                           Auger
Julian Bream, lute
The Monteverdi Orchestra, conducted by John Eliot Gardiner: Marilyn Sansom, cello; John Gray, violone;
    Nicholas Kraemer, chamber organ; Robert Spencer, chitarrone

          Antonio Vivaldi *Concerto in D*
             Carl Kohaut *Concerto in F*
          Antonio Vivaldi
             (arr. Bream) *Concert for Two Lutes*
           George Handel
             (arr. Bream) *Concerto for Two Lutes*

Lute: David Rubio 1967

Julian Bream   RCA   London, Walthamstow Town
                                ARL1 1181   Hall/Rosslyn Hill Chapel
                                                         Prod. James Burnett; eng. Bob
                                                           Auger
Julian Bream, guitar
The Monteverdi Orchestra, conducted by John Eliot Gardiner

          Joaquín Rodrigo *Concierto de Aranjuez*
          Lennox Berkeley *Guitar Concerto*

Guitar: Jose Romanillos 1973

1976
The Lute Music of John Dowland   RCA   England: Wardour Chapel,
                                     RL 11491   Wiltshire
                                     ARL1 1491   Prod. James Burnett; eng. J. W.
                                                           Bower
Julian Bream, lute

          John Dowland *Captain Digorie Pipers Galliard*
                       A Fancy
                       My Lord Chamberlain, his Galliard
                       Resolution
                       Mr Langtons Galliard
                       Forlorne Hope Fancy
                       Sir John Souches Galliard
                       Captain Pipers Pavan
                       My Lord Willoughbys Welcome Home
                       Galliard to 'Lachrimae'
                       A Fancy
                       Farewell

Lute: David Rubio 1967

1977
Julian Bream: Villa-Lobos   RCA   England: Wardour Chapel,
                                RL 12499   Wiltshire
                                ARL1 2499   Prod. James Burnett; eng. J. W.
                                                           Bower
Julian Bream, guitar

          Heitor Villa-Lobos *The Twelve* Études *for Guitar*
                             Suite Populaire Brésilienne

Guitar: Herman Hauser 1944

214

1978
'Live'　　　　　　　　　RCA　　　　　　　　New York, Avery Fisher
　　　　　　　　　　　　　RL 03090　　　　　　　Hall/Boston, Symphony Hall
　　　　　　　　　　　　　ARL2 3090　　　　　　Prod. Peter Dellheim; eng.
　　　　　　　　　　　　　　　　　　　　　　　　Edwin Begley

Julian Bream, guitar

　　　　　　　　John Johnson
　　　　　　　(arr. Bream) *Pavan and Galliard*
　　　　　　Georg Teleman *Parti Polonaise*
　　　　　　Fernando Sor *Fantaisie, op. 54*
　　　　　　Gabriel Fauré
　　　　　　　(arr. Bream) *Dolly, op. 56*
　　　　　Johannes Brahms
　　　　　　(arr. Williams) *Theme and Variations, op. 18*
　　　　　Claude Debussy
　　　　　(arr. Batchelar) *Reverie*
　　　　　Claude Debussy
　　　　　　(arr. Bream) *Golliwog's Cakewalk*
　　　　　Claude Debussy
　(arr. Bream/Williams) *Clair de Lune*
　　　　　　Isaac Albeniz
　　　　　　(arr. Llobet) *Castilla*
　　　　Enrique Granados
　(arr. Bream/Williams) *Spanish Dance no. 2*

Guitar: Robert Bouchet 1964

1979
Music of Spain, vol. 1　　　RCA　　　　　　　England: Wardour Chapel,
　　　　　　　　　　　　　RL 13435　　　　　　　Wiltshire
　　　　　　　　　　　　　ARL1 3435　　　　　　Prod. James Burnett; eng. J. W.
　　　　　　　　　　　　　　　　　　　　　　　　Bower

Julian Bream, lute

　　　　　　Luis Milán *'El Maestro' (1535)*
　　　　　　　　　　Pavana I
　　　　　　　　　　Pavana V
　　　　　　　　　　Pavana VI
　　　　　　　　　　Fantasia XXII
　　　　　　　　　　Fantasia VIII
　　　　　　　　　　Fantasia IX
　　　　　　　　　　Tento I
　　　　　　　　　　Pavana IV
　　　　　　　　　　Fantasia XVI
　　　　Luiz de Narváez *'Los Seys Libros del Delphín de Musica' (1538)*
　　　　　　　　　　Fantasia V
　　　　　　　　　　Fantasia V
　　　　　　　　　　La Canción del Emperador
　　　　　　　　　　Fantasia VI
　　　　　　　　　　Arde, coraçon, arde
　　　　　　　　　　Ya se asiente el Rey Ramiro
　　　　　　　　　　Conde Claros
　　　　　　　　　　Guárdame las vacas
　　　　　　　　　　Tres Diferencias por Otra Parte
　　　　　　　　　　Baxa de Contrapunto

Lute: David Rubio 1968

Julian Bream

1980

Music of Spain, vol. IV: The Classical Heritage	RCA Digital RL 14033 *ATC 14033*	New York, RCA Studio Prod. John Pfeiffer; eng. Edwin Begley

Julian Bream, guitar

Fernando Sor	*Fantasia, op. 30*
	Fantasia, op. 7
	Variations on a theme of Mozart, op. 9
Dionisio Aguado	*Adagio, op. 2 no. 1*
	Polonaise, op. 2 no. 2
	Introduction and Rondo, op. 2 no. 3

Guitar: José Romanillos 1973

1981

Dedication	RCA Digital RL 25419 *ARC 14379*	England: Wardour Chapel, Wiltshire Prod. James Burnett; eng. J. W. Bower

Julian Bream, guitar

Richard Rodney Bennett	*Five Impromptus*
William Walton	*Five Bagatelles*
Peter Maxwell Davies	*'Hill Runes'*
Hans Werner Henze	*Royal Winter Music, Sonata no. 1*

Guitar: José Romanillos 1973

1982

The Music of Spain, vol. V: The Poetic Nationalists	RCA Digital *RL 14378* ARC 14378	England: Wardour Chapel, Wiltshire Prod. James Burnett, eng. J. W. Bower

Isaac Albéniz	*Cataluña*
	Mallorca
	Cádiz
	Granada
	Sevilla
	Córdoba
Enrique Granados	*Dedicatoria (from op. 1)*
	Tonadilla: La Maja de Goya
	Danza Española no. 4
	Valses Poéticos
	Danza Española no. 10
	Danza Española no. 5

Guitar: José Romanillos 1973